Workbook Practical

How To Do The Work

A guide to Dr. Nicole LePera's Book

Recognize Your Patterns, Heal from Your Past, and Create Your Self

The Handbook on Holistic Healing

Genie Reads

Table of Contents

How To Use This Workbook

Hello there!

It is with great pleasure to see that you have taken an interest in the book "*How To Do The Work*" by Dr. Nicole LePera. If you have been searching for a deeper and more holistic way to heal yourself, then this would be the right place for you. Espousing the belief that the mind and body are intricately linked, Dr. LePera takes us on an insightful journey where we are shown how to utilize that mind-body connection in order to cleanse away our deep seated trauma and allow real healing to take root.

This workbook is meant to enhance and highlight the ideas and concepts mentioned, so that it makes it very much easier for you to take action and implement what you have learnt from the book into practical, daily usage. With the aid of this workbook, resolving traumatic issues and opening the door to holistic healing becomes much easier through the step-by-step guidance and systematic approaches highlighted within. Equipped with the knowledge and practical skillsets developed through the workbook's exercises, you will be able to overcome many issues previously thought insurmountable and become a warm healing light for yourself as well as many of the folks around you. In order to absorb quicker and with a lasting impact, it is vital that you answer all the questions presented in the workbook, and answer them sincerely. Only by digging deep and giving honest answers will you be able to flash light on what truly matters to you, and get the opportunities to effect lasting positive change in your daily life.

The workbook will also feature important summaries of each individual chapter, which will be integral in helping you answer the questions contained therein. As such, for the time constrained folk, you do not necessarily need to read the main book before answering the questions in this workbook. All the crucial points have been condensed and captured for your attention. For the folks whom have already read the book, the afore mentioned salient concepts will serve well as quick reminders and gentle nudges when you are doing the questions.

Whilst attempting the questions found in the workbook, please take your time to go through it carefully. This portion is an area where speedy reading can be set aside and replaced with thoughtful ruminations. The questions will encourage you to reflect and think, sometimes very deeply, before you jump in with any answers. It will be of great benefit to you if the answers supplied are colored with the honesty of thought and tinged with sincerity. After all, no one can be as interested in your welfare as your own self.

Done in this careful, constructive way, you will be able to harness the positive change created and see it reverberate throughout many aspects of your life. For some, the honest answers may create self criticism. Take heart, know that you are not alone, and that by just the mere act of acknowledgement of mistakes made in the past, that itself is a very important step forward.

You will want to come back to these questions again after your initial foray, say after a period of 4 to 8 weeks; there really is no set in stone time length, but it is highly recommended to have at least a space of 4 weeks between the first and second attempt at the questions. This second try is really to let you see the progress you have made, both in thoughts and actions, and also to think of different angles to the same questions with your new life experiences.

You can really repeat this process as many times as you find useful. The key is always honesty in the answers and an indefatigable spirit for self development and progress.

May you be well and be happy.

Introduction

Dr. Nicole LePera, author of the book, *How To Do The Work: Recognize Your Patterns, Heal From Your Past, and Create Your Self,* seemed to have all aspects of her life under control. One might envy how she leads her life with high efficiency until you look a little closer, a little deeper. Unbeknownst to the rest of us, the only reason she works endlessly is to distract herself from underlying internal conflicts.

Amidst her achievements and success, Dr. LePera realized that she had been running away from dealing with her genuine emotions. She was not happy, neither was she content with her life. This realization that she had was what pushed her to change. She started by nourishing her vessel – her body – by eating healthy food and doing regular exercises. Once she could see (and feel) the positive changes, she turned her attention to improving her mind and soul. She learned that to truly discover one's true Self, you must have a good balance of mind, soul, and body – which was how the basic principles of holistic psychology were established.

Not long after, she started *The Holistic Psychologist* where she shared her story, knowledge, and continuous journey to self-healing. To her surprise, thousands of people reached out and related to her. Eventually, her book was published and it managed to help more people who were in need.

This workbook on *How To Do The Work* aims to guide its readers on their path towards finding the sweet balance with regard to their overall wellness which includes breaking bad habits, healing from the pain of the past, and creating their best Self.

With the workbook's comprehensive chapter summaries, the readers will find themselves immersed in life-changing stories and inspiring testimonies. These narratives are also supported by Dr. LePera's tools and methods developed via different fields that range from neuroscience and psychology to spirituality and mindfulness practices. The chapter summaries are followed by engaging activities and reflective questions that will guide readers in their self-healing process.

Now, take a deep breath and close your eyes. Try to picture an alternate reality that looks different – but better – than your life. If you can successfully create a wonderful image of what you're aiming for, then you're ready for anything. But if you see nothing just yet, don't get discouraged. This workbook will help you. Let's Get To It

Ch 1: You Are Your Own Best Healer

Summary

It's a cycle: You wake up one day and decide that today's the day that everything will change. You'll start working out, eating healthy, waking up early, etc. But then, in a few hours, days, or weeks, you might find yourself feeling uninspired and demotivated. The mind starts being pessimistic which is closely followed by your body simply refusing to move. You'll become frustrated with yourself and give up. Then, a few months later, you might find yourself starting the cycle once again.

The sad part is that most people already know what to do to start bettering their lives yet they feel *stuck*. Many desire to change but only a few are courageous enough to transform that knowledge into work. This is the type of trouble that brings them to Dr. Nicole LePera's office and most of the time, they ask the same questions: "Is something wrong with me? Why is it difficult to change?"

Dr. LePera is able to relate to the turmoil of her clients as she experienced it first-hand. She grew up in a seemingly picturesque American household but behind closed doors, they were far from perfect. Her mother suffered from phantom illnesses and was constantly in pain while her sister actually battled a life-threatening sickness. To top it all off, none of them really talked about these problems and other negative matters – emotional avoidance at its best.

There was a time in her pre-teens when she dropped the golden daughter role and started partying like crazy but no one called her out for it even when every family member was aware. The danger of emotional avoidance is that all the bottled-up emotions and feelings will pile up and eventually, burst. One random day, her mother saw a note that showed proof of her drinking, her mother broke down – threw things around, and started screaming at her (as if it was the first time she heard about it).

Her life experience brewed her intense passion to understand why people behaved the way they do which is why she pursued psychology. Along the way, she encountered cognitive behavioral therapy (CBT). It's a goal-oriented and highly prescribed approach wherein a client is required to focus on one matter at a time to identify the fault in their thought patterns that will ultimately lead to understanding their behavior. It emphasizes the impact of your thoughts on your behaviors. However, this approach, although proven effective, can be a bit rigorous and stiff when actually used.

Dr. LePera also explored psychodynamic techniques. These are philosophies stating that humans behave the way they do because of internal forces. She was particularly drawn to this theory. Eventually, it led her to understand the power of the subconscious and how it heavily influences a person's motivations and instincts.

While looking more into this theory, she started treatment groups for people who suffer from substance abuse. It was when she realized that addiction is not limited to physical matters such as drugs, alcohol, sex, or gambling because emotional cycles are addicting as well. Emotional addiction can be seen when someone is seeking or avoiding specific emotions to cope with trauma. The more she studied addiction, it became clear to her that there is an obvious link between the mind and the body.

She started to include unconventional factors in her private practice. Though her clients gained new knowledge and self-awareness, the progress was slow which also affected Dr. LePera's confidence. The frustration she experienced pushed her to dig deeper and she had a profound discovery: all of her clients who reached out to her for psychological solutions also suffered from physical symptoms such as irritable bowel syndrome, autoimmune diseases, and more.

The Western medicinal practice treats the body and mind as two distinct entities: psychiatry or psychology for the latter and the other different branches of medicine for the former. They have deemed it unscientific to treat them as one. On the other hand, the Eastern culture and indigenous tribes practiced medicine with respect to the connection of body, mind, and spirit.

René Descartes, a French philosopher birthed the literal separation of body and mind with the concept of mind-body dualism. This notion is still strongly practiced to this day. Modern medicine focuses on symptoms, quieting them without treating the underlying illness. Psychiatric solutions usually compose of antidepressant prescriptions, without truly understanding the patient's real trauma. There is also the theory of genetic determinism which simply states that you are meant to inherit all the positives and negatives from the previous generation – basically saying that you don't have any choice in your future.

On the brighter side, Bruce Lipton, an American biologist, pushes the study of epigenetics, which is the genes' ability to adapt to their environment. This *new biology* changes everything – especially *change* itself. You go from being choiceless to someone who can stop your family's generational cycle. Dr. LePera had a dysfunctional family growing up which led her to believe that she was also meant to be somewhat problematic but epigenetics proved her belief to be wrong.

In unraveling discoveries of epigenetics, Dr. LePera also encountered the placebo effect, which is used to describe the ability of a substance to counter the symptoms of an illness. It confirms that the mind has the power to create physical changes in the body. One strong case study of the placebo effect involved depressed participants who believe they were taking antidepressants, which were basically just sugar pills. They all reported improvement in their health.

There's also a negative version of the placebo effect, which is known as the nocebo effect. It happens when pessimistic thoughts make the body worse. One documented case of this effect happened in the 1970s when a doctor mistakenly informed a patient that he had cancer and had only three months to live. A few weeks later, the patient died and his autopsy showed that he had no cancer at all.

Regardless of its positivity or negativity, both effects are testaments of how interconnected the mind and body are. Dr. LePera married her academic, traditional knowledge with the newly researched facts of mind-body healing to establish the basic principles of Holistic Psychology. These are the following:

1. Healing is an internal event that happens daily. It requires your strong commitment and accountability to do the work.
2. Holistic Psychology focuses on the choices you make that will allow your self-healing.
3. The tools used in the holistic approach are practical but it's the act of change that makes it difficult. It needs you to be consistent in the daily choices you make to maintain the change that you want.
4. It is empowering to take responsibility for your mental well-being.

Lessons

1. It's a common struggle to feel "stuck" when you try to break out of your bad habits and unhealthy behaviors. Most of the time, it's a matter of science and not just sheer will or the lack thereof.

2. Cognitive Behavioral Therapy (CBT) is an effective and traditional method of approaching such problems revolving around unresolved trauma. However, its principles are too rigid and sometimes miss out on other underlying factors.

3. The mind and body are connected and should be medically treated as one. It's proven that there are better results in using the mind to heal the body and vice versa.

Issues Surrounding the Subject Matter

1. Are you struggling to keep promises to yourself? Are you having trouble creating new (healthy) habits? Why?

2. Do you find yourself overwhelmed with internal critical thoughts? Why do you think so?

3. Can you identify your emotional, physical, and spiritual needs? If not, why do you think you're struggling to do so?

Goals

1. Understand the feeling of "stuckness" when you're trying to change your routine for the better.

2. Understand how the body affects the mind and how the mind affects the body.

3. Identify the recurring patterns of your "stuckness" that causes you to drift back and forth.

Action Steps

1. Create your journal as inspired by Dr. LePera's *Future Self Journal*. Choose or purchase a notebook. Design it if you wish to.

2. Write your name and choose a quote that resonates the most with you. Or you may even create a reminder for yourself. Just a little note that will keep you going.

3. This will be your notebook of small promises. It should start with your consistency in updating this as needed.

Checklist

1. Acknowledge that you are repeating the same habits that lead your life into the same downhill troubles.

2. Keep an open mind for the new lessons you will gain in this workbook. You may have to unlearn a few beliefs along the way.

3. Prepare yourself for the coming challenges as you will be making decisions that may or will scare you.

Ch 2: The Conscious Self: Becoming Aware

Summary

Jessica sought Dr. LePera in an attempt to try again after previously experiencing failed therapy. At first, all she wanted was someone to vent to. During their first few sessions, Jessica just talked about everything that affected her week negatively – just minuscule, unrelated events. Later, Dr. LePera noticed Jessica's chronic anxiety and her need to be a people-pleaser.

When things frustrated her, Jessica drowned herself in numbing mechanisms such as smoking pot, drinking excessively, and doing other drugs. As they worked on her issues, it was obvious that she was *stuck* in a cycle. She'd go to therapy with Dr. LePera, then the doctor would tell her the things she needed to work with, and Jessica would promise not to cope with substances but week after week, she never committed to this.

Along the way, she met someone who became her long-term boyfriend. Unfortunately, due to her unresolved conflicts, the man became the recipient of her frustrations. She kept reliving the same toxic cycle from picking random fights and saying hurtful words to feeling guilty and drinking to cope which would restart the cycle again. After two years of weekly sessions, Jessica said she wanted to quit therapy again.

Many suffer the same loop as Jessica in different scenarios and settings. Looking at the bigger picture, the main reason why you're failing to commit to change is that you don't understand the true connection between your mind and body.

Before you can start with the complexities of Dr. LePera's whole-person approach, you must first go down the nitty-gritty path. In the literal sense, consciousness simply means being awake but to move forward, you need to understand its deeper meaning – a state of open awareness. The whole-person approach will not be effective unless you will learn how to see the internal world within you.

When you're awake, you assume that you are *conscious* but are you really? Dr. LePera discusses that the conscious mind is not hindered by your past. It's practical and progressive. However, most people are living on a script. You follow a routine that is so repetitive that you don't even notice it and you truly believe that it's the truth. Unbeknownst to all, it's just your thoughts and not the true you.

Going back to Jessica, her indecisiveness was a manifestation of her monkey mind. The Buddhists used this term to describe the state where you never stop thinking until all your thoughts jumble together senselessly. One moment, she loved her boyfriend and agreed to marry him but the next moment, she hated him and wanted to run away from him. Her thinking mind had her trapped in a reactivity loop.

The only time you can truly see yourself and *within* you is when you are *conscious*. This could unearth underlying matters that are influencing the choices that you make. So, when you find it difficult to change your habits or behaviors, it's not mere failure but rather it's because you are living on the same script, a repetitive pattern that makes you run on autopilot. This means that you're unknowingly letting your subconscious make the choices for you.

You run on autopilot because of how you were conditioned as a child. Conditioning is a process of ingraining beliefs, patterns, and thoughts over the years into your subconscious. When you force yourself to awaken from autopilot, there is a natural resistance from your body and mind which is known as the homeostatic impulse.

Your subconscious prefers what is *known* which is why it loves staying in its comfort zone. It pushes you to repetitive behaviors and habits, regardless of their nature, good or bad. When you try to go against what your subconscious wants, your homeostatic impulse will take over and cause you to return to your comfort zone. It's an automatic response of your body and mind.

The resistance can either be physical (anxiety or agitation) or mental (pessimistic thoughts). This is your subconscious' way of telling you that it's uncomfortable with the changes you're trying to make. Failure to understand this concept could lead to self-pity and self-blame.

Going back to Jessica, her anxiety was increasing as her wedding day was around the corner. In one of her sessions with Dr. LePera, she mentioned the sorrow of not having a father-and-daughter dance. This happened five years into her therapy with Dr. LePera and it was the first time she had mentioned her father. That was how deep she buried her grief, she was equally surprised that she had not mentioned her father's death in any of her sessions.

Because she didn't face her grief and instead kept it inside, it affected the way she expressed her emotions–hatred, stress, and frustration emerged to cover up her underlying sorrow. She got trapped in a loop of these unexplainable, negative feelings. But because of the upcoming wedding, the topic of her departed father kept coming up. Finally, she saw how she was overly focusing on the surface stressors to distract herself from her repressed grief.

Dr. LePera helped Jessica discover how to utilize her conscious awareness to free herself from automatic responses. Jessica found physical movement the most useful for her, specifically yoga. In this activity, the mind sets the direction that the body follows which is essentially powerful in what she wanted to achieve. It was really effective that she took it as far as training to become a yoga instructor. She realized that the more she engaged in its practice, the more she learned to live *consciously*.

There is significant liberty in accepting that you are just a thinker of your thoughts and that not all of your thoughts are true. Your mind is a naturally powerful tool. Dr. LePera urges you to be truly *conscious* and not let your thoughts run your lives toward the wrong destination.

Lessons

1. People cope with unresolved trauma through numbing mechanisms including, but not limited to, excessive alcohol drinking, taking various drugs, sex, social media, and more.

2. Your body is resisting change because it has been conditioned to follow a fixed routine.

3. When you don't face the traumatic incident head-on, it will manifest in other things. It can also be buried behind your thoughts and emotions but will show up when affected by a *trigger*.

Issues Surrounding the Subject Matter

1. Why are you defaulting to certain mechanisms to cope with trauma? How did you encounter this mechanism in the first place?

2. What are the habits that were conditioned to you? How and why?

3. Why do you internalize your traumas? Why is it difficult to confront issues?

Goals

1. Identify and acknowledge your most common and repetitive numbing mechanisms.

2. Identify and acknowledge the traumas that you discarded or kept hidden.

3. Discover how to build your *true* consciousness.

Action Steps

1. Build consciousness by following the simple steps below:

   a. Allocate one to two minutes of your day. Choose to do an activity and focus solely on whatever you're doing.

   b. Observe every moment of the activity you've chosen. If you're doing dishes, for example, feel the soap, the water, the scent, and so on.

   c. After a minute or two, acknowledge that you have this time for yourself.

d. Repeat this exercise at least once every day.

2. Open your journal and use the prompts below. Here is where you start promising yourself.

   a. *Today, I will practice...*

   b. *Today, I am...*

   c. *I am thankful for...*

Checklist

1. You can opt to set alarms at random times as a reminder to consciously set intentions based on the promises you made using the given prompts.

2. Don't be too hard on yourself when you find yourself over-worrying or stressing out. Breathe and open your journal to remind you of your journey.

3. If you need inspiration on how to create your self-promises, you may check the web.

Ch 3: A New Theory of Trauma

Summary

Christine diagnosed herself as a self-help addict. She had read all the books and attended all the seminars and workshops worldwide but nothing changed. Her main issue was a physical matter – her immense hatred for her belly – which started in her early teens. Because of this, she tried to observe her food intake. To her surprise, she could not remember anything she ate for the day. She couldn't even pinpoint its taste or texture.

In medical terms, Christine coped with dissociation. It happens when a person disconnects from the environment because of a stressor. This is most common with adults who are suffering from unresolved childhood trauma. During their sessions, Christine opened up about the sexual abuse she suffered that started when she was just nine years old. Apart from that, her mother used to make fun of her and even urged her siblings to join in.

Because of the trauma she faced and not having anyone to confide in, she endured the pain alone. When the sexual abuse occurred, she learned to separate herself from the event – shutting everything down. This conditioning was retained until she reached adulthood. She could not remember her food intake because it is directly related to the part of her body that she hated.

By definition, trauma is the aftereffect of a tragic experience or event. A crisis like this is powerful enough to completely change a person's life. The Centers for Disease Control and Prevention established the Adverse Childhood Experiences (ACEs) test. According to research, the higher your score on this test, the higher the odds of unfavorable life events such as acquiring chronic diseases or a higher probability of substance abuse.

Although it can be helpful, the ACEs framework fails to see the whole picture. It does not account for the range of spiritual and emotional traumas. If you take the ACEs test and get a low score, you might gaslight yourself into thinking that you're not traumatized, just like Dr. LePera when she only scored 1 out of 10. There are a lot of people that can't identify a single traumatic moment (or events) that drastically changed their lives. It's not always an obvious situation.

You are most vulnerable and reliant during childhood which is why it's vital to have a strong guide from your parent-figure. A healthy parental relationship gives a child security and lets them live freely. A child needs to make mistakes and decisions for them to develop self-trust. It doesn't reassure them that they won't get to feel all the negative feelings such as grief, pain, anger, etc. but it helps them to prepare for these negatives in the future.

However, if a parent-figure has unresolved internal conflicts, they are not in good shape to take care of themselves and their children. Unfortunately, projection is quite typical for parent-figures with unresolved traumas, making their children the unknowing recipients. Everyone who knows a kid can confirm that children love copying others' actions, behaviors, etc. This is why it makes projection to children more dangerous because it's already the beginning of conditioning.

Dr. LePera used to think that she had a perfect childhood and it was not because of some childish idealization. This was taught to her, ingrained in her memories and feelings. She grew up with her needs denied and she carried this habit onto adulthood. She overachieved to cope with her unresolved trauma, which she didn't even know existed.

The first step of your healing journey is to identify your wounds – your trauma. Below are the six archetypes of childhood trauma. Keep in mind that you don't need to fit into just one type. You may relate to more than one of them and that's okay.

Archetype 1: Having a parent-figure deny your reality

Most of the time, children are comfortable opening up to their parents about something that made them sad or uncomfortable. But when the parent-figures gaslight them into thinking that they've got it wrong, it crushes their intuition. You are unknowingly teaching a child to reject their "gut feeling," which greatly affects their self-trust.

Archetype 2: Having a parent-figure who does not listen to or see you

One of the human's deepest needs is to be acknowledged, so what could happen when a child grows up ignored? It may come off as severe neglect or a subtle act of not seeing a child's passion or talent. Once a child grows up not being *seen* or *heard*, he or she could find it hard to trust their intuitive needs and reject them completely.

Archetype 3: Having a parent-figure who projects their life through you

Stage parents often fall under this category. Although some genuinely mean well, some push their children to live their dreams for them. Children who grew up with this kind of set-up often become perfectionists because of fear of disappointing their parent-figures. It would be difficult for them to be truly happy because they weren't given the chance to explore their likes and dislikes, as their parents dictated their lives.

Archetype 4: Having a parent-figure disrespect your boundaries

Children establish their boundaries clearly but some parents rarely give them importance. One of the most common incidents is parent-figures reading their children's journals which could lead to the child thinking that it's okay to give up boundaries when it comes to love or they could go the opposite way and keep secrets to themselves.

Archetype 5: Having a parent-figure who hyperfocus on physical attributes

You can see this archetype in parents who obsessively comment about their children's weight or manner of dressing – all for the sake of their kids looking flawless 100% of the time. The child could take this as an act of love, therefore live by the idea that love depends on someone's physical appearance. It's also unhealthy if the parent-figure shows different and opposite personalities within the home and in public as it wrongly teaches the child that it's acceptable to have *pseudoselves* – also known as *pretend selves.*

Archetype 6: Having a parent-figure fail to regulate their feelings

Some parent-figures, as most adults, find it difficult to sit in their emotions. It's sadly common to look for some kind of distraction rather than face it. Half of them may project their emotions inward, like some sort of withdrawal while the other half may direct them outward, making them highly volatile toward others. Children can bring this behavior toward adulthood which means they'd be living in the extremities of their emotions and have no in-between space.

According to two revolutionary psychologists, coping is an approach that must be learned to handle deep turmoil in the mind and body. Humans cope differently – that's a known fact.

But there are actually two categories of coping strategies: adaptive and maladaptive.

When you're the type of person who faces your problems and issues head-on, you're using the adaptive coping strategy. This type requires a ton of effort from the doer as it needs you to be active and conscious. It's difficult to master when you're not properly taught or guided.

On the other hand, maladaptive strategies of coping are those you acquire from your parent-figures, depending on which archetype you fall under. These are negative ones – drinking excessively, avoiding emotional reactions, etc. But the most commonly reported are dissociation, extreme rage or anger, and people-pleasing.

All humans have baggage – unresolved traumas. What differs is how each one deal with them. Resilience is taught at an early age, this is conditioned to children so if your parent-figures failed to do so, you will cope as how you know. This is why you must deal with your issues face-to-face moving forward. The first step toward healing is acknowledging the baggage you're carrying and you start from there.

<u>Lessons</u>

1. Dissociation is another coping mechanism where a person disconnects from their environment while the traumatic incident is happening.

2. A person's childhood years are vital because this is when a child is most vulnerable and adaptive. Regardless of whether it's a negative or positive environment, the child will absorb everything.

3. Adaptive coping strategies are those techniques where a person faces problems and issues face-to-face while maladaptive coping strategies are those inherited techniques that are often negative.

Issues Surrounding the Subject Matter

1. How do you describe your traumas? How do you deal with them?

2. How would you describe your childhood? What adjectives would you use and why?

3. Which coping strategy are you more familiar with? Why do you think you're prone to turning to this type of technique?

Goals

1. Identify what category your coping mechanisms fall under.

2. Establish what archetype(s) resonate with your childhood the most.

3. Identify and acknowledge your childhood wounds..

Action Steps

1. Prepare your journal and list down the different prompts to help you narrow down the possible archetypes to which your childhood trauma belongs.

    a. Archetype 1: Having a parent-figure deny your reality
        i. Remember if your parent used to give invalidating responses when you share your input or idea about a subject.
        ii. Use this prompt: *As a child, when my parent-figure(s), ___, I felt___.*

    b. Archetype 2: Having a parent-figure who does not listen to or see you
        i. Remember if your parent-figure(s) are too busy to acknowledge you.
        ii. Use this prompt: *As a child, when my parent-figure(s), ___, I felt___.*

    c. Archetype 3: Having a parent-figure who projects their life through you
        i. Think back if you received comments or messages that didn't describe you or rather, described a family member.

ii. Use this prompt: *As a child, I received the messages about myself:* (List them down)

d. Archetype 4: Having a parent-figure disrespect your boundaries
   i. Think back if your boundaries were crossed by your parents, like reading your journal, etc.
   ii. Answer this prompt: *Do you feel safe enough to say "no"? How would your parents react?*

e. Archetype 5: Having a parent-figure who hyperfocus on physical attributes
   i. Remember if you used to receive comments about your appearance as a child.
   ii. Answer this prompt: *What are the common messages you had about your appearance?*

f. Archetype 6: Having a parent-figure fail to regulate their feelings
   i. Think back to how your parent-figures express their emotions.
   ii. Answer this prompt: *Do they usually shout or give the silent treatment? Do they name-call or blame when mad?*

Checklist

1. In answering prompts, allow yourself to explain and dig deeper rather than provide straightforward responses.

2. Be honest with yourself and view your childhood from a distance, without judgment.

3. You may resonate with more than one archetype and that's okay. There's no wrong or right answer.

Ch 4: Trauma Body

Summary

Dr. LePera experienced various symptoms of dysregulation over the years. She suffered from dissociation, anxiety, random headaches, occasional brain fog, and constipation. Not knowing any better then, she attempted to have them treated as separate entities – just fixing the symptoms but not the problem as a whole. She even experienced fainting a few times in public. She knew something was wrong with her nervous system but only acknowledged it when it was her body giving up.

Based on the ACEs test, it is proven that there's a higher chance to acquire psychological and physical diseases when you experienced childhood trauma. The main cause? Stress – which is, unfortunately, the general state of people with unresolved problems. But, stress is not just a mental state, rather, it also threatens homeostasis which covers the emotional, mental, and physical condition.

As you encounter a threat, either imagined or real, your brain's amygdala will be activated. Then, it will send signals to the rest of your body as a sign of attack which will push the body to a fight-or-flight mode. This is what happens when you're stressed.

Stress can be categorized into two: normative and chronic. The first type, normative stress, is what a person normally experiences in a lifetime including birth, job-related issues, marriage, breakups, and death. The human body can develop a robust response to counter these stressors and allow the affected person to return to his or her baseline.

On the other hand, chronic stress is one everyone wants to avoid because it is persistent and constantly present. When you're under chronic stress, your body cannot return to its normal state. It continuously sends inflammatory signals 24/7 which eventually weakens – or worse, diminishes – your body's capacity to respond to real dangers like illnesses or diseases.

Stress can easily affect all of the systems in your body which is why you may feel like you can't eat or digest food properly when you're anxious or stressed. This could lead to diarrhea or IBS (irritable bowel syndrome). Unfortunately, once your digestive system fails to function smoothly, the rest of your body will feel the impact and get sicker.

The vagus nerve, also called the *polyvagal*, connects the gut and the brain. Its sensory fibers branch throughout the major organs of your body from the brain stem. When your body is in a homeostatic balance, the vagus nerve serves as a *neutral break* which allows your body to be calm and sociable. But if the polyvagal is activated, it becomes defensive and it will manifest through fight-or-flight responses.

The autonomic nervous system, responsible for a body's stress response, assures that the body's resources are distributed appropriately. When your body reads a situation as safe, the parasympathetic nervous system activates and prompts the body to relax. When this happens, you can be your genuine self – free, happy, and peaceful. You are in your *social engagement* mode.

On the flip side, when the autonomic nervous system detects a threat, the sympathetic system activates. This is the polar opposite of the parasympathetic. In this state, your body is also hyperaware. It activates your stress responses and causes you to either fight or flee. The most known patterns are listed as follows:

- Struggling to create meaningful relationships with other people
- Having little to no emotional resilience
- Difficulty doing high-level cognitive acts such as planning
- Having trouble focusing

Sadly, you cannot willingly control your fight-or-flight responses. This is an involuntary, automatic response of your body. There is no one to blame, especially not yourself. The same way goes with the third, least known, stress response. It is medically termed *immobilization* or in simpler terms, freezing.

The vague nerve has two different passageways. The first one consists of both social engagement and social activation. But when the other passageway is activated, your body freezes. It shuts down. This happens once your body feels like it can't survive. A therapist named Justin Senseri provided this illustration: "If you see a bear and your mobilization mode is activated, your body pushes you to either run or fight. But once the bear is on top of you, your body could surrender and act dead."

Freezing is what happens during dissociation mode. Those who enter this state psychologically escape their bodies. This also explains why some can't remember their traumatic experiences.

To understand this concept further, imagine that you are at a party that you are overly prepared for. You took your time choosing your outfit, fixing your hair, and even practicing what you'd say to your peers. But because you're already under chronic stress, the moment you enter the party, you feel as if everyone is looking and laughing at you. As this happens, there are three possible scenarios:

- You will argue with everyone. (fight)
- You will leave the venue. (flight)
- Or, your body will shut down. (freeze)

The truth is, human connection is a basic need. As they say, "no man is an island." However, if your nervous system is dysregulated because of unresolved trauma, you will struggle in connecting with other people. This will keep you trapped and unfulfilled as you have no means of satisfying your basic need. But why does this happen? Why are adults with unresolved childhood trauma prone to repeating the same mistakes and reliving the same trauma?

There is a concept called co-regulation, which explains how sometimes a person or an environment transfers its emotion onto you. As you've learned by now, you are conditioned by your parent-figures during your childhood years. If you grew up in a calm environment, your body system will internalize and mirror this. However, if you grew up in a chaotic home, your body's version of normalcy is disengagement, overreaction, and rage. This will also make it difficult for you to return to your safe *social engagement* mode.

When you are used to a negative environment, your body and mind become conditioned to the trauma response associated with those experiences and it solidifies the pathways of your brain. In simpler terms, your brain will *long* for those feelings – regardless if they are good for you or not. This is how you get emotionally addicted.

When you encounter a strong emotion, your body's immobilization or activation mode is triggered. These states are supposed to be uncomfortable but for those who are stuck in an emotional addiction loop, this rush makes you feel good. With other addictions, such as to sex or drugs, your body would eventually seek a higher dosage to satisfy its needs. The same goes with emotional addiction; which is why your subconscious would lead you to situations like toxic relationships, social media fights, and the like.

Everyone needs to comprehend why and how the nervous system dysregulates because it leads to a realization that this is simply out of conscious control. These behaviors are merely automatic responses that were ingrained in your mind because of your traumatic experiences and lack of co-regulation.

In the following pages, Dr. LePera shares several tools that are also included in the workbook portions of each chapter. You will learn how to use the vagus nerve in a way that will help you, rather than do you harm.

Lessons

1. Nervous system dysregulation is a terminology used to call symptoms that originated from repetitive activation or expanded stress periods.

2. There are two types of stress: normative and chronic. Normative stress includes those normally experienced in a lifetime–birth, death, breakups, etc. Meanwhile, chronic stress includes those lasting traumatic issues that are persistent.

3. Co-regulation is an event where a person or an environment transfers emotion onto you.

Issues Surrounding the Subject Matter

1. When faced with a sudden, stressful situation, what do you usually do–freeze, fight, or flee? Describe a recent event.

2. Do you have personal experiences with co-regulation? How did it happen?

3. Do you believe you're suffering from chronic stress? Why?

Goals

1. Identify how quickly your body can return to its normal state of balance.

2. Determine what activity allows your body to return to its homeostatic state.

3. Understand how your nervous system works and how it affects how your stress responses.

Action Steps

1. Observe yourself. When a person faces a stressful situation, his body will face it head-on then it will go

back to its baseline homeostatic balance. If your body cannot return to its balance, then you may experience different symptoms.(see the symptoms below in the Checklist segment) Do this weekly.

2. Try to restore balance to your nervous system by following any of the practices below. Take down notes of how you felt before, during, and after each practice you tried.

    a. Look for a smell, visual aspect, or taste in your environment. Focus all your senses on that matter.

    b. You can do a visual meditation. Close your eyes, breathe deeply, then imagine a white light. Assure yourself that you're at peace and secure. Do this three times a day.

    c. Be with nature. Go outside and engage with the natural environment. Reset your body.

Checklist

1. Be objective as you observe yourself. You need to ensure that you can capture the real and honest reactions of your body without prejudice.

2. Use this list as a guide of the different symptoms that you can use in Action Step #1.

    a. Psychological and emotional symptoms: guilt, fear, self-blame, numbness, wanting to be invisible

    b. Physical symptoms: insomnia, migraines, digestion issues, muscle aches or tensions, exhaustion.

    c. Social symptoms: avoidant relationship patterns, no boundaries, or overly strict boundaries

Ch 5: Mind-Body Healing Practices

Summary

When you start to understand the basic aspects of the polyvagal theory and your nervous system, you can finally start addressing your problems and push your shame away. Just like Dr. LePera, the behaviors, and habits you have were learned responses that helped keep you alive. As you've learned, the human body can learn and mimic dysregulated coping methods. On the bright side, it can also unlearn these ways and learn a new, healthy path toward recovery. You can use your body's power to heal your mind and vice versa.

Ally, one of Dr. LePera's clients, was suffering from multiple sclerosis and eventually realized that she had negative responses to the new medication that was given to her. She started her self-healing journey by keeping little commitments to herself and trusting herself to see her own trauma responses. She recalled how she was bullied during her childhood. She listened to her body's reaction to the sadness and fear and sat with her emotions without judgment.

For the healing to start, you need to listen to your intuition and let your body lead you to what it needs. For Ally, it led her to music. From singing to playing instruments such as the violin and guitar, and even writing her music compositions. In addition, she also tried yoga which helped her body relax. Most importantly, she gave the needed attention to her nutrition. She didn't know it at that time but every change she made helped in returning her body to its ideal balance.

The key to self-healing is to understand your body and learn how to utilize what your body needs and reconnect with your true *Self*. This starts with acknowledging that even though the responses of our nervous system are automated, there are methods to boost your vagal tone and manage how you respond to stress. To achieve this without intervention, you must find out how to stimulate the parts of your autonomic system that is within your control.

There are two methods of healing: top-down and bottom-up. Top-down processes are those methods that require your brain to direct your body toward healing while bottom-up processes are those where you need to utilize your body's power to influence your mind. But both of these practices work effectively. In these processes, you stimulate, test, and shape your vagus nerve in a controlled and protected environment, you can ultimately develop resilience. This is fundamental in the journey toward self-healing.

First, you must listen to your body's nutritional needs. According to research and Dr. LePera's experience with her clients, this necessity is often left unsatisfied. Most people eat as an obligation or as a habit and sometimes depend on their feelings. About 500 million neurons travel in the gut-brain axis, which is one of the pathways where information is exchanged between the mind and body. The vagus nerve is part of the messenger group that sends signals from the gut to the brain and vice versa.

Your stomach also houses the enteric nervous system (ENS) which is a network of nerve cells. These said cells communicate with the rest of your body – sending signals and chemicals. The ENS receives the information from the gut microbiome which makes neurotransmitters, as the food you eat breaks down, that send messages to your brain. This eradicates the previous notion that only the brain creates neurochemicals.

Further, the dysregulation of the gut and nervous systems affects your digestive process negatively which also impairs your body's ability to absorb properly. As this happens, your body will be incessantly deprived to the point that you will always feel hungry, regardless of how bountiful your diet is. And once you have a problematic eating habit, everything else will get worse. You could develop a condition called gut dysbiosis, wherein your internal system favors viruses and bacteria. According to studies, this can cause diseases identified as *mental illnesses.*

One way to better your gut health is to eat whole foods that are rich in nutrients. Each meal is going to be a chance for better nourishment and healing. Another popular approach is to follow intermittent fasting. Based on studies, planned intervals or fasts give the body a healthy break which gradually improves its systemic processing. But be careful, this isn't advisable for those who suffer from eating disorders.

Once you've catered to your nutritious needs, you need to shift your focus to your sleeping patterns. It is extremely dangerous to have inadequate sleep, especially for children. As you sleep, your body is automatically in its self-repair mode which is highly beneficial for all your bodily organs and systems.

If you're having trouble sleeping, you need to push your parasympathetic system into relaxation. Alcohol and caffeine are both the greatest barriers to getting a restful sleep. According to Dr. LePera, it's best to limit coffee intake before noon and alcohol three hours before your bedtime. It's also important to have a consistent routine to cool down your body right before your target sleeping time.

As you've learned by now, your body's autonomic nervous system is in charge of involuntary, automatic behavior and habits. On the flip side, there is a body system that is still partly within your control – the respiratory system. You can deepen and slow down your breathing which leads to your heart rate decreasing and your mind settling down.

The art of *breathwork* exercises your autonomic nervous system, Dr. LePera described the activity as doing planks for the vagus nerve. Once you use your breath to tame your arousal system, it's like you're telling your brain that you're in a safe and calm environment. This message will be shared with your other bodily systems. This is also an example of a bottom-up process.

Take *The Iceman* Wim Hof as an example. He pushed his breathing to its limits and won a Guinness World Record for swimming under ice, taking more than an hour of an ice bath, and running a marathon barefoot and shirtless above the Arctic Circle. To get to this level, he practiced by inhaling through his nose, exhaling through his mouth, and holding his breath. This technique engages your lungs and expands them, widening their capabilities in breathing.

Now, think back to Jessica from Chapter 2. Remember how she tried yoga and reaped its benefits? According to Dr. Stephen Porges, author of Polyvagal Theory, activities, where your body and mind are linked in a healthy place, allow your body to expand your stress tolerance.

Physical exercise has a number of benefits. It decreases the chances of acquiring dementia and cardiovascular diseases. It could even slow down your aging, deepen your sleep, and improve your overall mood. You need to understand your body and mind and harness their joined power by challenging your limits. You will develop resilience as your vagus nerve reads that you can withstand stress.

As you work your way from eating properly, sleeping enough, learning breathing techniques, and doing physical exercises, you might wonder, what's next? The next (and last) one discussed by Dr. LePera is undoubtedly the hardest. As adults, very few do things out of joy – just doing something for the sake of doing. One way to achieve happiness is through play.

A popular playtime activity for adults is singing. This activity stimulates your vagus nerve, among other things. Remember that the polyvagal connects to your muscles including your vocal cords and larynx. When you're safe and sound, your voice simply sounds different. You can hear an expanded range of tones.

You see, your body is truly amazing. By now, you should accept that you are *not* meant to be sick just because of your genes. Anything can change, even your destiny. Understand that human cells are capable of adapting to their environment. In doing these practices above along with the following tools to be taught, you can push yourself to the limit and widen your window of resilience.

Lessons

1. You can utilize your body's natural resources as tools for your self-healing journey.

2. Bottom-up practices are those healing methods where you use your body to heal your brain; meanwhile, top-down is the reverse of it where you use your mind to heal your body.

3. You need to heal your body by doing the following: eating properly, sleeping enough, practicing breathing and physical exercises, and being truly happy.

Issues Surrounding the Subject Matter

1. How often do you eat food that is good for your body? Why is it important to have a healthy relationship with food?

2. Do you struggle to sleep enough? Why does sleep affect your daily activities and overall mood?

3. Why is it difficult for adults to be genuinely happy?

Goals

1. Unlearn the dysregulated coping techniques you were used to doing.

2. Learn the different methods of top-down and bottom-up self-healing.

3. Understand how to properly take care of your body and mind as a whole.

Action Steps

1. Practice the breathwork technique that Dr. LePera usually uses.

a. Do this activity on an empty stomach (nighttime or morning).
b. You may choose to lie down or sit comfortably.
c. Take a deep from the lowest portion of your stomach.
d. Then when you feel like you can't take more air, hold your breath for 2 to 3 seconds.
e. Exhale slowly without any force then repeat about ten times.

2. As you practice the breathwork technique above, use the below journal prompts (bolded statements to remind yourself of your intention.)
a. **Today, I will be practicing** deep belly breathwork that calms my body and gives me peace and safety.
b. **I am thankful** for the chance to develop a technique to regulate my body
c. **Today, I feel** grounded and calm.

3. Pursue your happiness. Search the web, ask your trusted friends or family, or revisit old activities you used to enjoy. Do something for yourself.

Checklist

1. In doing things that make you happy or have fun, remember to stay away from any possible triggers that would pull you back to your conditioned patterns.

2. There will be days that you don't feel like doing the breathwork routine. Forgive yourself when you miss a session or two, but try again for the next time.

3. In terms of monitoring your sleep and nutrition, you may also include trackers in your journal.

Ch 6: The Power of Belief

Summary

People tell *stories* to themselves in order to live, like a way to protect themselves from the truth. Children do the same since they're not mature enough to understand that their parent-figures have lives outside of what they know. For example, if your mother raises your hand at you, you think that it's because you did something *bad* instead of thinking that maybe she has problems controlling her anger.

You tell these narratives, also called *core beliefs*, about yourselves, your past, your future, your relationship, and everything else – all based on your experiences. Dr. LePera believed that she was unwanted, and not *considered* by everyone else, especially her partners, because that's what she felt from her mother during her childhood.

Beliefs are not learned overnight; they are developed over the years, made up of different thought patterns. The more you think of something, the more you are likely to believe it – your practiced thought becomes your truth. Core beliefs are those that are consistently validated, which is why it becomes your perception of your identity. It usually comes from your home, community, parent-figures, and other childhood experiences. Sadly, most of these are affected by trauma.

When a core belief is established, you experience a *confirmation of bias*. To understand this concept, take Jane for example. She grew up with the core belief that she is *not worthy*. One day, at her job where she was recently promoted, she was called out for a minor error she made in her report. It wasn't even a scolding; it was just merely a supervisor telling her that she missed something and should double-check next time. But to Jane, it wasn't as *simple* as that. She immediately thought, "*Of course, I screwed up, I'm not worthy of this new position.*"

This bias is ingrained in your brain, and just like your autonomic nervous system, this is out of your control. A lot is happening in your mind and the world around you. The reticular activating system (RAS) is in charge of filtering your subconscious by using your beliefs to identify what information should be prioritized to align them with your practiced thoughts.

The RAS filter is also used by the brain as a form of defense. Dr. LePera has met people that truly believe their childhood is all sunshine and rainbows and they ignore the possibility of hardships. There is no perfect childhood in real life. To acknowledge this is essential for you to deal with your unresolved trauma that stems back to your childhood.

Childhood innocence is the core of your authentic *Self*, Dr. LePera refers to this as the *soul*. At this stage, you haven't established your core beliefs yet. It's where you are continuously learning and are receptive to the people and environment around you. Around this time, your neurons communicate with one another through brain waves which makes you who you are – your emotions, thoughts, behaviors, and movements.

As you are born, your neural pathways are hyperactive as it tries to understand the strange and unfamiliar world. Further, this is influenced by your immediate and macro environment. In this period of intense need, the presence or lack of comfort and safety leaves long-term effects on your mind, body, and soul.

The absence of parent-figures will lead to a child's hunger physically and emotionally. As a child, you have one main objective: to receive love. This will satisfy a child's need for security, nutrition, and care. When all of these are given by your parent-figure, your brain is in its best state to develop.

Your parent-figures are also your models in learning how to connect with other people, navigate your environment, and cope with stress. This is your earliest experience with co-regulation. If your child self wasn't taught this regulation, you will get stuck in a flight/fight/freeze mode, which makes your child brain suffer. Below, you will understand how this works in every stage of childhood.

From conception to age 2

The infant's brain is in its slowest brain wave cycle but with the highest amplitudes. This is called the *delta* state. Although critical thinking is not yet possible, the brain is acting like a sponge, absorbing everything it can.

Ages 2 to 4

There will be some development and the brain waves will gradually switch into the theta state. This is the same state wherein adults enter hypnosis. But for children, this is the time they focus internally. In this stage, the children cannot comprehend or view anyone else's perspectives but their own.

This is also where the child enters their egocentric stage. In childhood, *egocentrism* is where your brain fails to grasp the difference between yourself and a different person. You *literally* cannot see that there's a perspective other than what you think is true.

Around ages 5 to 7

Your analytical mind becomes activated. Although there will be still struggles in identifying what's perceived and real, this is the stage where children can form rational thoughts and understand the concept of cause and effect.

Around ages 7 and above

This is followed by the child's brain entering the beta state. It is the fastest brain wave with the lowest amplitude. You become more engaged, critical, and logical with your thoughts. This is where you're progressing slowly to an adult mind. However, during this part, you have already garnered your core beliefs and absorbed the subconscious conditioning that you will carry on into adulthood.

Eventually, as the brain develops more, the needs also become more specific and complex. This is not just about physical and emotional, but also spiritual. Dr. LePera listed three needs to have a *whole* soul:

1. To be listened to

2. To be visible

3. To freely express your true Self

When these are not met, a person can develop a core belief that they are not worthy of these needs. They could lead to overcompensating by exaggerating some parts of themselves that are appreciated by other people and denying themselves the basic needs that were not given to them before.

Apart from your parent-figures, your core beliefs are also affected by a broad environment. The educational system is a good example as it mostly focuses on a one-way method of teaching that pressures the student to be at the *top* to be validated and recognized. Then, there are these peers who judge everything: your style, interests, behavior, etc. When you've internalized the belief that you are everything that they say you are, your RAS will look for proof that will confirm this belief.

You already know that beliefs do not form in one night, which means they cannot be corrected this quickly, too. You need to work it out to truly change how you perceive yourself. You must meet and acknowledge your inner child and learn which is your most authentic *self*.

Lessons

1. Beliefs are thoughts that you constantly practice. Meanwhile, core beliefs are those that have been conditioned to you since childhood.

2. The core of your authentic *Self* is your childhood innocence. From infancy to age 7, a child absorbs everything around them – good or bad.

3. Emotion regulation should be taught to children but if not, they will most likely get stuck in fight/flight/freeze modes as adults when responding to trauma.

Issues surrounding the subject matter

1. How do you see yourself? What are your thoughts about your person?

2. How do your daily experiences attribute to your self-beliefs?

3. Why is it important to control your beliefs?

Goals

1. Establish your existing Beliefs Inventory by identifying your daily thoughts.

2. Eradicate the negative beliefs you have about yourself.

3. Create new, positive beliefs about your person.

Action Steps

1. Reflect on your daily thoughts (which are also your beliefs). This will be your *Beliefs Inventory*. Use the prompt below.
    a. *While I observe my thoughts today, I noticed the following:*
    b. *About myself:*
    c. *About my experiences:*
    d. *About my present:*
    e. *About my future:*
    f. *About other people or my relations:*

2. Based on the inventory you created, identify what you want to change. Then, think of its positive opposite and write it as your new belief.
    a. *Old belief:*
    b. *New belief:*

Checklist

1. Beliefs are just practiced thoughts. It's okay if you don't know what your beliefs are. Just focus on what you're thinking.

2. Use your new belief as your daily reminder or life mantra. It will allow you to practice the thought until it eradicates your negative belief.

3. Accept the fact that you will struggle in practicing your new belief and that is normal. But don't stop repeating it as you will slowly believe it at your pace.

Ch 7: Meet Your Inner Child

Summary

Anthony, Dr. LePera's client, was branded an outcast; the *black sheep* of a Catholic family. He grew up with rigid lessons of what's right and wrong, specifically the *sins* that could guarantee him a path to Hell. He always felt like he was *inherently* bad. It started when he was sexually abused by another boy, who was also abused in his home. Anthony blamed his *badness* as the cause of the abuse.

Then, it was further validated when his father became emotionally, verbally, and physically abusive when drunk. In an attempt to escape the maltreatment, he began hanging out with older neighborhood boys. Sadly, one of these boys started abusing him sexually, again. Anthony was made to believe that *he* was "asking for it" and that he had fun in their encounters.

With his intuition, he knew it was wrong so he tried telling a family member but instead, he was dismissed and blamed. While this was happening, he was sent to a relative due to the escalation of his father's abuse. This led to Anthony secretly drinking as well. At some point, he showed an obsession with sex, collecting all kinds of pornographic materials. Although he isolated himself, he still attended Church where sex was taught as something *sinful*. This, again, validated the wrongness Anthony felt about himself.

When he was given the chance to move away for college, he took it as a hope to begin anew, without addressing his childhood trauma. When he reached adulthood and began working, you wouldn't notice anything different about him. He was a successful stockbroker on Wall Street. But then, he still suffered from the same issues. He usually engages in meaningless and physically aggressive consensual sex with women he met online.

The stress of leading a double life (one of which was hidden from anyone else) got to him and he suffered a breakdown. He was losing hope of *normalcy*, claiming he was *unfixable*. When he finally got around to addressing his inner conflicts, he met with a supportive trauma therapist, and for the first time in his life, he talked about everything. But the pain did not end in acknowledging its presence. It was then, he knew, it was time to reconcile with his inner child.

Before you can grasp the concept of meeting your *inner child*, it's important to gain insight into your earliest attachment bonds as a child. Your relationship with your parent-figures is the foundation of the adult relationships you have (or had). Mary Ainsworth, a psychologist, outlined four attachment styles that show in the infant's first eighteen months.

Secure

Infants who have a *secure* attachment style may cry and get upset when the mother leaves their sight but these infants will overcome it immediately. This is seen in infants whose mother figures have created a stable environment wherein he is free to interact and explore.

Anxious-resistant

Infants with this attachment style are visibly distressed and stressed as their mothers leave the room. As she re-enters their sights, they aren't immediately comforted and would remain clingy. They might even throw a tantrum as punishment for their mother leaving them.

Avoidant

Avoidants do show little to no response to their mother leaving and returning. These children do not look for their mother's comfort, and would even blatantly avoid them. This reaction, or the lack thereof, stemmed from a disconnected parent-figure that lets the children do everything on their own, even dealing with their emotions at a really early age.

Disorganized-disoriented

Those who fall under this style are confusing and unpredictable. They either show no reaction at all or on the other hand, show extreme signs of distress. This is the rarest among the four identified attachment styles. This is a product of the children who suffered from severe neglect and abuse. Because they were used to immense unpredictability, their body does not know how to properly react.

The examples above just involve the direct parents, but in recent studies, the attachment theory goes beyond a child's parent-figures as it already included the whole family unit. It's also important to note that failure to establish a *secure* attachment style would lead to difficulty in forming adult relationships with everyone else. Although not keen on labels, Dr. LePera emphasizes the importance of your attachment style since this will help you in identifying the culprit of your trauma.

Dr. LePera read the work of John Bradshaw who was also a therapist. He spent his hours talking about the inner child in people who suffer from substance abuse. Coupled with her extensive research and Bradshaw's work, Dr. LePera realized that each human has a childlike part. This part is liberated, always wondering, awe-inspired, and most importantly, truly connected with the person's genuine *Self.* But when not given enough attention, this childlike part also acts out selfishly. Unresolved *inner child* wounds are carried to adulthood.

To further dive deeper into the concept of the inner child, Dr. LePera presented a list of archetypes that describe common personalities that emerged from childhood. You may resonate with more than one archetype.

- The <u>caretakers</u> develop their self-worth by neglecting their needs and focusing on prioritizing others and their needs.
- Achievement and success drive the <u>overachiever</u>. Validation is needed to cope with low self-worth.
- In contrast to the previous one, the <u>underachiever</u> believes that the only way to receive love is to keep themselves small and invisible.
- <u>Rescuers/protectors</u> fiercely try to save everyone else from their *weaknesses*. They see other people as weak, dependent, and helpless and constantly need him.
- Those famous people who seem to be like the <u>life of the party</u> are not showing their true colors. They ensure that everyone else around them is happy because it's the only way to receive love.
- The <u>yes-person</u> completely lives for other people because they think they need to be selfless to receive love.
- Growing up with a caregiver who is flawless, a child might become the <u>hero worshipper</u>. They can't decide on their own and need someone else, a superior one, to follow around.

Creating childhood fantasies is one way of defending oneself against unsatisfied childhood needs. One common example is imagining one of your idols coming to save you from your home. Nancy, one of Dr. Lepera's SelfHealer online community members, shared how she imagined her favorite band doing this for her and the satisfying feeling she would feel. As she grew older, she dropped the band but placed her ex-boyfriends and crushes in this role. Of course, none of them lived up to her fantasy and she'd end up where she started. Don't get it wrong: daydreaming is *not* entirely bad but *what* you imagine is what matters.

The first step in starting your *inner child* work is to acknowledge that your inner child is within you and undeniably present even in your adulthood. Even if you have little to no memories of your childhood, there are still ways to access your inner child. Then, the second step is to accept that your inner child was hurt–and still hurting. Doing so allows you to eradicate shame, disappointment, and self-blame.

What is your goal? Remember that in doing this, you're not about to solve everything that is wrong in your life. You just need to learn from your inner child. When someone criticizes you, how does your inner child react? When someone laughs at you, what does your inner child say? Listen to what your inner child is trying to tell you. Recognize its hardships, struggles, and experience and give it credit.

Going back to Anthony, he felt as if he was not worthy of love, that he was just *bad*. He coped using the ways he knew, not really helping his inner child. He realized that among his vices, he also practiced another way of coping: silence. He never spoke about what happened to him. This meant that his inner child never got the chance to be heard. Now that he understands the concept of *inner child* work, he lets his inner child and every other part of him *speak the truth*–breaking the cycle of shame and unproductive coping practices.

Lessons

1. There are four attachment styles: secure, anxious-resistant, avoidant, and disorganized-disoriented. These four describe the different ways how a person expresses and seeks love.

2. There are <u>seven</u> archetypes of the inner child. These archetypes describe how you manifest your childhood in your adult personality.

3. Creating and hoping for childhood fantasies is another way of coping mechanism that allows the person to play pretend rather than deal with his/her problems.

Issues surrounding the subject matter

1. What attachment style do you relate to the most? Why do you think so?

2. How does your family's treatment of you when you were a child influence your adult attachment style?

3. What do you feel toward your inner child? Before reading to the next activities, what would you want to say to her/him?

Goals

1. Access your inner child.

2. Understand your attachment style.

3. Learn from the reactions and emotions of your inner child.

Action Steps

1. Based on the inner child archetypes above, choose one that resonates the most with you. You may relate to more but you need to choose one first and then, you can revisit the other archetypes one at a time.

2. Open your journal and write a letter to your inner child (depending on the archetype you've chosen). For example: *"Dear Little Caretaker Nicole..."*

3. Check-in with your inner child multiple times a day. Let *little you* feel acknowledged and heard.

Checklist

1. You might struggle in choosing just one archetype. You can select the one which is most frequently activated. Or simply, use your instinct.

2. Be kind to your inner child. He/She is not at fault; they were just affected by the environment they grew up in.

3. If you wish to take up a guided inner child meditation, you may reach out to the nearest (and trusted) expert in your area.

Ch 8: Ego Stories

For some reason, Dr. LePera was always triggered by a pile of dirty dishes and silverware in the sink. Sometimes she'd burst and throw a fit (fight mode) or turn into a one-liner expert (freeze mode). Regardless, it always ended up with a fight against her partner. It may sound weird to others, especially if viewed without context, but for Dr. LePera, this is an *ego* story.

You see, one's ego is defensive and strong because it is protecting the *inner child's* emotions. Ego beliefs are also ingrained in your brain over the years which is why it's difficult to fight them back. In Dr. Lepera's experience, the fact that her partner left unwashed dishes in the sink meant that her partner is not *considering* her. This is Dr. LePera's core belief as a child: her mother did not consider her. So, this act is a direct validation of that belief which is why her ego would defend her in ways that she knew how – fighting or freezing.

The ego only believes in itself. In reality, what Dr. LePera thought is not really the case. The dishes weren't there *because* of her. But just like core beliefs, when you listen to your ego, you start to identify it as the truth. Another example is if you pull yourself out for the candidates for a job promotion because you want to avoid the possibility of rejection. This can happen if you were constantly rejected as a child.

The ego always acts like a bodyguard, hostile and defensive to threats. Below are some ways in which the ego can manifest:

- False bravado (over-confidence or narcissism)
- Black-and-white thinking (just right or wrong–no in between)
- Extreme emotional response
- Highly competitive (other's success is your loss)

When there's a fusion of your thoughts, opinions, selfhood, and opinions, these manifestations show. It will feel like other people's comments are all directly about you and not a distinct topic you're talking about. An opinion against something you love could rile you up and it would make you feel like you're being attacked by the other person. In simpler words, everything is personal to you.

As children, you were taught that you should be acceptable to everyone; this became a survival mechanism. You push away your true personality, your true identity for the sake of societal acceptance. When you continue to push away your true *Self* because of shame, you will most likely project the same emotions toward others. This is why people have ego stories.

The *ego work* starts with introducing yourself to your ego. In this step, your goal is to separate your *ego* as a different entity– not you. You need to observe it with no judgment, just witness its presence. The next step is to initiate a safe encounter with your ego. This process aims to push you out of your comfort patterns. Without knowing your ego, you kept on doing the same behavior and thinking the same thoughts. Now, you are going to create new patterns, healthy ones.

The third step is to establish a name for your ego. Silly as it may seem, doing so allows you to completely differentiate yourself from it. Dr. LePera calls hers *Jessica*. At times when she is about to throw a fit because something triggered her, she'd say "Jessica is making a scene again." Finally, the last step is to meet your activated ego. By now, you should acknowledge that you are *not* just your ego stories. This means that whenever your ego gets triggered by something or someone, you need to practice stopping before reacting. That way, you can think of a more appropriate response to this trigger.

When you begin to develop your attentional controls and try *self-witnessing*, you need to master observing your habits and behaviors objectively. Your *shadow self* is made up of "unpleasant" parts of yourself. Your ego fights to keep your shadow self hidden from the public eye, no matter the cost.

Once the ego is left alone in full control, the human mind avoids, dismisses, represses, or puts down everything. When you understand how to view yourself with honesty and compassion, you can take control of the wheel.

After Dr. LePera realized the connection of the dishes to her *inner child* wounds and understood how her ego created a story to protect her, it allowed her to see the dishes as they are. In a space of a few years, she now enjoys washing dishes. Even if she can see her ego pissed, she tells herself, *You are considered*. To further strengthen her journey, she created a fun ritual about dishes that made her happy.

The important goal of ego work is to develop your inner consciousness and acceptance of your ego. You need to make your choices every day to face it, just like how Dr. LePera chose to face and do the dishes. However, *ego work* cannot be used in oppressed environments. As an alternative, you may empower yourselves and the people around you with survival tools you will learn along the way.

Lessons

1. A human's ego is defensive and strong because its role is to protect the wounded inner child.

2. The ego's personality is conditioned over the years, but most especially during childhood.

3. Your ego and your *genuine* identity are separate and different.

Issues surrounding the subject matter

1. How does your ego manifest itself? What situation triggers it?

2. What is your ego protecting you from? Why do you think so?

3. How are you going to face your ego and shadow self?

Goals

1. Meet your shadow self.

2. Differentiate your ego's identity from your *true Self.*

3. Develop inner consciousness and acceptance of your ego.

Action Steps

1. Take time out of your day to reflect to meet your shadow self.

2. Use the following prompts below to engage with your shadow, and ask yourself the following questions.
    a. *When I'm jealous, what do I think I lack that the other person has?*
    b. *How often do you advise others?*
    c. *How do you speak about yourself?*
    d. *How do you speak about other people when they're not present?*

3. Follow the *ego work* discussed in the chapter summary above.
    a. Acknowledge that your ego has a separate identity from you.
    b. Initiate a safe meeting with your ego.
    c. Create a name for your ego.

Checklist

1. The conditioned responses of your shadow self are not learned overnight; therefore cannot be unlearned easily – and that's okay.

2. As you start doing this ego work, you will be more conscious about its presence and work. Allow yourself to be objective when you observe its works and behaviors.

3. Recall your ego's name when it starts acting up; it allows you (and the people around you) to establish the differences.

Ch 9: Trauma Bonds

Summary

Dr. LePera recalled that in her growing years, she was always *bored* and would look for something *exciting*–the cortisol roller coaster. In the romantic relationships she had in adulthood, she looked for that same level of stress. She'd act withdrawn from her partners and would later panic if they were starting to be distant.

One of her ex-girlfriends, Sara, gave her the *high* she was looking for. At some point in their relationship, Dr. LePera felt that Sara was cheating with a mutual friend. Sara dismissed this and told her that she was being *paranoid.* Dr. LePera accepted Sara's words as if it was her reality because this is what she was used to as a child. Then, one day, she found out that her suspicions were true. More than the fact that she was being cheated on, Dr. LePera felt frustrated that she let someone else ruin her reality.

This proves that attachment theory does not end in childhood. Researchers Dr. Phillip Shaver and Dr. Cindy Hazan proved that the attachment styles you received during early infancy to childhood serve as your foundation in adult romantic relationships. If you had supportive bonds in childhood, you are most likely to have the same in adulthood. Likewise, if you experienced abusive or distant bonds as a child, you will also seek the same *comfort* as an adult.

Trauma bonds, originated by Dr. Patrick Carnes, are problematic relationships where both people have unstable attachment styles. In this bond, your *neurochemical* expressions manifest. As with the other concepts you've learned, trauma bonds also stem from your childhood. You were conditioned into this when you were young and you reiterate the same behavior, actions, and emotions as you reach adulthood. But this isn't just visible in your romantic relationships, it can also show in your familial, peer, and professional relations.

Here are some usual indicators you will see in *trauma bonds*:

1. In certain relationships, you are unaware of your needs or you're aware of them but they aren't met by the other party (or parties) in your relationship.
2. You are obsessively drawn to relationships that you know will end up in problematic situations.
3. Due to the lack of self-trust, you're letting the other person decide your worth for you based on their perspective, fully ignoring your authentic *Self*.

If you're stuck in a trauma bond, you would do anything to stay in it. You engage in self-betrayal acts because you truly believe it's the only way you can receive *love*. It is an addiction. You equate genuine connection with physical and mental activation because this is what you were used to. When your mother gave you attention as a child because you were misbehaving, you could be intentionally acting out just to be noticed.

The stress you feel in an unhealthy relationship is coming from thinking that *you know better*. Regardless of the red flags and collective warnings from your family and friends, your highly powerful subconscious won't allow you to depart from the trauma bond. Though understandable, there is no reason for you to feel shame to be stuck in this kind of situation. *Trauma bonding* is not something you can easily part with. You need to *do the work* and give dedication, and time.

Similar to the other tools introduced in this workbook, the first step in doing the work to break your trauma bonds is through self-witnessing. You will have to go through the checklist below that is interconnected with the parent-guide archetypes from chapter 3. In doing so, remember that you are not required to fit into just one archetype. But it will help you identify which of these you truly resonate the most with.

Archetype 1: Having a parent-figure deny your reality

As a child:

- Your thoughts, feelings, and experiences were not validated by your parent-figures.

As an adult:

- You don't acknowledge your needs (or are not fully aware of them).
- You rely on other people to make decisions for you, including your needs.
- You blame everyone else for the choices that you make.

Archetype 2: Having a parent-figure who does not listen to or see you

As a child:

- You were neglected by your parent-figure.
- You believed that you had to hide your true *Self* to be loved.

As an adult:

- You pick partners with loud personalities; those people who are at the center of attention.
- As a result, you hate your partner for the same reasons that you were attracted to them–their *bi* personalities.

Archetype 3: Having a parent-figure who projects their life through you

As a child:

- Your parent-figures indirectly or directly told you their preferences for you (and did not ask you what you truly want).

As an adult:

- You depend heavily on external guidance to give you feedback or opinion on every decision you make.
- You feel the need to talk to one or more people to understand what you're going through.

Archetype 4: Having a parent-figure disrespect your boundaries

As a child:

- Your parent-figures go beyond boundaries by telling you to do things you're not comfortable with. (Example: being polite to an adult you don't feel safe with)

As an adult:

- You revoke your need to cater to everyone else's priorities.
- You ignore your boundaries or limits, letting other people walk over you.
- You don't understand why you're being taken advantage of (even if it's because you're the one letting them do so).

Archetype 5: Having a parent-figure who hyperfocus on physical attributes

As a child:

- Your parent-figures obsessively comment about your physicality–clothing, weight, hairstyle, etc.

As an adult:

- You constantly compare yourself to other people, especially with physical attributes.
- You are overly focused on how you present yourself in public, and even go to lengths to hide your true Self.

Archetype 6: Having a parent-figure fail to regulate their feelings

As a child:

- Your parent-figures often withdraw or explode when they feel something because they don't know how to deal with their emotions properly.

As an adult:

- You lack emotional resilience and adaptive coping techniques.
- You may handle your emotions by detaching from the world.

- You distract yourself with physical matters–
  substances, social media, etc. because you don't
  want to *feel* your emotions.

In going through the archetypes presented above, your main
objective is to understand what happened to you before, how it
affected you, and how are you coping in your current adult
relationships.

Dr. LePera and her current partner, Lolly, founded their
relationship with trauma bonding. The former decided to date
casually again after her divorce and was drawn to Lolly's
confidence and self-assurance. However, Lolly also had some
unresolved childhood trauma. This resulted in her having an
anxious attachment style–she was scared that Dr. LePera
would stay, but at the same time, also scared that she would
leave.

Lolly lived in extremities. One day, she's loving and overly
caring while the next, she's detached and withdrawn. This
behavior activated Dr. LePera's trauma responses in return. It
was a constant back and forth. But over time, with their joined
desire to grow together and individually, they made the
conscious decision to *do the work* together.

They both did journaling, worked out together, maintained
morning routines, changed their nutrition, and committed to
doing the work. But this does not mean that their relationship
is perfect–because there's honestly no such thing. As Dr.
LePera said, true love is not always a feel-good situation. There

will still be boredom, unsettlement, fear, and other negative emotions. But the key to succeeding and becoming happy together is to be consistent in working on yourself and be dedicated to changing for the better.

Lessons

1. Trauma bonds are problematic relationships where both people have unstable attachment styles that lead to recurring patterns.

2. It is difficult to end a trauma bond because it is rooted in what you were used to as a child.

3. Attachment theory is not just applicable to children, but rather it is carried on to adulthood.

Issues Surrounding the Subject Matter

1. How will you know if you're trauma bonding with someone?

2. Why is it difficult to leave someone when you know the relationship is no longer serving either party's best interests?

3. How did your relationship with your current (or most recent) partner begin?

Goals

1. Understand how your past experiences with your parents affected your adult relationships and coping mechanisms.

2. Acknowledge that there are wrongs in your relationships that need to be addressed and corrected.

Action Steps

1. Revisit the archetypes pertaining to your parent-figures which are also discussed in the above chapter summary.

2. Answer the <u>checklist</u> provided below and select those where you related with the most. Again, as with the other archetypes, it may be more than one. But for now, just choose the topmost.

3. List down what you've chosen in your journal. Based on what you know about the archetypes, answer the prompt below which shows the similarities of your adult experiences to your childhood traumas.

    Today when [insert the triggering situation], I felt _____ and I reacted by _____

Checklist

1. If you need more explanation on the archetypes, you may check the summary of chapter 3.

2. Use the prompt presented above for each archetype you related to so you can reflect on them one by one.

Ch 10: Boundaries

Summary

Dr. LePera said it was particularly interesting to introduce *boundaries*. She has clients who were so new to its concept that they would most likely reject the studies revolving around it. One of these clients is Susan who approached the doctor because she noticed her difficulty in connecting with other people. Susan, however, kept on insisting that she had a very healthy childhood, a close-knit familial bond, and stable parents – a picture-perfect family.

But as Susan practiced self-witnessing deeper, she realized that her over-admiration of her mother was, somehow, a facade. When she left their family home, Susan's mother kept calling her multiple times a day and would make her feel guilty for not answering the calls. She would also visit Susan's house unannounced. This behavior revealed some similar instances in her childhood. Susan shared that her mother would enter her room and read her private journals. Though she knew it was wrong, she did not complain about it back then.

In adulthood, she was her friends' *emotional sponge*, especially one of her friends in particular. This friend took advantage of her and vented to her about her problems at any time of the day. Susan, on the other hand, couldn't bring herself to reject the call as she would instantly feel shame and guilt.

When you grew up in an environment where you can't express your thoughts distinctly, you are prone to *groupthink*. You wouldn't have developed the initiative to set boundaries and *think* for yourself as you would always depend on someone else doing it for you. This dynamic is called *enmeshment* where there is no concept of separation. This is also a *trauma bond* that you will carry on until adulthood, as seen in Susan.

In a beautiful irony, genuine intimacy includes not just reciprocal sharing but also the establishment of healthy boundaries. By implementing these boundaries, you will learn that you have a space where you can express your genuine *Self*. You need to understand that boundaries are essential because they protect *you*.

These *walls* you build keep you away from undesirable, unacceptable, inappropriate, or inauthentic situations. Inside these walls, you're liberated to truly express what you feel, think, and do what you must. If you never established boundaries as a child, you probably struggle with saying "*no*" as an adult. As a result, you apologize repeatedly and overexplain.

One thing that must be re-evaluated is the concept of *niceness*. It's somehow a widely known notion that when you're being nice, you will be loved, liked, approved, and accepted. With that, you continue to say "*yes*" to everyone else. However, this should not be the case. Having boundaries is not being *not nice*, rather it's about setting clear limits, knowing what you want, and learning how to communicate these properly.

Boundaries, however, are not the same for everyone. While some struggle to establish them, some set up highly *strict* boundaries that are almost impossible to satisfy. With that, Dr. LePera shared a diagnostic tool below that can help you identify where your boundaries fall under:

- <u>Rigid</u> - struggles to ask for help; few intimate relationships; afraid of rejection; overly private
- <u>Loose</u> - cannot say "no"; oversharer of private information; highly affected by others' opinions; constant people-pleaser
- <u>Flexible</u> - self-aware; good communicator of needs; know when to say "no"; ability to regulate own emotions

While identifying your boundary, you also need to understand that you need to set these for *yourself*. It's not about providing a guideline for other people's behavior around you. As said early in this chapter, boundaries protect you. It should give you a space where you can appropriately communicate and express your needs. To properly do so, you need to set three types of boundaries.

Physical Boundary

When you have rigid physical boundaries, you are most likely denying yourself your needs and sexual desires as repression. On the other hand, if you have loose physical boundaries, you might be overly concerned with your physical attributes and you're highly affected by other people's perspectives on your appearance.

This includes keeping a clear boundary of what you are comfortable talking about or not (such as your sexuality, etc.) This also pertains to your physical needs – sleep, nutrition, and movement, to name a few.

Resource Boundary

When you have loose resource boundaries, you act like Susan, always available to everyone who "needs" you. On the other hand, if you have rigid resource boundaries (for time, for example), you only participate in *scheduled* activities and refuse to adjust your schedule even when it's needed.

Lack of flexibility in setting boundaries isn't helpful because if you're too rigid, you are confined in a certain space that won't allow you to be truly you. While if you're too loose, you let everyone else walk over you.

Emotional or Mental Boundary

In having too-rigid emotional or mental boundaries, you are only believing in your beliefs and ideas–refusing to listen to other people's perspectives. With that, you pull yourself away completely separate and distant from the people around you. On the other hand, if you have loose emotional or mental boundaries, you are always participating in groupthink and failing to have personal worldviews.

With flexible emotional or mental boundaries, you're able to create a safe place for your emotions while letting others enjoy their boundaries at the same time. You're not required to please everyone else.

You might wonder what are the manifestations of having little to no boundaries as children. Two behaviors commonly shown in adulthood are emotional oversharing and emotional dumping. These usually happen because of experiences you had with intrusive parent-figures who wanted to know everything about you.

Emotional oversharing is where a person tends to talk endlessly, sharing meaningful and meaningless ideas. This is automatic and cannot be controlled by the speaker which is why it is often followed by a feeling of shame. On the other hand, emotional dumping happens when a person *dumps* her emotional issues onto another person, without having regard for the listener's emotional state.

Now that you've learned a lot about the types, kinds, and effects of having and lacking boundaries, it's time to do the work. Of course, as always, you need to start by defining your boundaries. You need to step back and observe your life and notice where the limits are lacking. Then, spend some time nit-picking over your relationships with other people. Identify where your boundaries are most commonly crossed.

As you've identified which parts of your life lack boundaries, it's time to set them and communicate them properly. When you start making the changes, it's important to provide clarity to the persons involved. Ensure to let them know your reason without overexplaining it. Focus on using objective language and stating clear facts. Good communication also entails appropriate timing. Learn to read the room and only initiate communication when both (or all) parties are emotionally ready.

Last, but definitely not least, you need to learn to maintain your new boundaries. This is the difficult part because it requires consistency and determination. You need to be careful that you're not constantly defending your boundaries to other people, especially yourself. It's a good time to remind oneself that boundaries are there for you, to protect your peace. There is no going back.

Lessons

1. Boundaries are important as they provide you space to meet your needs while respecting others' needs, as well.

2. The lack of boundaries could cause you to be exhausted – physically, emotionally, mentally, and resourcefully.

3. There are three descriptive types of boundaries: rigid, loose, and flexible.

Issues Surrounding the Subject Matter

1. How do you feel when the topic of boundaries is brought up? Can you relate to it or not? Why?

2. How would you describe your boundaries using the descriptive types above? Why?

3. Can you relate to either emotional oversharing or emotional dumping? How so?

Goals

1. Understand the importance of boundaries and the effect of having too less or too much of them.

2. Define your existing boundaries (or the lack thereof).

3. Establish new, healthy boundaries to meet your needs.

Action Steps

1. Define your physical, emotional/mental, and resource boundaries.
   a. Observe which of these boundaries are usually crossed by other people. If you can't identify one, that's okay – there are those who haven't set up their boundaries yet.
   b. Use the prompts presented and do one for each type of boundary.

   My physical or emotional/mental or resource self feels unsafe or uncomfortable when _____.

   To create a safe space for my physical or emotional/mental or resource self, I _____.

2. Set your new boundaries and communicate them to the people around you that need to be informed. You may reuse or rephrase the sample paragraph below.

   I will start making changes so that [intention for new boundary] and hope you can understand. I imagine this is difficult for you. When you [the person's problematic behavior], I feel [how you feel]. If this happens again, I will [describe how you will react differently to meet your need].

3. Maintain the boundaries you've set. Be consistent and firm in your decisions.

Checklist

1. Setting and maintaining boundaries is the most difficult part of the self-healing journey. You will find yourself wanting to return to old patterns and behaviors and that's normal.

2. Continue to do the work even when it gets difficult. You need to make space to be heard, seen, and truly known.

Ch 11: Reparenting

Summary

In contrast to pop culture, *awakenings* don't happen in an instant and they're not at all *pretty*. Though these differ from person to person, they have three similar elements: they happen in natural set-ups; they connect to people in spiritual practice; and they are born from inner turmoil. Being *conscious* of your *subconscious* is uncomfortable.

When Dr. LePera was in the middle of her spiritual transformation, she felt lonely as she pulled away from most of the people in her life. But what she learned is that she needed to fully comprehend her needs (physical, spiritual, and emotional) before she can create genuine relationships with other people.

If you had supportive parent-figures, you're most likely comfortable with expressing your needs and reaching out for help when needed. But if you were raised by emotionally immature parent-figures, you might have a hard time communicating your needs which would manifest in tantrums and defensive or selfish acts.

Reparenting is the process where you take the position of becoming the wise parent that you needed as a child. It will help you relearn how to meet your unsatisfied needs in childhood. In this part, you are responsible for teaching yourselves and guiding yourselves in the learning and unlearning process.

Though each reparenting process varies per individual, the general challenge is to silence your inner critic from disturbing the process and to move forward with compassion and self-trust. You need to ask yourself, "What should I do for myself today?" To help you understand this better, Dr. Lepera listed the common pillars for reparenting.

Pillar 1: Emotional regulation

You need to learn how to correctly navigate your different emotional states. This was first introduced in the book when you learned about the nervous system. One way to do this is through breathwork: deep belly breathing in regulating your trauma responses and self-witnessing your body's sensations.

Pillar 2: Discipline

Loving discipline is about setting boundaries for yourself and following through with them. You need to make small (or big, it's up to you) promises that you intend to do daily. This is the reverse action of self-betrayal because, in this step, you do the work and actively participate in it.

Commit to one thing that you have to do on a daily basis. But in thinking of a promise, keep in mind that it should be a loving act–not too rigid. You're also allowed to take a day off once your habits are confidently on track.

Pillar 3: Self-care

The third pillar goes hand-in-hand with self-discipline. But in this part, you will need to truly support your needs and value. You need to commit to an act where you are caring for your emotional and physical needs. Dr. LePera suggested that the best example of self-care is establishing a good sleeping pattern.

Pillar 4: Rediscover the inner child wonder

If you can't remember what was discussed about childlike wonder, it's about doing something for the sake of happiness in doing the act. If you grew up in a home where you're constantly taught what should (and should not) be done, you might've lived in a rigid behavior, removing all opportunities for play.

As an adult, you need to learn how to do things that bring you true joy, not just the secondary benefits (adoration, success, or money). You can listen to your favorite playlist, watch your favorite movie, sing, or dance.

It may not show in the pillars presented above, but reparenting is difficult and consistent work. As with everything else you've learned, this doesn't succeed overnight. Along the way, you will have some fallouts. You will have external judgers (your parents, peers, etc.) and you will face your biggest critic: your inner self. It's also possible to experience loneliness, as Dr. LePera did. But do understand that it is part of the reparenting process. The key is to continue and be firm in what you are striving to achieve. In the end, carry the belief that you will get to where you want and that shall become your reality.

Lessons

1. Awakenings are not how they show in movies. Real awakenings are brutal and oftentimes, hurtful.

2. Reparenting is a process of self-healing where a person takes up the role of a wise adult to meet the needs of his/her inner child.

3. There are four pillars of reparenting: emotional regulation, discipline, self-care, and rediscovering the inner child wonder.

Issues Surrounding the Subject Matter

1. How did you view awakenings before? Why do you think awakenings bring both pain and solace?

2. What are the challenges you're going to face as you try to become a wise adult parent-figure in your life? Why?

3. How are you going to start with your reparenting work?

Goals

1. Understand the true concept of reparenting.

2. Identify which pillar(s) of reparenting you need to act upon.

3. Establish and deliver your reparenting menu.

Action Steps

1. Open your journal and refer to the four pillars of reparenting as you create your reparenting menu.

2. In this activity, you only need to ask yourself one thing, "What do I need the most right now?"

3. In your journal, create a list of the things you want to give yourself in honor of the pillar you've chosen.

Checklist

1. Here are some examples of the things you can give yourself, depending on the pillar of reparenting you're taking.
   a. Emotional regulation
      i. Practice deep belly breathing
      ii. Express genuine emotional responses without judgment

b. Discipline
    i. Keep small promises to yourself every day
    ii. Saying "no" when you need to

c. Self-care
    i. Journaling
    ii. Sleeping earlier

d. Inner child wonder
    i. Singing or dancing
    ii. Learn a new hobby

2. You can choose to follow the list above or simply use it as an inspiration for what to include in your journal. Should there be any activity that calls out to you, feel free to write it down.

Ch 12: Emotional Maturity

Summary

Age and emotional maturity don't necessarily go hand-in-hand together. Some children are more emotionally mature than their parent-figures. Emotionally immature people often struggle to tolerate their emotions and react in such extremes – lashing out or detaching, no in-betweens. Children who grew up with emotionally immature parent-figures reported feeling a sense of loneliness or emptiness.

Years of conditioned living and unmet psychological, physical, spiritual, and emotional needs would lead to disconnection from your true *Self*. Once you start healing yourself, removing yourself from the problematic situation that you grew up in, you would most likely have a sense of *survivor's guilt*. However, if you can see that your loved ones are not aligned with the changes you need to make, it's best to accept it than fight them over and over again.

Emotional maturity comes with accepting all your emotions – the good and the bad. The goal of this concept is to be aware of your emotions and learn how to regulate them. You see, the body *naturally wants* to return to its homeostatic balance within 90 seconds after experiencing a stressful event. However, some people struggle with keeping emotions as physiological reactions and escalate them mentally. In this case, a 90-second reaction lasts up to days, months, or years.

On the flip side, you can also use the conscious mind's power to create a positive alternative. Dr. LePera had reconnected with her body, she finally identified the difference between stress and excitement. When applicable and appropriate, she transforms her anxious feelings into feelings of excitement.

Apart from labeling your emotions, you also need to learn how to return to your body's homeostatic balance within the littlest time possible. As stress and trauma are both parts of everyone's lives, your only option is to control how you react to them. One method of doing so is soothing, however, most soothing techniques were developed as a child. The goal here is to develop *proactive* soothing, not falling into the same coping mechanisms you learned as a child.

As an example, Dr. LePera shared how doing activities that are *relaxing* puts her on edge more, such as taking a long, nice bath or reading a good book. Meanwhile, when she's doing the opposite, like taking a walk, running, doing dishes, or any other activity that requires body movement, it releases her stress. The secret here is to find more than one *soothing activity* that allows you to do the same.

It's also important to honor the emotions that you feel. Do not dismiss them but rather, listen to them and acknowledge them without judgment. But when you start to develop emotional tolerance, you will also learn that your body only has limited resources. This means that you will feel tired along the way and might fall back into your coping mechanisms. You need to understand your limits and ensure that you're not pushing yourself way too much.

You already have ideas about how to reparent your inner child, but how about parenting your own children? As you learn how to improve your emotional maturity, you can also do the same for them. Ironically, you can only do this if you exert enough energy and time to ensure that you are well taken care of. Once you provide the needed attention, love, and care that you need, harness the wonders of your nervous system, meet your true *Self*, and practice emotional regulation, your child can embody these through co-regulation.

One thing you also have to accept is that you can't predict nor control your children's future. At some point in their lives, they will encounter problems that you can't help with. You need to teach them how to endure stress on their own. This way, your children will grow up to be adults who are well-equipped in handling whatever life throws at them to the best that they can.

When you get caught up in stressful instances that drain your body's resources, it challenges your emotional maturity. Dr. LePera suggested that self-accountability check-ins are effective in these cases. When you strengthen your knowledge about self-accountability, you will also build up your self-confidence. Most importantly, you're giving yourself space for the inevitable failure. But, because you are self-assured, you know that you can stand right back up.

Self-empowerment should be your main objective. When you do, you make the best decisions for yourself even if the world is constantly changing around you. You need to understand that achieving emotional maturity is as simple as checking off your bucket list. This doesn't happen in a snap, but it is developed over time with consistent work and self-forgiveness.

Lessons

1. Emotional maturity is not defined by age. It is about how an individual regulates their emotion.

2. The key to acquiring emotional maturity is to understand how your body returns to its balance with as little time as possible.

3. There are activities you may do to balance your body, however, it differs from person to person.

Issues Surrounding the Subject Matter

1. How would you rate your parent-figures emotional maturity? Why?

2. How would you rate your emotional maturity? Explain.

3. Why is difficult to regulate emotions? What emotions do you struggle in dealing with?

Goals

1. Create or rebuild the connection you have with your emotions.

2. Establish a go-to routine that allows your body to return to balance.

3. Understand emotional maturity and emotional regulation and their impact on your self-healing progress.

Action Steps

1. Free up your schedule every morning. It would be best to do the next step before breakfast.

2. Practice a body connection meditation.
   a. You may sit or lie down. Take a moment before taking a deep belly breath.
   b. Exhale slowly and feel the changes in your body as you take in and breathe out air.
   c. Think about one part of your body and feel all the emotions on this certain part. Start with your head and go down slowly up to your toes.

3. Write down in your journal how you felt before and after your meditation. Try to take notes as much as you can so you can see your journey.

Checklist

1. In returning your body to balance, you may use the following soothing activities: self-massage, moving, and writing.

2. Apart from soothing activities, you can also opt to do enduring activities such as engaging in breathwork, grounding yourself, and resting.

3. Do not pressure your body into returning it to balance. This will only agitate you more and would lead to undesirable results.

Ch 13: Interdependence

Summary

As you reach this last chapter, you might think that you've
finally reached the finish line. For this workbook, that may be
true. But for your self-healing journey, there is *no* finish line.
You see, being emotionally mature is a never-ending process of
acceptance and self-awareness. And as you grow, you will face
some challenges along the way.

Dr. LePera admitted that when she wrote the chapter of her
last book, she was also tested as she saw a stranger heavily
criticizing her work online. She hated being misunderstood so
she moped as a response. That day was a special one because
there was an event at Venice Beach. Her partner, Lolly, wanted
them to come together and watch as the waves aligned with
the bioluminescence neon produced by evening algae.

Due to her mood, Dr. LePera insisted on staying behind and so
Lolly went without her. Although this was mutually agreed
upon, Dr. LePera found herself angry that she was alone in
their house. An internal dialogue of self-pity started and for a
while, she let her inner child go through these emotions. Then,
she lifted her head and applied the tools that were discussed in
this workbook.

She started with breathwork. Once she had regulated her breathing, she followed it by self-witnessing and labeling her emotions. She listed agitation, disappointment, outrage, and so on. After doing so, she stopped to ask herself what should she do to cope with her emotions. In the previous chapter, she mentioned that she needed to create movement with her body to calm down. So at that moment, she decided to wash the dishes. While she was enjoying herself, she also realized that she wanted to be with her partner, looking at the ocean, and enjoying the moment – and that's exactly what she did next.

As she sat there beside the person she loved the most, she knew that it was not just a moment of emotional maturity but something greater. It was about how she reacted emotionally in presence of others. This is the most significant goal of *doing the work*: to create a genuine sense of togetherness.

Dr. LePera shared that the fundamental part of her healing was finding her *SelfHealer* community; it was the ultimate objective of her interdependent *Self*. When she had to make the conscious decision of cutting people who weren't beneficial to her life, she felt like it was just her and Lolly. For a while, it was what she needed. But eventually, her intuition pushed her to invite new people – the right ones – and be part of a greater world.

In 2018, *The Holistic Psychologist* was born on Instagram when Dr. LePera shared her story with the rest of the world. She received an abundant response in an instant. Lots of people related to her journey and craved a positive human connection. As more people joined her community, her confidence also grew.

For a time, Dr. LePera assumed the role of a teacher and imparted her knowledge with her newly-founded online community of *SelfHealers*. People from all over the world also shared the practices and tools that worked for them. The accumulated knowledge is reflected in the community's growth. Dr. LePera felt like she had found *her people, voice, mission, and true purpose.*

Humans come from a tribal culture with ancestors living with groups for several reasons: division of labor, safety, and mutual support. As mentioned in one of the earlier chapters, connection is a human need. Moreover, research had proved that loneliness can increase the chances of developing chronic illnesses and other autoimmune diseases. Unfortunately, the same can be said with *ambivalent* relationships, which are relationships that were formed in trauma bonding.

It's not enough to just connect with other people. You need to be around supportive people and have healthy friendships, partnerships, and community to have a happy, long life. *Interdependence* is a two-way street of *real connection*. To achieve this, you must be whole and authentic to *yourself.* This is the only way you can feel a sense of connection with your people.

It has been discussed in multiple chapters of this workbook that infants enter the world as sponges – absorbing everything around them. As you grow up and learn ways to survive and engage with the world, you learn about who you truly are and how you define yourself in relation to others. When you're on your self-healing journey, you need to reform the connection to your *genuine Self* that you once have as an infant.

It is normal that you may think it's impossible to return to such a state of vulnerability. Perhaps, a lot of you refuse to accept that this is the only way because of your sensitive ego. When you feel like this, it means that your body does not feel secure enough to understand the human's need for interconnectedness or the *collective "we."* Once you've learned how to manage your body states, it will allow you to fully appreciate the similarities that you have with the people you love and your community.

The moment you maximize this positive collective mindset, it will create an altruistic bond. *Altruism* is the direct opposite of egoism and this is what kept traditional tribes strong. When each individual can properly express their uniqueness, the greater whole's needs are easier met because everyone is productive and contributing. If today's modern societies do the same, they are also destined for more incredible things.

As discussed in the past chapters, co-regulation can occur when one person feels safe enough to share it with the rest of the people around him or her. It means if you feel safe, other people can feel the same, too. You need to express your true emotions without fear of being judged or misunderstood. When you continue to cultivate supportive relations while consciously engaging with your internal world, everyone else benefits.

Once you can successfully break down barriers, you become responsive to creating connection with matters that surpass human comprehension. The only way to do so is to keep your mind clear and appreciate the greatness of the world and its people. As you continue *doing the work* of healing your mind, soul, and body, you also welcome transcendence in its multiple forms. When you reveal your true *Self*, your awakenings will manifest. The best part? You're not just healing yourself. <u>You're healing the world around you.</u>

<u>Lessons</u>

1. Emotional maturity is a never-ending process of self-acceptance and self-awareness.

2. The ultimate goal of self-healing is interdependence.

3. You need to create healthy bonds with your people.

<u>Issues Surrounding the Subject Matter</u>

1. Do your comfortably set clear boundaries in relationships? Or do you need to identify them first and set new ones? Why?

2. Are you able to self-witness your ego and how it works separately? How?

3. Do you clearly state/show the intention of your actions? How?

Goals

1. Understand what work you need to accomplish to be ready enough to influence good emotions and positive energy in other people.

2. Create or be part of a loving, supporting community.

3. Heal yourself and heal the world with your influence.

Action Steps

1. Gauge your interdependence (or the lack thereof). Answer the following questions in the Issues section above. Write them down in your journal.

2. Based on your answers, identify which areas you want to improve. Create a list of promises you intend to keep for this activity.

3. In creating interdependence, you may follow the below guides:

a. *Today, I will practice establishing interdependence in my relations.*

b. *I am thankful that I can create more meaningful relationships.*

c. *Today, I've expressed my true self and connection with others.*

Checklist

1. Progress is not linear. You will have ups and downs along the way which is why you need to be kind to yourself throughout the process.

2. Looking for your *people* will be tough but when you find them, remember to always assess the relationship. If it does not serve you, you can either heal the bond or leave it.

3. In doing daily work, you may find the following reminders useful:
   a. For your body – Remember to eat healthily, have enough sleep, and practice physical exercise.

   b. For your mind – Continue to self-witness and be non-judgmental of your trauma responses as you try to unlearn them. Build a happy relationship with your inner child.

c. For your soul – Reestablish the connection you have with your deepest passions, wants, and needs. Express your ***true Self***

Epilogue

When Dr. Nicole LePera was writing the book, *How To Do The Work*, she struggled since she was still trapped in the remnants of her early childhood trauma which resulted in her not remembering much. What bothered her the most was that she could not remember this certain quote that caught her attention – this was the quote that made her research more on consciousness. Regardless how deep in research she got, she just couldn't remember it.

At this time, *The Holistic Psychologist* was growing more and more – its audience reaching the wide world. Then, the pandemic happened. Like many people during those trying years, Dr. LePera found herself unmotivated and she even stopped cooking. One night, she was with Lolly and another trusted member of her team, they decided to get pizza on Postmates. This time, they randomly selected a pizza shop that they had never encountered before, just relying on the previous buyers' reviews.

Eventually, the pizza was delivered to them. Dr. Lepera immediately noticed the cute lettering on one side of the pizza box and she could not believe it. It read:

"We don't remember days, we remember moments."

Cesare Pavese

It was the quote she was looking for. Out of the different pizza stores and the billions of famous quotations in the world, how could she think it was not some sign? It brought back her memories, all the challenges she faced as she started her self-healing journey. It was a manifestation of how far she had come.

Though she can't confidently say that this pizza box directly pushed her to the right path, she admitted that it brought her to make a conscious decision. It was to reach out to her family. In the past chapters, it was highlighted how she had cut off everyone from her family to heal her *inner child* wounds. It was in her interdependence state that she realized she still had to make the effort of reaching out, no matter how scary and difficult it may seem.

This started out with a letter where she wrote that she was willing to reconnect only if they (her family) was also ready and willing to work together. Although hesitant, her family agreed to try again. At some point, her sister started her self-healing journey, too. Then, Dr. LePera can finally communicate with her mother *without* feeling like it's her responsibility. She called her mother just because she wanted to, and she said it felt amazing.

You see, you are a powerful being and you can control your world using your energy and thoughts. There may be matters that are out of your hand but you can choose how to react to them. You can change your perspective about yourself and the world as you know it. You are fully capable of accessing your *true Self.*

You don't hold the future – that's a fact. But you have all the tools you need within you and this workbook as a guide. As long as you keep *doing the work*, you will achieve what you're aiming for.

May you be well and happy.

Made in the USA
Columbia, SC
28 February 2020

Terzetto is a work of fiction, formed or conceived by the imagination. Names, characters, places and incidents either are the product of the author's imagination or used fictitiously. Any resemblance to actual persons, living or deceased, events, or locales is entirely coincidental.

Table of Contents

If I didn't get paid to ride the rails you'd still see me on board as if I were. Checking cars for passengers who didn't like the idea of paying my salary, and dispensing valuable advice. I am paid for the first service by the railway company. The second by any customers who actually take my suggestion.

I hold nothing against those who searched for and found a free ride. It is within their right to do so. As it is in mine to get them off of the train by any means. I was once one of them. Perhaps there is still a bit of that old self somewhere deep down. I don't pay to ride the train either.

I was not an easy hire. The position didn't exist before me even. Sure, various members of the train's crew would patrol when they had time, but their success rates with lightening the load were dismal. I didn't respect their authority then. Because of those past run ins, don't respect it now. It's nice to see their Monday morning manner, all made up with curtain face, waiting on the simplest question so they can start the show. I knew a different side of them. A more emotional, less rational side. One where smugness became frustration. I am proud to say that none of my now colleagues ever hurt me during my mischief making.

I welcomed newcomers to the train hopping life style. As many as possible. I needed to know they were in it for the long haul. Many of my predictions were correct. The times I was wrong weren't so many that I could face accusations of guesswork. Through my guidance, a trail was blazed and a train hopping syndicate formed. We exchanged information about tactics the rail crew was trying. We sifted through scouts' reports once reunited. Knowledge and experiences were passed on to the greenhorns. Veterans, such as myself, Cole and Bonnie, would discuss theory.

Cole and Bonnie are nicknames I've given to protect identities. They could have just as easily been Bonnie and Cole. I can write about my own experiences, having been absolved by my employer for any and/or all of my past

recriminations. The big boss says charges won't be pressed against the nameless. I'd still prefer to use nicknames.

Cole, Bonnie and I all started rail riding for different reasons. Bonnie and I admired Cole's resilience to get as many free rides as possible. We had enough money to buy a ticket but chose not to. He chose to not have money. He came from a working class family working towards poverty. When he realized he could get by on less money than the rest of his family, he decided to do so and never looked back. Why work all day to barely scrape by when you can work on how long you can go without. If it were possible to work a job yet still focus enough attention inward to bypass physical limitations, he may have tried it. Starved but with no decrease in output. He's the creative one in our group. One foot on the train and the other jumping the platform.

Bonnie has a way with words. She hardly needs to use them, but in doing so is twice beheld. A politician's daughter, she could pluck a civilian off the street and have them believing they should be the one in office. When I first met her I felt an immediate connection. It was only after knowing her for some time that I found it to have only been one way. A chameleon relies on trust. Once Bonnie began to trust me I knew the real connection was forged. If I followed her example, I could also have nice words said about me after first impressions. It's something in the eyes. I think it's supposed to be involuntary. Bonnie has control.

I came into the world as green as the grass on the other side. Which is what I say to convince myself that the fight still needs fighting. Ask anyone on the street where it is they think a boxcar loiterer is going and see if they can give a clear answer. It was an even harder question for the loiterer. Most of us would say it was about the destination and not the journey. If we didn't arrive at the destination the journey would mean nothing. Our bucket list was ever expanding.

A scout had given the name of a small station he had visited which was very far off. Even further back is the time when he had. This station had a state of the art

communication system. The information passed by word of mouth and when it got to my group, we added to their blunder. Ended up one stop too far down the road. After that incident we walked back to the station we left. We had missed our chance at the next closest station. On the way, some swore they would leave the train life behind. I complained as much as anyone and helped to fill any silence, so that others could think of something substantial to say.

The trains are much emptier nowadays. Bonnie and Cole must have arrived at their destination at some point. I haven't seen them around lately. It broke both their hearts the first time they saw me in my official capacity. I allowed them more questions and time then I would have other offenders. That was before I had a lot of encounters under my belt. I was probably very direct. The fact that I can't remember more vividly proves that I left that old life behind.

I can be your friend and a conveyance, or your enemy and an irritant. It's how I need to handle situations. My motto is, by any means, which is extremely broad. Since my former adversaries had little success getting me off the train, I had little inspiration to draw from. I advanced in my career because I threw the rule book out the window, which should have already been done for me. There were no rules about a motto, so it's lasted

I was an enforcer but I was fair. If I had been too empathetic I wouldn't have been able to do my job. I did cheat myself occasionally with that one.

...

During my travels in the period of mishaps, I got a glimpse of an even older life that I use to live. I was a driving instructor up until that time, and partly throughout my sentence as a rail skipper. It seemed the old life was calling out to me with every car I saw. Pedestrians being picked up left and right before giving the driver's directions. I couldn't believe the occupation had grown so much in the time I'd been away. I later learned that the people I thought were like me were actually customers, paying to get from point a

to point b. It wasn't quite as easy as the rails but to each their own.

Now I don't always use force, and find myself doing so less these days when dealing with free-riders. I suggest they adopt the model of the paying customer and present my speech to steer them away from the train hopping lifestyle. After all, good talk doesn't last forever after first impressions. This is my second form of income. I give directions as to how to get a ride from me. Which if all goes well leads to them paying me to follow orders from point a to b. I modestly think I have an advantage over my competition but I remain humble so my other job is not affected. Not only do I have a seemingly endless supply of people in need of transport, I also know the best cars for the type of driving required. You would be amazed at how many cars are available when you work in transit.

I took care of the gas when I needed to, fueling up cars that others less responsible than myself chose not to. This wasn't the case with all the cars. Some I would drive until they were empty but find a fresh tank the next time I went to use it. Models that were fueled before complete exhaustion were my primary targets. However, their privilege made them less accessible to me.

The repeat customers I have will sometimes ask about my business model. How my garage can house all the vehicles, does fueling up cut away from profits and what type of maintenance each car requires. I tell them it's not worth the headache. Don't say much else. Why give them something more to worry about.

First, it would be irresponsible to give out trade secrets. Second, on account of my trustworthiness and charming disposition, people mistakenly find me enviable. If I were to give insider knowledge, the recipient may think it's the last piece of the puzzle and hope a career change will bring them closer to what it is I have. Lastly, without my background and the camaraderie shared with colleagues, I'm not sure the business model could have any chance of succeeding.

When people looked into Bonnie's eyes they saw something that can't quite be described. When people looked into my eyes they felt the need to try. Bonnie had people see her as she wanted. People saw me how they wanted to. Bonnie and I were both leaders. I felt sorry for the passengers I would shuttle around who thought it was an inner peace they saw in me. That was just eyes on the road.

...

My hobbies are few and lack of time my excuse. I work my part time for money and full time for purpose. Though if overworked the two are sometimes confused. The place I call home has been consistent throughout the years. I've had no problems with the city's water and am able to heat my residence rather inexpensively because of it's size. Some people might call me a hoarder. They don't see the method to my madness. It's easier to heat a space that is crowded. I'm rather purchase clutter than endlessly throw my money out the window.

Before I could justify my impulse, I was collecting keepsakes from my travels for validation. This may come as a surprise but any head of an organization knows how important a track record is. In the business we were in your word only counted for so much. We sacked the exchange rate. The most far fetched stories were believed if whatever minor detail that had affected the climax could later be shown as an object to the listener. Sending them over the edge. I didn't use the same trick twice and would retire the props to my house when finished.

Another difference between myself and the run of the mill hoarder is I know what I have. Whereas my counterpart is surprised when they find themselves lacking. I have a workman's knowledge of my inventory since I frequently move objects so that more space can be occupied. There's no correct answer to the puzzle. Which keeps stress to a minimum.

I'm not going to say it was always such smooth sailing. There have been moments during my time as a homeowner

where I've panicked and thought the house wasn't prepared well enough for winter. Running out to antique shops on cool fall days searching for anything that might be worth it's weight. Buying the furniture, and any objects that would seem nightmarish to knick-knacks, with coins rather than paper bills. Needless to say most of my purchases went out with the season and sometimes didn't even make the initial inventory sheet in spring.

I didn't intend to favorite what I'd collected from my jobs. Which isn't to say that I don't throw much of it out as well. All of the things from my formative days as a salesman have already served their purpose and mementos of my toll taking all ended up leading to the same thought. In the beginning I could ponder the memorabilia and if necessary use it as encouragement. Once I no longer needed the pep talk I was already too successful to be able to tell any memories apart.

...

I set my own hours. A noble way of saying I don't always get paid. I'm my own boss but since I can't pay myself, I have to rely on the honor system for my train gig. Intimidation, or threat there of, as a chauffeur. If I'm having a good work week I'll get paid for all the interference I've run, and not some lesser figure, which is common practice with bounties. The passengers will, if nothing else, have paid and hopefully not made a mess of the car or left any personal possessions. I can only guess what happens to anything left in the car, but am sure it'll be done by a stranger. I don't inspect the car after docking it. I usually try to ask the passenger to check that they have everything before leaving, but only after they've paid. If the question is asked too early, it's likely the passenger will be too excited to remember to pay after being reunited. The risk can have it's reward in the outpouring of gratitude from discovering taken for granted things. The natural reaction absent of monetary influence is a welcome change of pace. Having money is what you make of it. If one of my fares forgets to

pay at least they weren't thinking about their circumstances.

I report to a wonderful woman. The only fault one could find with her is that she surrounds herself with tarnishing people. Without their deceit and contempt, I'm sure she would find find a space to plant both feet firmly and give me what I deserve. I try to catch her alone but our rendezvous is often disturbed the minute I stop talking to hear her response. She talks very loudly when conducting business. There used to be many reasons for her doing so. Now there's only the one. She thinks it easier to continue at that volume than provide explanations to each of her employees that stagger in. I'm unable to sell myself as being as trustworthy as I am because of interruptions, and lose my place once my peers have swarmed in to pick apart the discussion. Even times when I was able to be fluent and was seen as sincere, moments I thought were private, during our next meet up I would learn we had in fact been overheard. That put me in worse spots since I didn't have the chance to defend myself when I was being slandered.

I don't stoop to the level of my peers. If I knew I was going to be short changed, one might think I need just inflate my numbers. That could work short term but any furthering of my career from that point on would be impossible. If I started being less successful it would surely be noticed how crowded the train was. More success and it would be even harder for my supervisor to believe the count I report. Also challenging me to find an appropriate number just outlandish enough. More problems would arise from any changes to the staff or any other variables provided by a workplace.

I mess around with enough numbers during my second shift. Not having any expenses towards the car, I calculate fares on a person by person basis. Determining how long it took from the time I hung up to me acquiring a vehicle, and the distance from car to pedestrian, sets the flat rate. Once the passenger is within earshot I tell them the fee, which can vary slightly from the number just concocted based on

the first impression. If they happen to not be of my train skipping progeny. After the base fee is agreed upon, I tell the customer they can be charged by the minute or the mile. Most go with mile on days I'm being difficult.

It is not uncommon for more than one customer to call on me at the same time. When this happens I'm put in a difficult position. In order to satisfy all parties I'm forced to speed, disregarding the safety of my passengers. There are less complaints about my driving than one might assume however. Most passengers are willing to believe the car is in the condition it's in because of a bond between myself and it, rather than seeing it for a replacement. If two passengers are riding together, by choice and not circumstance, I am also affected. Finding myself speeding to get them out of the car in order to free up more space. Conversely, if I only have one fare I may drive slower so that I can field requests while the car is out of the lot.

...

Hygiene has a prominent role in my life. More so now than ever before. Though I was never dirty, I was never the cleanest, and knew that my boxcar smelled differently than my neighbors. This wasn't a problem though once meetings between us higher ups started to be conducted in neutral places. When I began working for the enemy, or so would have thought the old self, I wanted my presence to be known long before I arrived. Of the hundreds of thousands of scents aboard a train, I found the most distinct was that of cleanliness. This isn't to say that trains are unkempt. If you purchased a ticket I'm sure there would be pleasant aromas abound, but in the circles I used to run in this was rarely the case.

After I had pledged allegiance but before I had become neurotic, for a few weeks I was type cast and my identity was mistaken. Some people have trouble remembering faces. Almost no one has trouble identifying familiar odors. It was some time before I could remove the sign I metaphorically wore as reminder of my past transgressions. The change of clothes and newly found attention to detail

helped only so much. Until my mind convinced itself that I was no longer a train jumper, my pheromones identified me as such. If there was any doubt I had left that lifestyle behind I would not be able to drive, or at least would never have a repeat customer.

While driving I keep the bottom half of my uniform but switch into a comfortable t shirt rather than the baggy long sleeve I don during company time. I had a more form fitting shirt but traded for one with more mobility. Since tactics have changed I've thought about going back to the original but still am found to be persuasive as is.

My coworkers have uniforms that are the same size throughout. They care for their dress and only replace it when a new one is issued. If only I were one of them. Asking for a new set never gets easier. Regardless of the fact that each request signifies how dedicated I am to the job, I am made to feel shame. It's an uncomfortable feeling when you expect it. I'd much prefer being kicked from the horse if ever I should feel so high.

...

Dear Bonnie,

It's me. One of your many admirers. If you haven't stopped reading by now perhaps my boldness will help separate me from the many. When we knew each other you didn't know my real name. God knows Bonnie probably isn't yours. That's what made you special. Forget being the daughter of one of the most powerful senators to ever ration mercy, it is your relationship with your secret and yourself that sets you apart. When you talked, we listened. When we were listening you knew your words were true. So many of us tried to develop a spiritual side. It seems you were born with one.

If you saw me today you probably wouldn't recognize me. I've changed the way I walk since I've stopped having the pleasure of hearing you talk. I don't have hair like I used to. Perhaps you still have all the wigs. Remember that one that didn't pass inspection on the factory floor that you got for a steal? What was it you said? Something like they broke the mold when they made this one. You may be molded in your parent's image, but there's no way they could pull off a wig like you.

I'd tell you to wish them both health but it may confuse you as to who I am. You never spoke much of your parents. I didn't bring it up for fear of rejection. If you got defensive at the question, you might have prematurely shut me out. I'm sorry if it's something you wanted to talk about. You were as hard to read back then as Marie's handwriting when she gave a signature. Yes I know Marie. I know we called her Venmo.

I dress a little differently now. How I wish you remember. I had that brown hat, and you called me an acorn that wanted to be a pine cone. Maybe we were all your little acorns. I had a green jacket that I would sport frequently. Do you remember a green jacket and brown hat? I didn't stand out much but I was always standing. I wasn't as important as you and could have chose to sit, but I followed your example. Did you know you were the measure

of man? It seemed you could do no wrong. Maybe we all were wrong for trying to mimic you.

It seemed there were birds that followed you around everywhere. Both literal and metaphoric. Those that tweet, and those that would tweet nowadays. I'm not online. Not since we first logged on to the internet at the same time. You were probably a lot of people's first simultaneous log on. Perhaps I can be more descriptive. You must get so many letters. I hardly had to ask around at all to find your address. But fear not. I never mentioned who was asking.

I've met a lot of people who were either down on their luck or regarding it in some other way. Depends what time of day you catch them. Or, if they are at the stage where they believe great things all seem to be happening, if you get a moment with them at all. Certain types will carry their past with them fresh, rehashing moments constantly and conflating actions for coincidences. Still others find merit in their ability to alter the course of their day, and with a little persistence affect outcomes in their life. Of course in order to do this they would need to stop once they've reached their goal, taking stock in what they did. From the stories I've heard, most people in the latter category either push on to the next goal or continue to make the first goal unattainable. They can't catch a break.

I jump on these opportunities. Figuratively if possible. I convince the lawskirter they're lucky to see me and build up enough of a rapport for them to hear my suggestions. If my words fall on deaf ears, I fall on my sword and switch stance. After sizing the party up for a second time, different intent from the first, I cycle through any peaceful options still available. If the concerned remains unresponsive after those advances, it doesn't last long. For either of us. Those are cases from work I don't take home, or wherever it is they want to go.

. . .

What I don't keep I leave behind. Rather, all things I could claim as my own are not always prized. Not exactly

following the lead of those informed who have finished with their paper, I move through pages without becoming any the wiser. I recycle the gently used objects by having them at the disposal of any passengers. The newspapers are distributed through the train station, so it is only with the shuttles I need provide this service. Hitting a runner with a newspaper wouldn't do much good, and I need as much good to come from those interactions as possible. Customers in car appreciate my taste, or at the very least admire the grit it is subjected to. The reading material is foreign, price and shock value factoring into that decision, but the selection available from me caters to every audience. News travels fast on a train.

Newspapers from foreign lands sell for less than the local papers, if even sell at all. I've been given many for free by vendors who are eager to find a place in the market. It would be rude to refuse. I wouldn't be comfortable saying I wasn't interested. Because of the vast amount of news that passes through my hands, it requires discipline for me to not browse the goods. Discipline to not learn something now that I could have learned then. The customer is always right, so when they bring up a topic I can genuinely give my thoughts. Then if it should lead to a debate, be ready to easily concede because I hadn't prepared an argument. Different customers have different needs and should be pacified as such.

I also think it's important for my passengers to be exposed to different cultures, so I don't have to witness their same reactions again and again. If they talk local after skimming the alien, they are much more likely to present a unique view. Also aiding in the formation of their new jumping off point is their belief in me as an intellectual. They have already judged the covers.

...

It's nice to have a job where I'm able to help people. What few complaints I receive that it's not my place to pass on advice are silenced by reminders that the upset lost their rights the moment they hopped the train. Though the rules

of engagement are not as loose as when at sea, I am still able to engage judiciously. I don't persist in setting an example, as it is their right to be hog-headed. Their face can be made to look as such. The story of the snout similar to that of the garden snake, evolving first through punishment before coming full circle and functioning in it's highest order. Cognizant of what is lacking, all attention is focused on getting back to a baseline impossible to remember, until it is ultimately passed and a new normal solidified.

Both animals when brought to mind cannot be imagined doing anything else than what we're accustomed to seeing them do. A snake doesn't feed from a troth, a pig doesn't use a forked tongue for smell. I don't believe this is a failing on the part of humans but rather a sign of the excellent state of the animals. They're aware of their limits and approach all tasks the only way they know how. Either the calculations are made for them subconsciously or else they are being extremely under-utilized.

I like to think I'm able to run on autopilot during some interactions. Not normally something to boast about, I have no qualms doing so because I think I learn from my mistakes. Therefore, so long as I don't make any while going through the motions, I can usually handle the situation. If while functioning in the trance-like state I do slip up, I will have no way of knowing and won't be able to improve on my autopilot for the next interaction. If by chance I return to the world of the conscious after a snafu I must be careful not to repeat the same folly next time. I can only learn about the mistake through deductive reasoning and whatever face the runner has ended up with. It is better to make a mistake and continue on than to blunder and get hung up on it. Blocking out sound helps me not correct.

...

Spending as much time as I do around trains one would assume my sense of time is exceptional. This is far from the case. I rely heavily on the schedules of the trains. If one of them is running late I believe I've already missed it. Consistency is excellence in this world. Since their time

keeping is excellent I figure they could never be late. Else they wouldn't be able to be excellent just by being consistent.

It's not a knock against the conductor, but it could be said their performance is actually lacking should they beat the schedule. If they leave the station not at capacity and move through the next stops in a similar manner, they will win the game their playing against themself but lose the audience along the way. Passengers would rather the train be early than late. As a contracted employee of the railway company, I root for the train arriving behind schedule, if only so that the customers it would have missed do not search for a free ride. Not many people follow my approach if they believe the train to be late and will wait longer than I do.

Time management is not a great concern. The time spent obtaining more bounties would be canceled out by the ensuing argument with my supervisor. Instead I go at my own pace and let the short straw fall into my hand. Since I am without competition in my field I'm also free from deadlines, but if my future were threatened by a likable headhunter I suppose I would end up sporting a watch.

...

There is, however, competition on the roads. I can't solely rely on my benevolent, boiling over character to secure fares. Customers may forget just how generous I was when I caught them, and I can't count on their memories to remain questionable. The easier it is to forget the easier it is to replace. I could be remembered incorrectly. I try to drive the point home while driving them home during the initial shuttle. Depending on how fresh our first interaction was, they may be too agreeable and the lesson is lost. It is better to get them after they've taken rides from a few others so they can appreciate the gift they've been given and follow the subtle prompts I present them with. It's always a gamble. Some customers have great long term memories, while others short.

I've mentioned the quality of the cars I drive as being an advantage over other motorists. That only goes so far for towards marketing. It's unreasonable to assume I am the only service that has vehicles of that caliber, so word of mouth about such objects would do nothing for my business. I tried using bumper stickers with my number on them but found all the calls to be too distracting, more than half not even propositioning my car. Most giving notes on my driving. The numbers didn't work so they were changed to letters, but by the time I came up with a word that could be just as easily remembered as a string of numbers, there was only one sticker left. I might have been better off ordering a new design from the start to spare me from all the rubbish sayings I then had floating around. When the new stickers came I was unsure of myself, and have yet to put them on anything other than departing train cars. I can't possibly be in all of the places the trains go at the same time, so am able to drive up price once they've left and I'm there, because of my being sought after.

...

Before I really start to break the eggs of this marketing adventure omelet, I think it's important I tell of an injury I suffered during an accident. I say it was an accident because up until that point I had chosen to be willfully ignorant of the capacity for skin saving my opponents had. I had come across mad dashers, well spoken anthropoids and violent offenders, but they were never in the same league. It took a little bit of all three in one eccentric ne'er-do-well to batter my ignorance. They saw the same world as I did but radically different. In a past life we could have been friends. In this life we weren't, which led to the initial underestimation.

The sales pitch failed before I even had time to mention I would be getting paid for the new transport. A chase ensued. I countered their solidified reasoning for why a train made more sense for the recreational traveller, with my own rehearsed sentences that became less coherent as the cramp at my side grew. We stopped running, and,

without getting into details that don't deserve to be in a story, I got a noticeable scar running from the top of my head to where head meets neck. It could have been worse. It could have continued off of my face. I was lucky I didn't have hair at the time. Even luckier that it had no chance of growing back. It would require finesse I don't have time to manage to cut the hair around the band. Both my jobs allowed me to wear a hat and may have even preferred me to do so.

...

You liked to allude to the golden ratio. Your face spoke for itself.

Mine needed to be spoken for. It is a simple face, Bonnie. Please remember. If you're starting to from a clear picture of what I look like. Stop. I need to first tell you that I have gained a little bit of weight. Not naturally or I wouldn't be so embarrassed. It seems to all have gotten stuck in my face. Heavy is the head that wears the crown. Yours. Heavy are the eyelids that carry extra weight in the face. Mine.

You never turned your face too fast. You never made it seem like it was dragging through time. A nod from your direction had all eyes glancing to see if it was you that bowed their chin. It never was. We all batted our eyelashes recognizing the mistake. Your eyelashes must have got more attention than some whole people do. You never let it get under your skin. At least from what I could tell.

I wasn't an angry person when we knew each other. So many faces are easily remembered if witnessed in fits of rage. It is a simple face Bonnie. Not expressionless but not soon to win any awards either.

Your face even looked noble in the rain. The rest of us battled with our eyes and squinted, but you still seemed to radiate. You could have sold overpriced umbrellas in the desert. Seeing you in the desert would take one out of the environment. Not entirely a mirage but definitely an oasis. If someone saw me in the desert they'd probably look for you. We worked together. Never in the desert but we possibly passed through. I know how you felt about job titles. We were closer to being on the same page than I was with Cole. You probably have a concrete image of him in your head. Cole was alright.

I'm driving much more than I used to. If only I could take you for a ride. It'd probably end in disaster though. You sure can wreak havoc. We all loved you for that. I myself was the staple periphery person. What sees and hears but doesn't say what they think. You needed no sidekick but I still felt competitive with Cole for the position. I was

somewhat of a leader. Who knows what Cole would have been had he stayed around.

If you remember Cole than you must remember Cole's girl. Cole's girl would lead you to her sister, Cassandra. The more people you recollect from those days the easier you'll be able to remember me. I don't want to say that I was a leader, unless that's alright, but I rallied the troops.

Without hope there is no tomorrow. Then it's just another hopeless day. Marketing is much the same. I strive to be heard about today so that in the future I will be known. Following examples of people I assume to run successful businesses, I have gotten my face onto benches around the city my home is in. Towns which I am not in are marketed to less because of my infamy. They may see a bumper sticker here or there. I brought specifications for a new design to the same factory, though to a different department. The end product is a blanket that when laid flat resembles nothing more than anything else cubist. When draped over a bench the images line up and show my face mid-wince. Because of the scar it hurts to smile.

It was recommended that I not leave the coveralls in the rain. I collect them while ferrying around, and give them a dry space in the car or ball them up and squeeze should I be on foot. If a storm is just passing through, I follow suit and leave the curtain any old place once it has subsided. No longer needing to move with the object through the rain to reduce exposure. While driving I set my standards a little higher, with the knowledge that I can leave it as it was should I despair and want to leave it just because.

I'm pretty good about following the linen laborer's advice. Haven't always been though. In the short period I wasn't, I was briefly blessed with good weather. When the sun's shine had began to decline in the middle of the day, and I still a head above the clouds, my prototype would have called me more than a fool if it had able to talk. I gave myself that distinction shortly after, discovering my jaw dropped and unwanted taunting eyes. Mother nature had

started a smear campaign. There is no winning against either, mother nature or smear campaigns, but I took the precautions from then on.

...

I come from a working class family no more than a train ride away. The first time I ran away must have been pretty significant. Where I ended up was where I established my base later in life. Can't remember exactly why. What prompted me to unpack my boots was my willingness to work. My parents thought I was too young at the time and when a manager called asking why I missed my shift, the parents were furious. They gave all the classics, citing we work so you won't have to and do as I say not as I do. I knew I was in no position to work so they wouldn't have to, so when I left I was unable to give them a taste of their own medicine with what I had been spoon fed.

It's hard finding a job during the day as a child. It's also just as hard to loiter around work sites during the night. It took a while for me to see what the adults saw, but I eventually returned home as clean shaven as when I had left. My timing was impeccable and I caught my parents in between shifts. When I made my appearance, the only response I got was concerning the take out. Whether they didn't remember the argument or had thought they had won, and my absence meant I was taking some time for myself, they were as carefree as they were projecting me to be. In that moment I welcomed the casualness and didn't mind having to sneak jobs while under my parent's roof.

It was a couple years after until I wholeheartedly fled again, minor disappearances not withstanding. This time it had nothing to do with work but rather my victimization from chemical imbalances and hormones. The journey meant next to nothing but the destination allowed for future journeying.

The final time I left my rat-racing parents was planned and came shortly after my first boxcar jump. I was a late bloomer to recreation and had my occupational timeline been reversed, I would have known you work so you can

play. Having gone without play for so long the decision was made for me and I became a drifter. I got it all out of my system though and now, because I am all business, work so that I can work more. Experience has given me the perspective to draw a line between discipline and neuroses.

...

I wasn't completely without occupation during my sabbatical and saved every cent I earned so I could continue vacationing. The difference between what I did and a regular job was mostly in my approach to saving. Where others worked so they could live a better life, I toiled so that mine could stay the same. I didn't know Cole was doing the same elsewhere. His approach to saving must still have been different than mine and regular job holders. What I did before was honest work, though it didn't have to be, but the opinions I gave through checkered boxes were sincere. I didn't ask as to why my views wanted to be heard or if my answers were on par with my peers. I kept my head down and my hands busy.

For each survey I completed I had the choice of receiving cash or coupons. At first I was fine with either option. One's for saving, the other for savings. In a moment of weakness and doubt not far from the start, I caught myself in front of a mirror with cut hands strained to contain all of the coupons. Rather than see the damage I was doing to myself, I doubled down and went to the store. The coupons had expired. The dried blood on a coupon for pizza crust should have told me so. It was strictly cash from then on, with an occasional entry into the lottery from the survey makers. This was the third option. Since it couldn't feed you unless you're marketing scheme took off, and your meals were billboard (bench in my case) to table, it was hardly ever chosen. What coupons I kept serve as reminders that I can always go hungrier.

I still complete the polls sometimes out of habit. There's something refreshing about context driven campaigns and am always excited to see how answers will be made to work for those in question. One in five

consumers prefer this while the other four said they don't care one way or the other.

I became one of the four consumers who didn't care one way or the other. At first I believed giving preference to certain brands would give me a better chance to be known to the lottery proctors. I won the drawing, which I like to believe was from a large pool, but because luck had everything to do with it, it didn't bother me much if it wasn't. I was given the opportunity to have my face with a slogan on future surveys. Four weeks prior and up until I won, I was pumping out forms carelessly, so something must have worked. I took more time on the surveys that had my slogan on them. The prize was always the same. In order that my advertisement not be replaced I needed to continue to better my chances

...

Being chose to be able to be chosen from other finalists who were picked to write quips and prose was an honor for me. You can only thank luck for so long before needing something more material. Anyway, luck had nothing to do with the judgement of our submissions. I don't know how many other contestants were picked apart but my slogan ran for a bunch of weeks. It went like this, 'when at market and eyes steer sockets, and suddenly your confused, remember your training and opine complaining, which brands are friends of you.' I didn't include my face because I thought it would be a strange thing to see while taking a form anonymously. The scar would make it seem like I was forced to be on the survey or that I was some act of charity. The message to trust the poll pushers to narrow your choices was already too much.

I knew my run was nearing an end when I found a survey through a different address and my slogan had been replaced. Not entirely removed but in the process of being fossilized. Taking the right third of my caption was the right side of a business card. The other two thirds arrived with the reprint. Some realtor who had ties with the big household brands bought my space. I suppose that's better

than being replaced by any other advertisement from that time.

...

It was easy to break ice with the realtor the first time we met. She knew who I was and I knew her character because of her stamps of approval. We both liked some of the same brands. She asked what my needs were and we were able to settle. She got me my current residence and a decent amount off the asking price. I didn't know her as well as I thought, when the last paper was signed saw no more of her in the house. The sold sign was eventually taken off my lawn and with that her presence no longer felt. I make cookies sometimes. I can't bring myself to look at a survey.

When I was a new homeowner I followed suggestions from my peers who themselves had just barely gotten their feet in the water. Veteran homeowners provided no advice, knowing I'd sink or swim and either way wouldn't be a bad neighbor for long. I caught myself about two years in suggesting something to a new homeowner I was interested in trying myself. Let them figure it out. Then figure out a way to get them to speak of their successes and failures.

My house hasn't failed me yet, in my inspection or dependability. I haven't failed it by expecting too much. There are only a few payments left to be made but it's held up its value so far. It's a good house to be alive in. I use it the most for sleeping. If my schedule permitted, and my salary had heating and plumbing covered, I believe I could be fully occupied with my artifacts. Shifting the balance of power in the house. Taking down my possessions or digging them up would be less pressured. I prefer being puzzled over content. Besides, what soldier wants to leave their troops behind. Everything has it's place.

I have a few bureaus for my clothes. Two stand vertically while the other is on it's side and is in case of emergency. I don't foresee myself having to leave in a hurry. I just like to know I could. The handles were adjusted so it somewhat resembles a filing cabinet, but open the drawers

and out fall the clothes. If I do end up on the run, bed bugs will just be another of my worries.

...

We didn't have houses during the days of the hub. I got an apartment shortly after. We spent some time together in Venmo's tent but I never showed you my quarters. I don't even know that you ever slept. It seemed everyone had a story about you at the end of each day. How you managed to be in so many places at once is astounding. Seeing as you never really left any of our sights. It's a good thing you didn't wear sunglasses or we all would have caught ourselves staring. It was better that we all knew that we were all looking so we didn't have to think much about politeness. I say we all, but maybe I can describe myself better to separate from the bunch.

Don't for one second think that I would ever lump myself in with that crowd. I never would do that to you. I'll tell you about my apartment so that hopefully you can form a better picture of the person that I am. It wasn't just me in the apartment. I had roommates. Let us not give them much thought. They thought my customs were strange. How could they not. They never knew you and the influence you had. The styles you affected.

Where I lived there were five rooms. I won't say how many were for daily maintenance. Each room came with it's own pros and cons. You probably could have rearranged some things and given each room a few more pros. How I kept them was neat and tidy. No personality. Call me old fashioned but a room is a place where you try to wait productively. Life is always going on outside.

I had a few sinks in my apartment. Two that were connected. One that was more of a washing basin than anything else. I used it for yard work, we had a communal patch of turf with a couple wild flowers and some annoying shrubs. My roommates from the other apartments would let their animals out on the patch. I didn't mind the animals. Paid no mind to the owners.

Didn't you used to mind the animals? Caring for them as Chrissie would her plants. Chrissie and Screaming. You heard from them lately? I wonder if she still tolerates him. I suppose she could set her schedule to his wondering when

lightning would strike. Make it easy to tend garden. You would be able to mind the animals to not enter a garden. Most animals wouldn't follow that suggestion. I think you could make it work.

The apartment had electricity. Big change from the hub. Are you living somewhere with power? It's amazing how fast your wants become your needs. Everything else in my life would be affected if I were the only one without power.

In the business that I'm in I don't need to know where the line is, only who has crossed it. It is not my wont to ask a fugitive whether they are one or not. The severity of the transgressions would vary anyway so I don't know that it would do much good. It's best to approach each situation expecting the worst. There will be time later to see if there's any validity to their claims of being good. In cases of the most wanted's, what is not said bleeds truer than what is. These are one-off run offs and their silence saves me the trouble of being an accomplice.

If the train mobility are only wanted for a warrant they usually take me up on my shuttle service. After wheels start rolling, they let down their guard a bit and come clean about their motives for a lift. I appreciate when they leave out not feeling threatened by me. Their stories always start by explaining how they saw me as prey during the first encounter. They were quick to take me up on my offer and were unaware of what I could do. They had been presumably been on the train to get away, but realized they could kill two birds with one stone if they stayed a minute longer to rob and commandeer. I think they change their minds about that when they realize how good a listener I am and decide to relate their plan instead of carrying it through. Those fares pay me but their good will seldom lasts. Their reason wasn't good enough for the correction and any continued spontaneity would force them to think on their relationship with people. Money doesn't require much thought.

...

I have never made a citizen's arrest. Doing so would require granting rights I cannot give. I've received no formal training as a citizen, and have learned as I go. Those citizens who do take steps in the first act usually become law wielders in the second. That is not my path. No arrests professionally or otherwise.

I have too much respect for those who hand out rights and their watchdog retrievers to soil either reputations with any self righteous sense of duty I might have. I don't have any problem making their jobs easier though, so long as my hand is unseen. If I do detain a fighter it is by way of limiting their mobility. This allows for the absence of handcuffs, and me as well when officers arrive at the scene. Thanks may then be in order but are filtered before they ever get back to me. Being unseen makes it hard to know when the stories are about you.

...

One of the more thankless jobs in business is to "get out there" so you can face character assassination. Someone has to do it but the more the merrier. If one person is wrong that's great. If a whole group are, then the opposed must really be on to something. There never used to be as big a fuss about air pollution. Now I am both hero and villain.

In the role of a hero, I rescue wayward travelers who are contributing to pollutants but not making contributions for the relief cause. They downsize, switch modes of transport, and if all goes well I am able to pay their dues. Dues that they would have paid had they bought a ticket. I am cast as villain for working with the train industry and hardly going a minute away from the smell of exhaust. These distinctions are self inflicted. If I were widely known as either, my work would suffer. Both, and I may be alright. As I am now. I can't change how other people see me, nor how I see myself. It is a thankless job.

...

During one of my lower points in life I was told that everyone has their own cross to bear. I relayed this sentiment to a rival minister. He knew the source before the word had even left my mouth. I was escorted out. I've been changing my load bearing capacity ever since.

I would shave off the cross or tack on to it, by the number of people in my life. Immediately after the, I don't share the same views as my neighbor premise, and me getting kicked off the church premises, I returned to the horse's mouth. There I was accepted. If in being so meant my presence was at least tolerated. We were all equal in each other's eyes. This led to competition.

Every member was their own judge, jury and executioner. The minister couldn't handle the workload and sermons became less and less interactive. Nothing was being accomplished when congregates expected all their experiences to be canon. Sarah needs to make a point and it is expected you're familiar with what she said three weeks ago. Sarah is progressing nicely but if she continues will have to be put out to pasture. The sheep cannot become the shepherd.

I started making friends once a damper was put on our individuality. Where before we were outcasts collectively grouped together, we then became a tribe who centered around the weakest link. The glue that we were so sure of was really starting to dry out, and the questions that could invigorate it were discouraged before ultimately being forbidden. Every member needs to walk out of the church having grasped the basic lesson plan. Should they comprehend more, great, so long as they don't attempt to learn more before others have a base comprehension.

...

There was once believed to be a book of Adam. No rib. Not a living soul can prove it ever existed and the ones who try can only say it's contents were unknown. It doesn't matter what it said but more that it was said, since everything was known and didn't need to be said. If it wasn't said then it's important that we at least believe now

that it was, so we know then that it didn't need to be.
Bonnie had a way with the eyes.

Bonnie was not of the religious archetype and
confessed if pressed to rephrasing the best. The way
disciples all speak with one voice though not in as many
words. Something to the tune of, I'm not religious but am
spiritual. The circles Bonnie made appearances in were all of
that mind. She never needed to stoop to be heard.

We were used to the wine but we always chose bread
over crackers. Cheese never made much sense to us floaters.
Some cows are religious as well. Goats have no trouble
talking about one third of the trinity.

Our gatherings were modest. If you had wine you were
in. 'Over there' they would give everyone a taste though all
had paid for a full meal. We tried to prop each other up.
They tried to shut us down. It's easy to see why Bonnie
didn't go to church.

...

Coal is supposedly making a big comeback. The news
was read to me. I have no preference one way or the other,
but if it will effect me, I'd like to remember where I was
when I first heard.

You can't get bored with fire. You can lose touch with it
and have to rekindle the relationship. The flames may even
try to bite at you, but woe are the foe to fire who are cold
when it's around.

There are posters leading into the locker rooms of past
coal shovels and tempers. Purgy was the nickname of Frank
Finnegan. He claimed it wasn't important what you put in
but what you left out. Followers of his model took out of
their predecessor's wisdom that it may be smarter to leave
coal out of the equation entirely. It's too bad Purgy is no
longer stuck around us otherwise we'd ask for his thoughts.

We've got a pretty good electrician on call, and a
plumber on staff certified with boiler and HVAC licenses,
but we do all miss Purgy. He was before most of our time so
there feels to be a real connection there. Purgy never
needed to wear sunglasses. He always had to wear a hat.

Purgy had a daughter by the name of Isabelle. Isabelle didn't spend much time around the tracks until her father passed. She would bring wine every time she did. If only she didn't prefer to drink alone.

A nice travelling salesman was by the train station one afternoon and saw Isabelle drinking at a time he thought much too early. He asked for the name before saying anything else. She rattled off as many top shelf booze brands as she could think of. The man was in love after that. The sound of her warbled voice didn't hurt either. He preyed on birds with broken wings. She put him in his place after she sobered up. She resumed drinking shortly after and they both fell in love with the cyclic chaos.

Isabelle and Sal Travers had three children. Two died in a coal mine fall and the survivor, who never was challenged one day of her life, went by the name of Isadora. Isadora only comes by the station to check in on her husband, who for some reason rejects the offer to work with his father in law and has set up his practice at a kiosk. Ostracized even from that community for not moving around too much. His whole shop would fit in a van yet he keeps it stationary. The whole family is cooked.

...

I don't want to say that the Travers family is unlucky. Many card players wish for them at their table. Isabelle and Sal are much friendlier than their daughter. They are superior grievers. Isadora is a grown woman but didn't grow much from childhood. It's not my place to speak of borrowed time, I never had siblings to lose.

Isadora's husband took her last name when they got married. Mr. Travers senior thought his daughter's fiancee was doing so to get in his good graces. The fiancee, Newt, just didn't like the name he was given. The father in law had good reason for his assumption, his name carried weight around the town. He was known to talk your ear off and able to sell you a shoe as replacement. Newt didn't say much. A big part of kiosk culture is to be seen and not heard.

Too many complaints and you're off the circuit. Let the product speak for itself and the stand speak for the product.

The first time Newt saw Sal's temper he knew he had found the perfect girl. Sal was a very old-fashioned man. He didn't like the choreography of the first dance on his daughter's wedding night. It was too well-prepared and when Sal saw his daughter, who looked very much like his wife, dancing with a man who appeared to have nerves of steel, it reminded him of how he'd been the opposite on his wedding night. When it was his turn to dance with the bride he over compensated and then again when he was walking back to his seat.

The words of encouragement from Isabelle were lost on him and he was not able to share the happiness with his daughter that she hoped from him. He eyed the groom suspiciously for the rest of the evening and upon seeing him leave early, followed him. Sal confronted Newt outside and thought that he was making a run for it. Newt said he was just taking a leak and wanted to do so away from all the guests. He said that if he was in the bathroom there would likely be people that followed him in there offering drugs, on that his last night of freedom. Sal punched him in the nose and said that Newt was a better man than he.

...

Newt's nose healed tremendously well, and now, if somehow you were able to be spared from hearing the story by Sal, you would have a hard time noticing it was ever spared. I buy certain things from Newt. He's a man of values.

Isadora would like to work with Newt at the kiosk but he doesn't think that a good idea. He tells her to save her hands for him. Isadora has mentioned wearing gloves but Newt can't think of any style that would be appropriate. Surgical gloves and the kiosk would seem full of contaminants. High end woman's wear and the kiosk would look inferior. Isadora has sat on her hands to spite Newt but they didn't lose their touch. Idle hands are the devil's plaything. Newt does alright.

I hope Newt never goes full gypsy. I'll hear him step foot in one of the cars long before I see him. You'd think he had control of the whistle. Either way, his nose looks good right now.

...

I've got a punchable face. Had to teach it how to punch back. I think it's going well because the hits don't seem to be as hard anymore.

...

I've heard that fighting is a skill. A skill is something to be envied. If no one cares about a skill then it becomes a talent. There are talented fighters and there are skilled fighters.

Flying is a hobby. There are people that fly for business or pleasure. If no one flies for business or pleasure then it becomes an instinct.

Instincts are rewarding. An instinct is something that is tried and true. If no one follows their instincts then they become untethered.

...

The first thing that I do in the morning is stay asleep. As the morning rolls on and I wake naturally, I check my watch to make sure I'm not still dreaming. Every morning of every day I do this. I want to beat the dead line.

Breakfast was never marketed to me as much before as it is now. I'm not guilted easily and am usually good about skipping that meal. Lunch isn't anything to write home about either. I really come alive during supper time. I've won quite a few roll eating contests since I've become employed. After one of my victories is where I learned that restaurants melt the butter slightly in the microwave before putting it on your meal. I stopped doing the competitions shortly thereafter. Dry bread is harder to eat when there's butter on a table close by.

I used to worry that I wasn't getting enough to eat until I started to notice I was getting better sleep. Then not eating became tasteful. To appear healthy because of a good night's rest is important in my trade. I'm rail thin.

Though I may be skinny there is plenty of muscle on my frame as well. There are many situations where I have to approach the suspect like a crisis averting negotiator, hands raised above my head. Nonthreatening. It may not sound like a work out but it takes a lot of focus to walk tensely and tersely. Plan B is where the real exercise begins.

...

It's easy to be threatening when you're not a threat to anyone's job. People will look the other way. Most times to a screen.

I hope that violent media does desensitize, otherwise there would be threats to my job. If people became sensitive to fight scenes they just might learn something. Better to let it wash over them so that the worst they could do is embarrass themself. Picking a fight an hour after watching the film in a place that would feel right for a movie. With a few drinks in and twenty minutes off the clock something tragic must occur. Another forty and the conflict is building. Ninety minutes gone and the violence has reached a climax. After two hours, a resolution. Until next time.

Pray the blockbuster isn't lackluster. Then there would be a threat to my job. If there wasn't as much action then the dialogue would matter. People may then think that their own dialogue was more important than it is. That any and all disagreements were worth fighting over.

These types of thoughts are apt to happen when one is driving. Nothing else to do.

...

I've been getting a lot of sun where I'm at. I don't know how you didn't burn like the rest of us in the days of old. Suntan lotion was hard to come by. We didn't have any vendors around the hub. Your skin never burned. You didn't smell like you were cheating. You probably could thrive in any environment.

You never saw much of me in the winter months. Our schedules didn't allow it. You needed to be in places where you could be seen. I needed to be in places that were very much unseen. I could have sent a scout to you. You knew about the places I was going. You were as traveled as the rest of us. Yet always close to home.

Your tent didn't change much over the years at the hub. I followed your example and soon a shabby shanty fab was started. I wasn't the voice of the campaign. No help there. Perhaps you remember my tent anyway.

It was as characterless as they come. Some posts, some tarp, some stakes, a few zippers. All mine. I didn't have a wash basin at the time. I didn't spend much time in the tent.

You probably won't be able to remember that I never conducted meetings more than a few tents away. I think your tent was out of that range. Cole's was too. We all had to make an effort to make an effort. If we had been around snow we would have had to follow the same path to the meeting every time. Our meetings were spontaneous. Any number of things could lead us to calling one.

If I still were calling meetings in the location I'm at, I'd ask for your secret to not get burnt. I wonder who is in your inner circle now. If you've heard anything abut the hub let me know. Please remember that I was once in your inner circle. I had a green hat and brown jacket. I was one of the first disciples to let my domicile reflect the living condition. I called Marie by her nickname, Venmo. I remember where she got the name.

If you remember my green hat and brown jacket, you might remember the signals we shared by playing with our zippers. You were the only one who could show the broken zipper signal. We all knew what that meant. We didn't need

to signal back. I don't wear anything with a zipper nowadays. It would make it too difficult to lead a normal life. Everyone I passed on the street I would suspect of conspiracy. I know what you used to say about them but there's still a part of me that can't help but go against your sage advice.

Cole had a firm handshake. At least, he liked hearing that was so. I stopped shaking his hand when I wouldn't pay him the compliment. I don't think it bothered him much.

He always told this story about how he broke his leg, and for the time it was in his cast the other leg kept growing. The broken one stopped. He said that's why he walks with his shoulder down. He wants to get out in front of it before he's asked. I think it's an act so that he can get a better grip because of leverage. I tried telling him that it doesn't matter how good the handshake is if a first impression is able to be made before that. Bonnie offered her hand delicately. Newt probably would tell Isadora to stay clear of Cole.

Cole had more friends than me. I didn't begrudge him for it. He was the railrunner's equal, while I became a sequel. Even before I left the top spot I still was left out of coffee pot table talk. Cole was a quick wit and could self deprecate as good as any other pile of. He was lucky he didn't believe any of it to be true. He had me going for a while but I think he's a decent guy.

Cole knew a girl who lived a couple train rides away. She came to the station one day in an econoline van. Cole must have really laid it on thick because they left the van near a forklift and never went back. Someone stole the license plate off the van and the rest of the parts were soon to follow. I always felt like I could have done more to preserve their memory. It was a different time. I was an indifferent person.

...

Bonnie's story isn't as mysterious. Or it wouldn't be, if she were not in it.

...

You never get used to people thanking you for your service. You learn to cope when they do not. I had a dentist in my car recently who stole advertisement stickers off of the newspapers. He could have had them had he asked. I wouldn't have considered it stealing had he said thank you. He'll get all the glory when he fixes some kid's teeth. The parent will thank him, as will the kid, who'll be advertising paper towels on their forehead.

It used to be common courtesy to be gracious. Goodness used to be a currency. I advertise judiciously to get in people's good graces. I even invade some people's personal space. Never while it's raining and seldom for more than about fifteen minutes. Never if they believe their space is violated. Most of my fares still come from my other job. I'm in their personal space for less time then. I decide how much space I need to give. I'm a better salesman than strategist.

...

The bank I go to is very discreet. They tell me to come after hours and wait to be let in. I wait across the street. I'm lucky if they hold the door open for me. Otherwise, I have to beat it to it's close.

The tellers are friendly people who don't believe a single word I say. I may have given up too much the first time I went there.

...

My uncle used to tell me dirty jokes. I don't try any of them when I'm with my customers. I do practice some out in front of the mirror. It's all in the delivery.

He lived to be damn near one hundred. It was hard for him to walk for the last twenty years of his life. I wish I could have continued my education. He had a power scooter.

...

If the powers at be stayed as they were, what would everyone else be up to? The pretzel stand vendor would have no incentive other than apprenticing hopefuls. The

apprentice would never stop learning. The day has yet to come when the power has shifted. Everyone has been busy.

I hear a lot from my customers about how they can almost taste it. How they can feel it in the air. They are always on their way to some destination. Every day seems like a holiday to me. Maybe that's why my appetite is so rare. You can't journey on a full stomach, but it's easy to wait for a meal.

I grew up in a time when a dinner only came around twice a year. There were great meals on a few more weekends. I can get take out from any restaurant now. I usually end up eating at the establishment. A busy body is an unstable mind. I can't drive for pleasure and business. Some things need to be waited out.

...

We sold t shirts before I sold the rights. Cole's girl would have been able to continue the venture had she not abandoned the econoline van. Bonnie got plenty of donations but couldn't get anyone to commit to a sale. It was a simple design on the shirts, as is the life of those chasing a free ride.

Any money I made I kept secret from my silent partners. If I was the simple face they chose the character to be based on, I deserved to have my space. We all shared the same head space. Money wasn't important to anyone.

There is still a poster with a face that looks like mine around the main hub. The shirts are mostly used for rags.

...

There was a barber who charged six clippers at once from a generator that took care of all of our hair. When we heard the generator power up, we knew the search for the power strip would follow. That the next day it would be we who'd be combed through. Bonnie convinced anyone that had long hair and wanted to keep it so, to cut it in the mirror by themselves. You're more likely to make a mistake early on and decide not to continue. Letting your hair grow back out until you can try again. She could have told them

just about anything over the sound of that generator and they would have listened.

Our syndicate's members all started with the same cut. It was different depending on whose advice one took. Unfortunately some bad home hair cuts led to standard balding and hair falling out in weird places. The side of the tracks that we were boxed in to wasn't the cleanest of places. I think some people's scissors weren't up to snuff. The clippers were always well taken care of. More so than the power strip which could have been kept in storage with them. Bonnie could have worn a wig and people still would have tried cutting their own hair.

Shaves were another story. The barber claimed that he had a steady hand when the generator was running. No one cared enough to try to prove him wrong. Any drastic changes made to facial hair were done with clippers. The barber had a weird look about him as he moved the clippers around the face without ever lifting them. He could talk your ear off if you happened to laugh when he was taking the only routes possible. I had a pair of scissors myself. I could have been in Bonnie's camp.

...

Daylight savings times meant shadow boxing or later sunsets. You can always shadow box while you're on a train but you can't always see a sun set. I don't change my clocks. Makes it easy to be disappointed or excited during times it matters. Like if I think the bank won't still be open or it seems late for a certain age group to be hopping trains. Brain games are good for the mind.

People often have reservations. This is what has been said as consolation to me. I try to get the reserved where I need for them to be but it never seems to be enough. A tip is worth a million, I had other plans anyways. It's a tricky business.

...

I thought about plowing snow when I was halfway across the country. Haven't thought much about it since I

came back. People say we're in a pissing match with the polar bears. We've got camels in our back pockets.

Some scientists are trying to speed up the evolution of the polar bear. They wear white lab coats and have bags where there eyes should be. I'm not sure the experiments they're doing are entirely safe. I should have asked more about that story. One of my fares probably switched careers after that ride share.

...

I don't trust under dressed scientists as far as I can throw them. There's nothing to grab on to. I don't mind doctors in jeans though. It would have been unheard of when jeans were first invented. Doctors still smoked cigarettes then.

...

We could have bought weed for the hub but we chose hash. We had a certain image to maintain. Plus bowl farts with hash would burn small holes in the t shirts, which gave the shirts a social grace. I quit that dope and gained a lot of weight in my face.

...

Keeping the weight in my face and nowhere else is one of the more difficult things required for my job. It is also thankless. I could no longer coast by with my simple face. I needed to see reactions from the people I apprehended. Since people were able to read me so well before, they seldom would change their expression when they saw me. It made it hard to move forward safely.

Suspects that wore sunglasses were easier to read. I could see my reflection in them and was able to know what I was going to do before doing it. I keep some distance when approaching sunglasses with a hat pulled low. Just thinking about it makes me tired.

...

I am like an arrow without a bow. I could do some damage if not for the bowlegged that throw. Their feet aren't in the right place at the right time. My feet are out of place when I tow the line.

The furthest distance between two objects cannot measure anything else within that path. Once the objects become tethered, measurements taken from either side in must be the same distance as the opposite side still connected. So the distance from me to the hub is the same as Bonnie, wherever she may be, to the hub.

Light is the head that has a halo resting upon. Heavy are the thoughts when one cannot see the halo. I imagine your thoughts were always light, Bonnie. Which isn't to say you weren't a deep thinker. I myself have perused the aisles of the super conscious. You were the overseer of all things conscionable. No one could see things for what they were better than you. You were impartial. We were all partial towards you for it.

You may not remember but one of the underlings once found a family of baby turtles. And what a family it was. Had they been able to grow old together they could have become friends. You told us to keep the turtles away from Marie. We all had a good time the next night after we didn't heed your warning. Sorry about that. It still was fun though.

At the party you thought there was something missing. Any party would be missing something if you weren't there. A part of you was and wasn't at that party. I don't think I wore the green jacket and brown hat to the party. It might have been viewed as disrespectful. I wore black. We all wore black.

The fire showed us what we'd look like if we played with fire. If we went against nature and lost. If nature wasn't quite done with us, so spit we back up for a later date. We could only look at the shadows for so long. We were all so young and fit in the days of the hub. Every day I look more and more like my shadow.

You probably look different than I remember you. Do you remember how you used to look? I know you said we can never fully see ourselves, some flaw in our programming, but please try to remember. Although your eyes were probably drawn to different things about yourself. We could never see you how you see yourself. You were always one step ahead.

I don't want to overstep or dance on any toes so let me try to describe myself before throwing stones. I've heard about myself that I used to be a glass house. I can tell you this is no longer the case. My exterior has hardened since I've grown weary of people that couldn't be you. My eyes

*have dulled from all the strain put on them seeing people
other than you. My ears have voluntarily deafened from
mistakenly looking when my name was called by people that
aren't you. My pace has quickened for attempt to run into
you. My tongue has gone dry from hearing people start to
say words that begin with a bo.*

*Please remember you said there's no I in team but
there is a mate.*

...

Sometimes I'm reminded of Bonnie in interactions that
have nothing to do with her. Not only would she never be in
the places I am, she also would never act the way I, or the
people I interact with, act.

There is a grocer who had orange hair. When the sun
hits it the whole store is aware. Aisles away at a different
time of day, the chance of her being eclipsed fills me with
dread. And shame on her boss for docking her pay. She
wasn't going to try to burn as bright as the sun. Unable to
afford artificial sunlight, she shaves her head.

I asked if she shaved it herself but she took a break as
she was putting food into one of the paper bags. Her
coworker wasn't much help but told me her name and how
I could find her online. I decided I would go back to the
store the next week.

After our break I saw her again at the same store. I
knew she thought me to be the strong silent type so I let
her have that and slammed my groceries down in front of a
different cashier. It was like swearing while being put on
hold. My groceries were bagged in under two minutes.

I got a reputation at the grocery store through
persistence. In an always changing environment it's hard to
be recognized but I played smugness perfectly and was able
to leave impressions. Seeing how highly I thought of myself
built confidence in others that I must be as I seem. I don't
offer my services while shopping. People are already
worried enough about getting their bags into their car. They
shouldn't be asked to put them in mine instead.

...

I don't think most adults should be allowed in grocery stores. And definitely not any children. Things have changed so much since the new shopping carts have come in. The thought behind the old models was that the store would be able to sell more of the products that were being pushed around in an open metal cage. They realized that it did nothing for the actual store and just increased sales of certain brands.

The new carts aren't see through. Both types of cart are still available. I'm afraid to use either one. I usually choose a basket. I don't ever buy pineapples in public places. Those show offs do make everyone else look better though.

Canned pineapples are fine but then you send the message that you are interested in going full pineapple or that you are unable to act your age. I buy ingredients while others buy precooked meals.

I think the carts that aren't see through are much sturdier than the ones that are. I've seen the see throughs tip over after collisions. A kid broke his arm because he was sitting in the front of the cart. Who's walking who type of thing. The kid was pulling on the shelves to get momentum and the mother, in her defense, had worn the wrong type of shoes to get any traction. Right before the crash her feet were practically dragging on the floor behind her.

How the owner of the other cart didn't budge is beyond me. The cart took the full impact of the hit and pushed back against it's lesser. The small man behind the big cart may have experienced some slight vibration in his hands on the handle but nothing beyond that.

Neither cart had pineapples in them and good thing too. The man probably would've went to the emergency room with the mother and son had that been the case.

...

I can't say that I've ever sent anyone to the emergency room. We would've paid good money to receive that type of treatment. Bonnie could usually find doctors wherever we were, but those who dealt in cash were even further

removed from the days when they would smoke cigarettes. I don't know what drugs they were on but they did a banged up job. We promised to fill the prescriptions they wrote but would usually leave them lying around the hub. It was for their own good. It was important to share with your doctor. The doctors still got paid when any scavengers would find them.

There were plenty of us that were after free rides who claimed to be doctors in the past. They could never be found in the room after an accident. Made it more of an emergency. I would do the same thing if I were in their position. I display an invalid driver's license on my rearview mirror during transport. I gained weight in my face so people wouldn't think I could scrap.

It felt much safer when operations were done in winter. Everything seemed sterile and the steam could be managed. The doctor's eyes never adjusted because of the drugs. A still picture could have talked. Too much or too little steam was always noticed.

Purgy had a saying that it's not what you put in but what you leave out. Doctors orders would have been to throw Purgy into the boiler.

...

I've got carrying bags used by food delivery services but they're usually mostly empty. They do keep things warm though so I've got some batteries stored in there. I don't necessarily need warm batteries but I also don't need to be a scientist to do science. The bags are a little too thick for any sparks to be visible but I'm sure they're there. Shrodinger may have checked on the cat eight times but decided to leave the experiment as is on the ninth. The batteries will stay in the bag. Food could be the control if I knew which direction I wanted the experiment to go.

Sleek things appear bold because the space around them has more chance to shine.

I try to see the disc around people's heads as cultures of old used to. I pray it wasn't cataracts that influenced art. I'd rather be patient if that was the case. I've tried kneeling

down when I talk to people who are standing in front of the sun. I can see where they're coming from.

I've heard that if you can imagine yourself with a fishbowl on your head you're halfway there. Then you have to anthropomorphize your thoughts. They'll have a will of their own. Thoughts, let's say you chose fish, will swim around the outside of your head. Inside of your sphere, outside of your corporeal body. Don't poke the glass.

...

It was once easy to surround yourself with good people. There are too many causes for that to be possible nowadays. The wealthy were the best at surrounding themself in good company. The poor had a chip on their shoulder. They still made the statues.

We didn't make statues but murals instead. I never did much painting. It is not the leader's way. Those days are gone. We have satellite maps.

Bonnie wouldn't let anyone paint her. Probably for the same reason she cut her own hair.

We made a posthumous mural of Cole and his ride after they chased their shadow away from the hub. One of Cole's eyebrows is off. I think the artist forgot to paint it and someone added one inspired by looking at his girl's. That mural doesn't take up much space. I don't know who commissioned it.

There's another one of Cole with me next to him, beside an anteater. That was during our rise to power.

...

There's a strange feeling to being retired from a job that didn't exist. It's part of the reason I went back to work. Gainfully self-employed. If you love what you'll do you'll never think about work.

For the love of money I would have sold my left most toe. That would have made me ambitious. Take a finger for my toe and I would need to do extra to prove my desire to work. Explaining the loss of the finger wasn't a workplace injury and that I wasn't afraid to lose another one. There is

no one that can make that deal for me. No one would buy it anyways. It's not worth trying.

...

Music would make a good currency if it were relatable. I've heard good songs while I drive but fear writing down the experience because it would take me out of it. Giving suggestions later doesn't pan out well because my fares didn't listen to the songs that came before. It's like falling off a cliff without walking to the edge. My left most toe is worth just as much as any suggested music.

If I could bottle up my feelings and sell them as medicine I think I would. I've definitely felt laughter. There's a time limit that comes with it. If you don't start to feel self conscious when your smile starts to twist then you can extend the allotted time. Tolerance for pain is also a factor. The come down is brutal. Nothing seems so funny as trying to get a laugh. This makes for a vicious cycle.

...

If you see my car on the street, you might mistake that driver for me. That someone has style but must not be able to keep up with the times. I sold my last car fifteen years ago. Still getting royalties from the modifications that were licensed. It seemed like a good idea at the time to install cameras around the outside. I was going to be selling it after all.

I wasn't concerned with the people that bought the car but instead the places they would take it. I figured we must have similar personalities so I wanted to know the spots I was missing. I did take a vacation in a town they visited once. At a different time of course. That town will always remember me for as long as the advertisement holds up. I haven't went back to switch it out. They haven't went back to the town to vacation. I never changed the batteries on the car after selling it.

...

I definitely have an on and off switch. I don't let my work life carry into my personal life. That would be bad. I'm not sure how people do that. There will be times when I

pick up a fare and they are on the phone while I'm trying to add to their personal life experience. They don't realize that they won't get that time back but they most certainly will get longer work hours.

I also can't apprehend rail runners in any old place. Even if I know who they are and they know a skinnier faced me, I'm out of my element.

...

I don't mind having dogs in the car during my fares but appreciate when I'm given the heads up. A chauffeur always keeps their head forward. A dog being wrestled into the car may not make a sound until I've started driving. The dog doesn't have to be so nervous if I know it's there. I give it a thin lipped smile when I see it and a real toothy one to my customer. I give the customer the treats while maintaining eye contact with the dog. If the situation calls for another snarl I don't miss it.

Those customers are sometimes better trainers with their dog than my others. The free runners spend a lot more time with their dog but don't always train them correctly. I can't negotiate with a dog. Those dogs know how to attack but not much beyond that. On one follow up appointment there was a real turn around with one of my clients.

A dog that I had to kick in the balls because it's owner couldn't stop me from chasing after her was much more behaved when it met me in my second domain. The girl had improved much as well. She was able to dissuade me from chasing her when she called and asked for a ride. I was the one who suggested she bring her dog. I had seen commercials like that while pumping gas.

She said she digged the rig and I said it ain't like that. As with most of my repeat customers they have no direction. They were on the train so they wouldn't have to think. She asked me where an employee could find work. The dog barked before I could answer.

Her name was Clara and she had been an exterminator in a past life. The dog didn't have a name but came to come. Clara and Come had similar interests and were never apart.

She tried to leave the dog with me when I brought her back to the train station. It did help me find her to give it back. She gave a big tip and said she was just about to put up posters.

I saw the posters a week later while I was pumping gas. I took one of the tags off the print out and called Clara from inside a restaurant. I asked how could she not tell me that he had a name. I got a lot of sympathy hugs when I hung the phone up.

Clara is on her way to owning roller skates. She gave me some business from people she met at the dog park. They all warned that the dog wouldn't like the sound of the wheels on the pavement but she's going through with saving anyway.

...

The restaurant I was in when I made the call was vegan. Those people all feel a strong connection with each other through their shared suffering. We can't help but feel their pain. We are connected with them in misery.

...

I support shared suffering. If you can't bear the burden alone it's a smart move. I try to make life simple for my customers. They don't affect me much. I did gain that weight in my face though.

My apartment is cluttered. I find I can save on heat in the winter that way. I don't have much company. The company I do have also likes to be warm. We all had warm feelings towards you Bonnie. It didn't matter how you felt towards us. But you were more than your average person on a pedestal. It appeared that you truly cared about us and the others. Maybe it was the politician in you. Maybe it was that you really knew politicians despite all of their outward appearances.

My cost of living comes at the cost of living. I have a business now. I'm a shuttler. One of the first shuttlers to grace this wonderful land. There have been distant relatives before me. I could close the distance to their relatives faster than they could create more. I'm quite the driver. I don't recall ever seeing you drive. Not that we needed to all that much around the hub. It would be a shame if your lack of driving came from being born with an induction spoon in your mouth. Don't get me wrong, I would appreciate shuttling you around if you ever gave me a call. There is such joy to driving though. The eyes of the people in other vehicle's takes on a whole new meaning when you're behind the wheel.

It wouldn't surprise me if you were a master driver. How else could you be in so many places at once? Your skill with a map was impeccable but mine with a schedule could match that. I can't figure for the math. It was we three, Cole, you and I that never missed a train entering or exiting the yard. Even if you were able to switch trains effectively you would never reach the car rental place in time.

I don't rent cars myself but believe I and my colleagues have an understanding. I use their cars and don't interrupt when they complain about them being void of gas the next day. I use their cars and I let them feel like they are somehow more superior than I because of my lack of transportation. If they knew how readily I am able to find transport we may lose the understanding that we have.

You understand all this, Bonnie. All of our thought processes around the hub began to converge. I almost need not say anything in these letters.

...

I hear a lot of people telling stories where they make the person that tried to oppress them sound simple. It's a strange way of talking and sounds like what one does when they are asleep and are dreaming of yelling. I guess that's taking the high road of bitching. The low one would be snappy and biting. One is cruel through mimicry while the other is forward with it's insults.

I don't ever try to diffuse these situations, especially if they are on the phone, but I do ask them to read me the news from the foreign papers once they regain their dialect. The finance section is the most entertaining to me. One can't ever tell who is ahead or behind.

...

I lost my ass when I tried investing. I got rid of my smart phone shortly after that. I had a set of rules and I was very disciplined while trading. One of my stocks was priced much higher than the other one. I went by the percentages and not the dollar figures.

People were really angry when I lost my money. They couldn't believe that could happen to such a nice guy. I couldn't believe when I saw them on the train years later. They thought they were even nicer than I.

There are ways to get ahead in the markets but I chose to look at the microcosm. If you stare at a screen for too long the numbers start to change.

...

Some people in the neighborhood are friendly with each other. I'd be more inclined to being so if I wasn't constantly being berated with requests. It comes with the territory when you have a simple face. I will get around to cutting my grass. I promise I won't miss trash day next week.

I spend more time at my house than I used to. My neighbors think that makes me relatable because they also could go out but choose to stay home and enjoy the simpler things. We live in a gated community. The people here are guarded.

...

The trash truck is an eye sore to some and a sight for sore eyes to others. Anyone can paint the truck any way they like. Best to ask permission first. I don't add anything to the conversation.

Someone painted an eyeball being weighed against a block of gold. I think that was done by a tall woman.

...

I keep chalk in my locker at work. My hands are calloused but I'm able to get an even better grip on the train seats because of the chalk. I can propel forward and balance myself should I leave my feet for a kick. If the chase leaves four walls there are a lot of slippery things on the outside. Sometimes the slap leaves just as big a mark as a punch.

...

I received almost no punishments when I was growing up and coming of age. Which isn't to say I wasn't deserving but may have been too smart for my teachers. They disciplined me more regularly than my parents. The parents knew that almost everyone they had known growing up had turned out alright. The teachers never really grew up, out of college they may have even reverted. My parents are two of my biggest influences. They're starting to not do alright.

Physical discipline was the only kind of punishment that worked on me. I have a lot of patience for conversation. If you don't respect your handwriting then it's very easy to write lines. Instead, a ruler to the knuckles time after time. My parents would take away my toy trucks. Those teachers would have put the trucks in the attic, if only to talk about me behind my back.

If my parents weren't around to catch me in the act then they wouldn't discipline me after the fact. They believed that I was my own person and didn't have to be

the person I was around them if they were not around. I carried that in to every interaction I have now. You can be yourself when you're alone but be who you are around me when I'm nearby.

...

When I first saw how far we'd have to walk to get to the detention room I was stunned. Next thing I remember I had my hands folded and was standing in front of the class. The proctor said that those who stand with their hands behind their backs already look guilty and people are usually hard on them. I confessed my transgressions after introducing myself. Everyone said my name in unison but no one remembered it after the hour was up. That's one problem with going through the motions.

I remember there was one kid in detention with me who was named Vlad. He was five foot tall, weighed one hundred pounds and couldn't have been older than thirteen. His mom was the proctor. He was allowed to do whatever he wanted. It was antagonistic. Those were the days.

...

Those without a fighting spirit are already broken. And if it ain't broke don't fix it. So if you are inclined to fight you're perfectly healthy. Those who give up don't last long.

...

Research shows that no one needs to know anything. The people polled were very well read.

...

It was a good thing we didn't print our own literature around the hub. Nothing is classified.

...

Two soldiers walk into a bar. Their was dead air on their radio. When communications were reestablished I picked up the signal in one of the electric cars. I headed towards the scene and found a charging station. Everyone had questions that morning. I salute those that got any answers.

People are getting bigger. I notice this driving the electric cars. Shadows look larger at the pump. I urge

customers to turn on their hotspots when the charge is running out. They usually walk the rest of the way. GPS takes up too much bandwidth.

If I do pump gas it's always with gloves on. I don't let customers grab the steering wheel unless they too have gloves. Most asked for a ride for a reason and there aren't many complaints. The rubber disposables in the back are free for anyone to take. It's all factored into the final cost.

...

If you spend enough time on a train you're bound to hear an accordion. Don't fight it, it's just your brain trying to cope with the ordeal. Somewhere in your subconscious you've connected the two.

The wheezing takes me back. Some of our base lines were such that you knew a steady cough meant so-and-so was doing fine. Some's poison is crickets, others passing cars on the street, but what put me to sleep was the rhythmic battle for air.

...

I'm quick to jump on people who cough in the backseat. I know I shouldn't but it feels like they're mocking me. Dry coughs really set me off. Forgo contentment for a quick release. No your cough doesn't break the silence, it pollutes it. I'd rather a slap on the head while I'm driving than a passive aggressive whisper.

...

The foreign newspapers made a huge deal about the illegal drug trade on the internet. We never had to go to such extremes. We did find people to meet in person through the underside of the web. The web will never stop growing now. We are stuck but not so bad as the domain dealers.

We had runners. They wove in between time wasters but were prone to getting sidetracked. Another reason we didn't use email. Roads are limited. Tracks can go over water. I didn't read much into the hype.

I stayed away from any of the serious drug takers. The recreational users experimented more. Most of the stories

we heard were basic when they reached Cole, Bonnie and I. Bonnie could be the best or worst part of your trip. She sifted through your insecurities. She hardly did any work.

One of Cole's nephews got ripped off through the internet. Cole through the modem out a window. If you know where to look you can still see it on your way to Seattle.

...

If someone says you haven't lived till you've tried this, consider them already dead.

...

I could have become an engineer. I think too literally though and when things were explained to me, if they weren't worded absolutely correctly, went right over my head. Being new to the task I didn't have the confidence to improvise and so never learned.

I've got experience driving and making amends for people. Repent is such an ugly word. There's no true north in a moral compass. I'd rather get tipped than played.

...

If I do have to put someone on retainer I get paid hand over fist. It's not stealing if I'm doing my job. As long as their hand touches the money first I should be good. Smelling salts provide opportunity for a rematch. Then it's double or nothing.

The quick nap doesn't provide much as a refresher. I very rarely have to give the money back. I let them sleep the second time. They're in my back pocket.

I leave a business card. When I was more crass I would leave the shirt off my back. I couldn't get away with wearing the shirt had I not gained that weight in my face.

...

People are allowed to smoke in my car but not if they're in the front seat. The windows are always slightly rolled down in the back. It's amazing how focused you are when you start to get annoyed. Too bad the focus is usually counterproductive.

...

I have a hard time eating food from restaurants because of all the variables. Even if I stick with one fast food chain, the packaging can vary from place to place and so can the utensils. If I sit down at a nicer establishment I spend so much time trying to appreciate everything around me that the food is wasted. Some of the best food I've ever had has been at a hole in the wall joint.

...

You know enough about trains to question where all the trash goes. Know enough about trash to know trains were invented in a time before trash morals were prevalent. Short answer is, we do with it what we can. Longer answer is there's never a shortage of food for the fire.

...

One good thing about moving through the country side is the lack of people. Anything that needs to be let loose from the train can be dumped just about anywhere. Any people close enough to care are usually too close. Anyone else sees it much too late. By the time the person can even wonder where the trash came from, we're already miles away and have been picking up garbage at each stop.

The waste containers are standard gray. The people that are encouraged to use them make them look better. The trash bucket has no shame compared to the person.

A lot of people look around after they've put something down. I don't ever ask what someone just threw away. If I could have used it I'm sure it would have been offered.

...

I leave my feet in dreams almost as much as I do chasing down prey. My job is of a predatory nature. My dreams give me hope that I can cover even more territory in the future. If I fly around too much I'm stopped by an unexplained weight in my legs. I've never seen what I look like in a dream.

The closest I've come to seeing my reflection has been while awake. It is important to see yourself in others. It is

more important that others see you for themself. What's the purpose otherwise.

...

If you can live with yourself you'll never need a room mate. If you can live by your self you'll never need a room.

...

Dottie was my landlord when I was living in an apartment. She didn't live there. I had her come by my place sometimes. I always turned the tv's volume way up when she was planning to stop by. That way she knew no one was in there with me. She would have heard competing voices otherwise.

Dottie says that a dollar saved is a penny earned. It's her way of saying that you'll never save enough money. She said misery loves company. She didn't trust banks.

I invited Dottie inside a few times when I had cooked too much. She understood I couldn't bring the leftovers to work. She was very good at selling apartments.

Her office was on the other side of town from the train station. She worked in the city proper but loved selling just about anywhere. The name of her business even had sell in the title. She didn't advertise her personal number. She already had me sold.

...

I used a landline phone then and I still use one now. I'll borrow someone's mobile if I'm in a jam, or rifle through the in case of emergency contacts if I'm in a more favorable position. It's not a crime if you do the time and I do my homework. I know the vital signs. The perpetrators are never in any real danger. Smelling salts prove that.

I don't offer the salt to any of my fares. Fear of them dozing off on me is never a concern. Most of the time they lead the conversation. If they have a destination they almost always stay awake. The reruns are accustomed to sleeping while traveling. I don't allow them a second dose should they be of the fight instead of flight or compromise type.

The runners that accept my offer for a ride without squaring up are good folk. I casually slip smelling salts into the conversation to gauge their reaction. If I see them on the train again it could be useful information. I'm getting better at reading faces I've seen before.

...

You always said the furthest thing from the truth was usually a surprise. I'm still not sure that I know what that means. Truth is, you didn't need to say sensible things. We didn't need to listen but we still always did. Your voice carried and the acoustics of the hub seemed to be built for you. Though you never joined in with the band, they would have loved to have you. Probably tell you to jump in anytime. They were a good group of musicians. Saying anything else would tarnish their reputations.

Your reputation preceded you. We always made sure of that. We wanted to make sure you would have the best interaction possible when meeting strangers for the first time. They might not have known, but probably did, how special you were. We didn't want anyone to waste your time. Giving a short biography of you was easy and ever changing. Your reputation was that of factotum. In real life you were so much more.

You may not remember the second time we met. In fact, you didn't. I asked if you remembered the joke I told when we first met. You said no. The retelling didn't go over very well at all. Perhaps somewhere in your memory you recognized the joke, which made it hard for you to laugh when you heard it again. I'll spare you from what I said. There's absolutely no chance that you'd enjoy it now.

Your laugh was contagious. And not because we all wanted to encourage you. Hearing it from a distance would make it feel like between we and you there was less distance. Hearing it face to face made us marvel how such a genuine sound could come from teeth so white. It was as distinctive a laugh as one could find. You seemed to be everywhere. The laugh assured us you were really there.

I never laughed much around the hub. Not for lack of trying. It just seemed that we could never get ahead. It was my job to make sure we did. I can laugh about it now, even if it is pensively. I think everyone managed to get away from the hub alright. Surely you left after Cole and his girl took off and I vanished into thin air.

Someone gave me a card reader but it got thrown from the train, more civil then being thrown from a car, after the transition to every card having a chip. It may be more secure, but the people who use them that are overly concerned with their safety scare me. I don't want to cater to their paranoia. Cash is my way before the highway. Their conversation is usually dull, lacks originality and seems to be prefabricated. If you don't have anything nice to say at least make something up. It's hard to drive listening to a take that's already been took for all it's worth.

Some times those people that pushed for extra security for their cards have a baby with them. They are already training the baby to rehearse as they do. It's not an exaggeration. They are training babies while they feel unsafe. It shouldn't be a problem until the baby starts to talk and listen at the dinner table.

It's better to act spontaneous than to be spontaneous. You can act like a baby is fully grown but you can't act like a baby. Babies have every reason to be scared of the world. Act rationally. Be scared of your baby.

...

I developed a sweet tooth when I learned that sugary foods digest differently. Can even cure stomach pains. Because of this I try to at least have one chocolate bar before going to bed. I get all the energy I need for the day from a meal at supper and whatever else is good to eat in front of the tv.

I watch tv so that I'll eat more. I'm able to get creative with those food choices because they are creative with the packaging. I spend much more time in the dry goods aisles than I do near any freezer. There used to be commercials on tv for just about anything. Now just about anything can be a commercial. Very few for tvs.

...

I have a laptop computer at my house. There's no internet. I use it for typing.

Eating food while watching tv has gotten me accustomed to subtitles. I have a foot pedal for my laptop

so that I can transcribe audio recordings. You can't download off a streaming site so I don't miss out much. Lectures are more my pace and can be bought in most major markets.

It takes a while to transcribe the audio but the foot pedal helps. When I'm done I'm able to load the product into a media player that utilizes a music visualizer. Although I can't see the performer the abstract art moves with the sound of the voice. I'm able to read the subtitles. I don't want to write much more about the lectures, they're too played out already.

...

We had plenty of people who believed they had something to say. I'm only saying any of this now because I'm so far removed. We didn't print any literature. What is left unsaid makes the world go round.

One of the better orators who actually stayed around the hub for while was Tertan. He was dyslexic but couldn't spell anyway. Going by the name that had given him so much grief throughout school helped to keep him honest. He never conceded in a debate.

The debates were philosophical, such as they are in any camp of degenerates, and they served no purpose other than entertainment. We knew we couldn't change anything. We were as sure of that as the train coming around the bend.

...

We never had to worry much about the train schedules. Most of us were already on board. Coal, Bonnie and I had taken care of that. If Cole, Bonnie and I were on board it should have meant everyone else was. In the rare case that the hub was without leaders, runners were left to fend for themselves and hope the car and time they picked were adequate. Those were few and far between. Cole, Bonnie and I didn't always travel together so didn't always see eye to eye. The inside of a train car is just as comfortable as the outside of four which have you boxed in. People had their crews. I was lucky enough to be in Bonnie's.

I think Cole must have put in a good word for me. One was about as much as you'd get out of him. Or, Bonnie sees something in me that I don't. It's hard to read someone who has reader's eyes. They're thinking about what you're thinking, while you can only think to hope you haven't thought anything damning. I don't know how much someone with them eyes gets paid but it should be much more than I'm getting. I couldn't get paid to read people. Gainful self employment wouldn't allow it. I wouldn't be able to set a fair price.

...

If you knew how to talk and didn't care if people listened, gambling was probably your speed. You couldn't talk yourself away from the table. There were some people who had more sway than your own conscience. I wasn't an enforcer yet. I couldn't help those who couldn't help themself. If I didn't know now that I didn't know then.

How I came to be regarded as a leader was momentarily questioned after I'd been standing around the tables for a while. As soon as they learned I was unable to play. Also, since I hadn't sat down. You can't fake it till you make it with cards. If there's any question in your eyes that you don't know how to play, how quickly they'll lie about your hand. Instead of losing to each and every subordinate who understood the simple game, my excuse was that people of my caliber played a different game. One that Cole and Bonnie would understand but not many beyond that. I made sure the game was explainable and believable but incomprehensible.

I do practice throwing cards. My goal is to get so good that I'll never have to show my technique. Just knowing what I have in my hand would give me the confidence to handle unstable situations.

I don't think a card can stop a bullet. You can't palm a gun though. Quick draw, hee haw.

...

Remember leap frogging as a kid? Now imagine throwing backpacks over fences as an adult. It's not how

fast you can run if you get to the drop first. The fences were so we didn't have to go around buildings. We cut through them instead.

Inside of the backpacks could be anything. We only ran when we hadn't planned. We never ran in the countryside.

...

You can get a good meal if able to look presentable. If you have enough time you can always get a good meal. Too much and you might over think your appearance. Out in our country in the country, where cities are smaller than some city's towns, you can find a good place to sleep. It's good to get out of the boxed cars every now and again, even if never quite free of their influence. You'll be charged more if you don't look presentable. Lodges aren't running a charity. No matter how bad you're in need of a room there will always come a price.

What makes a good place to sleep has a lot to do with the people who sleep nearby. If the city never sleeps you're probably not safe doing so either. There are places with unlocked doors. Awake people usually congregate in those places. Out in our country in the country where cities are smaller than city's towns lies the exception. Those are they that sleep whenever. Them are those who are always tired.

...

It's always smart to turn off the light when you're exiting a room. If you're in a sun room leave them off at all times. A full moon can be ruined by a spark.

...

Breathing in smoke isn't necessarily healthy but smelling fire does a lot for cognitive function. Incense is a masking agent. It is burned for the setting so that the characters will all be on the same stage.

I don't think burning incense is a power move.

When wood is being burned nearby, and it is controlled and has been for some time, a familiarity seems to be in the air. Ever since someone first drew smoke and a fire so that they could explain what they had seen, we have felt a deep affinity for that which first made us wonder.

...

We don't think much about lakes being thrown onto buildings. Poured on city blocks in a controlled manner. We do think about how much sand it takes to make a beach look significant in front of an ocean.

Most people nowadays give me side eye when I offer a plastic refreshment bottle.

...

Someone once quoted someone as saying that one man's trash is another man's treasure. One man's brand is another man's measure.

...

I met the new coffee making machine. His technique is pretty good. That's what he tells me. I don't drink the stuff. People of all ages try to brag if you put them in a corner.

I don't really introduce myself to people so I don't ever have to say my name. If someone wants to meet me, they'll probably have waited long enough to ask around and figure mine's out. I'm nowhere near being strong enough to say my name and tie it to a profession.

...

The business canvases are doing half my volunteer job for me. I still offer rides if potential fares don't run first. The land line has been ringing on to the floor. I need to attach it to a wall. Will probably get an answering machine first. That could get knocked over by the phone. A lot to think about in between fares.

If you've ever tried asking advice about advice you've probably stopped talking a long time ago. Questions like that seem to linger and answers will enter your thoughts during silences that could go unfilled. I'm not afraid to pose nonsense questions but only if it's to get back to something specific.

...

I always felt weird as a token kid when I exchanged money at an arcade. It was something about the warning that the tokens were non refundable which gave me pause. I may have been more likely to not think about the

consequences had I not been reminded. I overcame that and eventually felt good about spending money to make money. The prizes were special because the vendor said so. I couldn't be told otherwise. I was a token kid.

I won a watch during a time when I was very ambitious. Other children at school had chipped in to make a football team and ended up winning money when they won one tournament. I bought tokens. I was too competitive at that age to form a squad. There were only so many prizes and I didn't want to know anyone that had the same toys. Sometimes my choices were made for me and I would walk in the shoes of someone who had a better exchange rate than I. Whatever prizes they claimed were the ones I sought.

I don't think I know anyone that grew up to work at the arcade. Someone must have because the money exchange kiosk is still plugged in. The arcade has a sign out front that says tokens are now refundable. You won't get what you paid for them but the arcade could really use some returns.

...

They say you forget things as you get older. How it seems I remember you better with each passing day. They also say you don't miss something until it's gone. I never thought I'd miss the hub but the possibility of you being there has me longing. I imagine you must be running the whole operation now. Perhaps you believed you should have from the start. That could explain your lapse in memory. If the whole time I was around you don't believe I contributed then it's a shame on me for not knowing. My face is so simple to read. Your's makes mine look ridiculous.

I'm glad to have a ridiculously simple face in most situations. The present one excluded. If you saw me now you'd probably have an easier time remembering me in the future. Not because we would have had more encounters, but on account of the weight I now carry in my face. I carry the weight for those who never read the nutrition label on what they were eating. For the stuffed but never full. I wear the weight for those who have long since ate their share, but still believe a better taste is out there. Until I make a move so you can see my face right, you'll never remember my face but anything light.

When I was around you at the hub my face wasn't exactly gaunt. However, that is the closest word I can use to describe it. It didn't quite match the rest of my body but whose does in time of stress. I tried to make the load easier for you. If you didn't notice than I either did my job really well or it was a job that didn't need to be done. I still wouldn't have minded doing it, if only to have you on my mind. Your words were spoke in such a way that it made you voice extremely hard to remember. Your inflection was always right and the wisdom always warranted, so our brains always taxed. You could have sounded like anything. We had to repeat what you said in our heads with our own inner voice just to comprehend. It was still a good voice to have in your head while working.

Some things you are never too old for. Other things old people shouldn't do. I hope I'm fried before I get old.

Everyone wishes to convey how young they really are on the inside. I'd have an excuse to make other people believe it. An old man and an infant walk into the bar.

They say that taste is first to go. Not too concerned with that one. Eyes and ears don't stand a chance. The nose has a lifetime of experience and smells start to mean more. Touch seems to be more sensitive but you've already lost touch of that sense and it's just your body telling you that it's not running properly. Hot and cold are not subjective.

...

If you whistle while you work with your tongue behind your teeth, and you hear a whistle overhead, write a letter to your hard hat to bury along with your tongue, and put the two to bed. It's strange to never not hear the sound your breath makes.

...

The runners taught the lucky ones how to whistle. It is in their nature to tire of huffing and puffing. They had a lot of time on their hands. They were very fast.

They would bring back new whistles for our ears and the experienced whistlers knew how hard it was to produce the sounds they made. The feeble tone was the most challenging. Having it heard was next to impossible.

A strong whistle could mean a number of different things. We talked strategy while warming up. The runners would jog in place. The sound of their footsteps led our heads to mirror theirs. Left, right, forward, back, up, down, crick, crack. None of us were able to think much about what we were saying. They probably retained more because their movement was forced, while our's was subconscious.

We could always yell if it came to that. We were never in town long enough for our voices to be recognizable.

...

I try to keep a calm voice when I'm talking to my passengers. I've already sold them on getting into the car. So long as their criticism is never constructive I'm able to keep my composure. Arguments for the sake of arguing can

be postponed. They can say whatever they want about the way I'm doing things if it's not true.

If they knew how the operation ran then I would have to listen. I could only listen if it was posed as a hypothetical and didn't remind me of my business. I'd be an open book then. Someone would close that book on me once they were done reading. I'd have to then open the book on them.

...

We accepted change along with anything else we could grasp. I keep a cup in the center console for any coins my fares need to get rid of. There are hand written I owe yous also in there. Those from people whom I couldn't read their cards. The future with I owe you debtors is uncertain.

Change is good for gambling. Anyone that tries to take the money and run usually leaves a trail to their hideout if they make it that far. The energy we ask of the batteries may be more costly than the quarters we wish to find using flashlights after a flee. Catching the runner was the top priority so coins would get trampled down into the mud. Being thorough involves working overtime.

I can throw a card faster than someone who has been losing at a table can run. I never had someone to catch.

...

The cars I drive cannot be caught. Pictures are taken of the cars when I go through toll lanes. The ez-pass signals that I've paid and the footage is deleted to free up space. Still worth getting my money's worth on the off chance it isn't, though chances are a robot won't get my humor. I'm not sure where the drivers of the other cars need to go that they would choose to give up their privacy. My own customers are from all walks of life.

If I'm called for a ride and the customer wants the conversation to lead to somewhere, I sometimes take them on the toll roads so that I may be inspired. Some state license plates have artwork behind the number and letter configuration. Those states need all the help they can get. The people that requisitioned to be their sponsor even

more. The plates provide food for thought. I go with my gut after inspiration strikes and take the customer to whatever connection I make.

...

I'm not ready to use a bean backed seat cover yet. I think it would skew my customer's perspective. It may even bring on relapse in the salt smellers, who, seeing me travel in luxury because of my pain and the support the cover provides, will long for the cars of old. Better not to give them the idea.

...

When you're in a cargo car there is not much space to manoeuvre. It usually took about an hour and a half for one of us to settle in for a ride. Once you found a comfortable spot you couldn't believe how much better it was then what you normally subject yourself to. Train cars are pretty stable when they move so you didn't have to worry about falling in your sleep. You learned pretty quickly not to sleep on the floor on windy routes.

There are no windows in those cars and the free runner's journey is nowhere near as important as the destination. The destination never seemed to come and it might have had to do with the lack of change in scenery. If you spend eighteen hours a day around coffee beans it's hard to appreciate what's around you when you are without.

...

They say if you teach a man to fish you can probably teach him to do other things. After a while you can teach that hobbies, no matter how fulfilling, lead to nowhere. Couple the sentiment citing the hobbyist's counterpart, the businessman, with their take on being self taught.

Bettering oneself is a hobby. Money is the measure of man.

...

We had a trick at the hub that would get semi favorable dogs towards us to eat out of our hands in nearly

no time. If the dog was questionable we put the food on the ground until it was comfortable.

Since the generator was used to charge the clippers and very few other things, we got warm using blankets and layers of clothes. If someone were laying down with a blanket over their body and a dog was nearby, that person would pull the blanket over their head and hold it maybe sixteen inches above themself. If the dog came over it would investigate the man made cave and find kinship with the architect. It was simple but effective. With such good results we tried it every chance we had. It'd have been crazy not to.

...

We only socialized with dogs around the hub. When we traveled it would have been irresponsible to form any connections around the country. The taste of honey is worse than none at all. We couldn't bring any dogs on the train anyway. We volunteered to be human cargo, they did not.

...

It's easier to imagine a train carrying cargo than one carrying hundreds or thousands of individuals. If you see a train passing by and think your life is important, it's hard to imagine all those passengers you measure yourself by think the same thing about themselves. The passengers think the same about the people they pass as is thought of them. Most of the tracks go through the country side.

Train passengers think less of people living near tracks. They don't think them practical. They have taken a train for pleasure. They themselves live near highways so that they can conduct business.

Country dwellers who live close enough to train stops are not seen as practical either because of the heavy tourism traffic. If you get off a train and someone isn't trying to sell you something, it's only because they don't have a prototype yet.

Houses near train stops all seem to be lacking in some regard. I can't put my finger on it but they all seem close to

crumbling. The people that live there must sell in order to take their mind off their living situation.

All this can go unnoticed by sitting in a cargo car.

...

I try not to mix business and meetings. Time is money. Since I'm the only one in my department, and have no one to conference with concerning matters that only concern the would be us, if I'm given an agenda, I'm able to answer any questions with finality.

...

Purgy helped to organize the union for the district the hub was located in. When I was still running in circles, I would've been helped tremendously had I known his story. It was Cole, Bonnie and I when our time came. Purgy left out a lot of candidates to be representatives. Purgy put in long hours looking at mug shots. They would have been able to be headshots if not for the bad lighting.

Purgy chose two representatives to head the union in the district. Sam and Hank were the names that they called each other. No one ever enunciated when they called them. They always responded anyway but to the untrained ear it sounded like someone was about to say something but had broken off.

Union representatives have two voices. Outside and inside. They wear corresponding hats.

...

Bonnie could almost make you believe she advocated fair wage. I'm not sure what Bonnie believed herself but we all believed in her. She was our Purgy.

...

Great expectations come to those who wait. Wait too long and they'll be forgotten and cannot be resumed with the same vigor. With your expectations lowered when whatever is set to happen, happens, you'll be able to objectively rate the experience. If your great expectations are not forgotten you may be disappointed.

...

I've only woke once to the walls closing in. I was in one of the cars and I must have been really tired because I didn't hear the door open. I woke to bags of rice being pushed into my sides. The workers loading the car must also have been lacking because I wasn't noticed. I make more noise when I'm asleep than I do awake.

...

Degenerates used to be able to find work by being test subjects. The medicine was developed and worked wonders for our kind. It wasn't marketable to the general public. We got paid with the medicine.

There were plenty of home remedies that took up shelf space. Capsules would have been easier to swallow and taken up less space. If one of the recipes called for swallowing a spoonful of cinnamon we could do nothing but accept. The pharmaceutical companies must have had a stronger brand.

A lot of us had foot problems. We carried all our problems on our backs.

...

I speak of our tribe as a collective but we traveled light and mostly alone. Those of us that paired off, or were already such, and knew their partner's body better or as well as their own, were able to travel together. The time it took to find a comfortable place to rest their head was reduced because of help from the expert observer.

...

If you are asked to hold a mirror up for someone that person may want you to leave. A friend needs to be able to inspire confidence.

...

You can never be too over confident. Once the line is crossed there is no going back.

Unless the source of the confidence is identified the big foot will always go back for smaller shoes.

...

Clowns show that they aren't big enough for their own shoes. Some people feel insecure around clowns.

...

We didn't have a masktasker. We weren't that kind of organization. We all gathered around the hub but no one was in it for anyone else. We didn't need disguises. We all could see through each other.

We forbid masks around the hub. It was a way to keep out tourists. Anyone that was truly committed to getting a free ride knew that they had to show their face. If someone did managed to get lost and trapped between the boxcar walls we helped them by showing their way out.

If they found their way back they couldn't say they got lost again. A hand helped wants to bite to prove it's still capable. If you ride escalators all day you'll end up mad at the stairs.

...

There was a pickpocket on one of the outer fringes of our society. He was in constant competition with one of the adopted dogs. The dog didn't even notice him. The man dug up the dog's burial sites and moved whatever objects were stored away. He would transfer the objects to a new spot. The dog always found the loot quickly. The man smelled just like the dog.

...

I am nowhere near the tracker the dog is.

...

Around the world, you said. It's nothing but a big blue ball, you said. Us that were privy knew this was how you slyly slid in a dance was coming up. Everyone else thought you were making plans to travel. If we believed anyone could accomplish that feat it would be you. You had a head start growing up on a military base. Forgive me if the details aren't correct.

It felt like we were in the service every time you gave a command. How ready and able we were to please. How void of thought and focused when we knew what goal you wanted to accomplish. How thoughtful we were upon completion. It always gave me a rush. I hope it was also good for you.

You were a people pleaser, a people person, and a person of the people Bonnie. When you were alone you were a person of interest. In crowded places you were as if on a pedestal. If on a boat, you outdid the figurehead. Only when sneaking onto a train were you not eye catching. I've seen you do it but that was only because we worked together. Let your pride not be hurt.

Maybe you did notice me observing your furtive movements. I was probably the only one who ever did catch you. Perhaps that will help you remember. I almost certainly wasn't wearing the brown jacket and green hat. No decorations or medals to speak of either. You hopped shortly before I usually did, so I might have been wearing my running gear.

My running gear was tan camouflaged. It threw others off my trail who assumed I couldn't possibly be going to cold climates dressed as I was.

The best guesswork is subjective. Time is relative. Guessing correctly relatively fast, if able to be affirmed immediately, leaves most astounded.

I was able to correctly identify a wanted criminal. I was pulled from off the street and when I came to was looking at five people who'd have killed to be in my shoes..

My memory was a little foggy at first but the more the suspects stared at themselves in the mirror the more I remembered. I never followed up with my supervisor from that day.

...

I have never sat on a jury. Never wanted to, so decided to never give myself that chance. No need to say I'm impartial to November reign. You cannot vote to convict if you are not registered to vote.

...

If you saw my advertisement on a park bench in all it's grandeur, your first thought may be I probably voted for so-and-so's party. I'm too good at picking to ever want to have a record.

...

Bonnie's late uncle was recently in the news. He wasn't as big a success as his brother-in-law but was just as good a family man. He ran a hardware store. Their slogan was, if it ain't broke, you probably bought it here.

I've thought of writing to Bonnie recently. I've even thought of reconnecting with the old scouts to see if any new hubs have popped up. All it takes is four trains and a novice at the switchboard. There is still time yet to think of what I'll say. It's important to have reasons for your future actions.

...

There is a rush to get new laws in the books. Artificial intelligence is on the horizon and the powers that be are not at bay. Every election year there will be a few clauses that can be voted on and will be passed. I'm not sure if the goal is to help or hurt the artificial intelligence. I'm sure they'll let us know when they arrive.

Everyone kept their distance at the hub so there was not much law breaking when we were together. If you are mostly only concerned with your own self interests, as is everyone else around you, there is hardly ever conflict because both sides know where the other is coming from.

We know where artificial intelligence comes from but not where it's coming from. Not yet.

...

I obey the rules of the road when I'm driving. I approach every rotary as a self driving car would. I blink twice as a courtesy to people whose eyes I feel on me. I brake more gradually when I have passengers in my car. I avoid deep puddles so I won't need to swerve. I treat other drivers with respect.

I learned how to drive by watching old movies. I learned that if you are constantly self correcting you're able to stay on the straight and narrow. If I wasn't so heavily influenced I may not feel the need to have passengers in the car.

Between fares and on my way to the hubless tracks I drive solo. I usually have my best thoughts about music during those times. I appreciate the art form for it's own sake and I can't pretend to look for connections with passengers at every interesting lyric. The radio has seen better days. It's good that it can't listen in on me.

...

Some people say that you're favorite music is that of when you were younger. Others say that it ends up being that which you discover. Some people prefer terrestrial radio while others are their own curators. Living is easy with eyes closed.

...

I think it was around the time Bonnie was acting as midwife to Sister Nancy that I met someone for the first time. She had been around the hub for a few months but never said much. The way she looked at me I knew she didn't believe the hype. She returned to camp after a brief stint of absence and I was the first one she told that she had got cochlear implants. Once she heard the sound of my voice she understood why I was revered. She traveled less after that fact. People she thought were her friends became her enemies and her enemies, friends. The world around her suddenly looked different.

...

All of my senses have faded over the years. Some faster than others. Others catching up in next to no time. Smell being one of the underdogs.

We all looked for our first free ride with bright eyes and speeding hearts. We knew towns by the restaurants within them and our noses knew us. Spend enough time around moving vehicles and your nose starts to beat itself up. It's hard to find the same excitement for an old favorite when your senses don't oversell it. Pizza shops may smell great but provide no positive visual stimulation.

Ears have heard too much screeching. Eyes have been in the dark too long. Fingertips are raw from work. Still trying to acquire taste.

...

After spending time with the cargo you become very familiar with ingredients used in preparing meals. All the time you spend looking for a suitable place to sit pays off when brands seep into your consciousness. Because your primary concern is looking for the space in the cargo car that will have you, all the labels you can't help but notice while searching take a backseat but are not forgotten.

I don't cook in my apartment. I used to when I lived there but I felt I had something to prove to myself then. Once I reached the place I wanted to be and had no one to share my success with, I lost interest in cooking. When every meal you makes tastes good to you you lose your appetite.

I don't ever encounter uncongenials actively eating. Even if food stuff ingredients are surrounding them they don't test my patience. It's one thing to search for a free ride but never look for a free lunch. I imagine if I ever came across someone engorging I could expect a fight.I don't think they'd be the type to run and probably wouldn't want to argue after a meal. I have not yet done battle with a full stomach.

...

You're not supposed to go swimming until at least a half hour after eating. Then any food in the water won't look so appetizing. The food near bodies of water will send you running. What eats the food served near bodies of water hasn't been tested for edibility. What eats the flesh of people in bodies of water hasn't been vaccinated against. Unofficially there are lots of species in the food chain.

...

I was taught as a child that our bodies are like pyramids that house great persons already dead. The eyes are windows to the soul. Something looks back out.

...

Bonnie could win any staring contest. She knew when you were going to blink before you did.

...

I've tried staging contests for my fares. In one competition the winner of a no entry raffle won the opportunity to set up my outgoing voicemail. It doesn't sound like much, but it was a chance for someone not widely known to the circles I run in to be heard. This was after I had already gotten my face seen by people who looked away from waiting passengers at the bus stop to avoid awkwardness. When I had won a contest of my own. After that.

I gave notes as to how I thought they should sound. I knew how the people they didn't know thought and what would be appropriate. A few winners quit early. The voice I went with was gravelly and finished their work. They went on to do voices for network television children's shows. I kept the recording to this day. Similar sound bites are available but none which advertise my business.

...

Every time I drive a fare I get better at my job. If I were a perfectionist I wouldn't be able to learn from my mistakes. Conversation is not as simple. If I'm unable to keep up with foreign affairs I may find myself in a hole and digging deeper. Losing streaks can go on for weeks of conversation time, a few days in the ride share profession.

They say that brevity is the soul of wit. It must be this way otherwise favorable opinions would turn. You can be the most intelligent person in the world for ten minutes but not ten hours. My fares average about thirty minutes. If I wanted to appear intelligent I would play music. I try to draw out conversations. It's not entrapment if there's no ill will.

On the other side of town, in what I consider my farm league extermination duties, I do try to keep suggestions short and simple. If I try to be too over persuasive I end up seeing the holes in my approach. A fine observation to be made in retrospect but not easily hidden face to face. Out of breath from the sales pitch, the ensuing chase is taxing. Very few who do not accept my offer the first time end up fighting with me the second time. They don't see the point.

With great whit comes little brevity.

...

If you have your ducks lined in a row you're probably in the coop. If your time card is spotted you've probably been working hard.

...

I don't believe in taking days off from work. There's too long until I retire.

I don't have any positive role model retirees in my life and that has me worried.

...

Woe to the worrier, the warrior wanes tragically.

...

I ask my fares to wipe their feet before getting in to the cars. Cargo civilians to not make me peel them off my shoe. Neither party listens, which is how I know there's a little bit of both in both of them.

The fares I ask so that they may feel like their entering my home. The civilians so that they'll know how far my hospitality extends.

...

I remember you mostly with your hair down. You did have nice ears though. All the better for hiding I suppose. It was a constant struggle between Cole, I and yourself to keep runners out of sight. When I think back on those days, I can't believe we pulled it off. Sure we lost some runners because where we temporarily hid them was no longer accessible. They should have known the spot was only temporary. Don't be too hard on yourself, Bonnie. An old seeker can't teach the newly ignorant anything.

You taught us all more than you know. How you did so is beyond me. Every day there was a lesson to be learned. We learned that from you early on. Your feats were spoken of around the hub. When I wasn't in uniform or my green jacket, I was very inconspicuous. I'd tell you the stories I heard about you but the brilliance would be lost in the written word. I'm sure some made their way back to you anyway. All rivers lead to the ocean. All oceans were between you and us.

We modestly tried to close the distance. I for one was as friendly as the environment would allow. Cole never did wrong. Scouts made sure you were the first to know. Underlings met you in the middle. The dogs gave their best howls when they saw you approach.

You were a string of lights in a tunnel. A ton of life in the rubble. If it was discovered the world revolved around you it would come as no surprise. All of our heads were spinning whenever you were around. Sorry if the work ever suffered because of this. Sorry for all the interesting takes runners had on tasks, trying to impress you. A job well done was done for you.

I remember that was always how you said you liked your food. Well, done. Of course! So simple yet the absolute closest thing to the truth. I would like to be able to eat my food please. We all ate fast around the hub. Blame it on our pasts. When asked what you thought about your meal you'd repeat your slogan. Different emphasis. Also when asked how your food was. It was as if you were so involved in the experience that no other words could come to mind. But to

use the same two words effectively for three different questions. Bonnie, you were something else.

The train station has no use for recreational vehicles. Otherwise I'd use one. To have a house on wheels is any rail runner's dream. We are content just about anywhere so long as the journey was over. To realize your dreams stifles both notions. I could live the dream without having to live asleep. Anyways, the rvs would probably be noticed if they disappeared from the lot.

...

I once joked to one of my coworkers about their car. I was lucky they didn't take me seriously. I'm vigilant about checking the miles I put on and am lucky my peers are not. I wouldn't be the prime suspect for the joy rides. My coworkers know how many hours I put in. They don't know much about my past.

My supervisor knows enough about me to do her job. Anything more and I'd have her on the hook for harassment. I don't mind her though. Most of my coworkers are alright as well. They don't get in my way and if they do are quick to move. Their view of me is obstructed, as every proper workplace should be.

I don't take their doughnuts or coffee. Not even when it's offered. I appreciate someone spending money on me but I can't keep up with the charades. I'm not envious of the expressive faces of my coworkers when they take the first bite but am not totally at peace with it either. To explain how I lost my sense of taste usually takes longer than finishing an appetizer. They don't have time for me if I don't have time for a doughnut.

My supervisor doesn't partake. Just as I didn't partake when I was leader. The offerings are different but the meaning of the word no is the same.

...

I look like the kind of person that can say no to fun. The kind of person who doesn't know how to say yes to a good time. You know the type if you are one. We make the best

excuses. Excuses so grandiose that if we could just continue the story could be the life of the party. I've tried telling simple looking people this secret. The look on their faces.

...

If you see the gas station you've gone too far.

...

I have some experience interviewing for jobs. The interviewer loves when they are asked questions about the company. They would like to move up the ladder as much as anyone. They can't change anything as a recruiter but can suggest to people who can. Whether or not those people remember the recruiter when they are at the summit, and the ideas they borrowed, is uncertain.

I didn't get the last job I interviewed for. The recruiter said I should write down my goals and try later.

...

When I first actively started to spot the metaphorical needle in the hay stack, that of the civilian hidden in the cargo, I reported to no one. My supervisor didn't interview me but we sat down for a consultation. We both had things to offer each other. She didn't hear it from me, but word had got around I was sweeping with a vengeance. She gave me authority she may not have had to give. She would look the other way.

When I was able to go unnoticed it was decided I could receive compensation and even take on bounties. Names weren't given but descriptions of the suspects and tendencies they may have were. Not all free runners flock to the same areas. Different climates for different primates.

The fares of mine that face forks in the road with every sign, sometimes believe a one eighty needs to be taken. Anything that reminds them of their past pushes them to move in the opposite direction. A reformed runner may wish for a ride to the beach after a lifetime of going to mountains. The waves being called back to the ocean is like the chairlift returning to the top. I still commend them for making the effort. The world is not hot and cold.

...

Contrary to popular belief is disliked fact.

...

Before I was able to sit down with my thoughts, and before I was looking for about an hour and a half for a place to sit, I spent some time apprenticing. I left before I became a master. A few years later I returned to the master and offered to learn for free for two weeks since I had given such short notice.

The trade is now completely done by machines, who do all the work for free. My master must be close to one hundred now. If I had been able to finish my training I would have a colleague. I don't begrudge my master for not trading with me.

...

I've seen a group of people follow a leader into a freezing ocean. They all followed a different leader out.

...

I am an influence now and leader may have been the wrong term for back then. It was me, Bonnie and Cole, and together we made a horse's mouth. I was left to do the public announcements. Bonnie's voice would have incited radicals. Cole never talked much.

From the passenger's viewpoint I cannot be seen as a leader. They can see my front through the rearview but my back is to them and I'm not leading into battle. A leader would never be that vulnerable. I am in their service but they don't think of me like that. Many young recruits didn't believe that sentiment at first either. 'If you really wanted to help than you would be nicer.'

Although I'm always in full view I still do a lot behind the scenes. I never know which car I will be driving off the lot, so I need to always have my reading material, music and refreshments ready. When the passenger's eyes glaze over I know I'm really in their head. The hope is that they'll later think about what they refused to then, when they were only concerned with paying the fare and getting out of the classroom that had become my car. If they paid more

attention to the car ride, the lesson wouldn't have had as much of an impact.

...

There's a saying to be the change you want to see in the world. The people you encounter who aren't ready for the change you want to see, will not understand you when you're out in public. You may get the authorities called on you. You will then need to be the change you want to see in an asylum. The people looking over you in asylum won't believe that any of the change you want to see is possible, and let you act however you wish. You may gain a following from your new peer group.

If the message gets across years later, and you are still on the inside, you will not be believed outside of your peer group that you had the idea first. Notes on your time will be of no help and consist of your supervisor's interpretation of your change. The world will have changed without you.

...

Free riders tend to zone out. The walls of their room are hidden by cargo and they have nothing to focus on. Having your body in a state of constant movement does things to the mind. It is more subtle than waves at sea, but trances do come out of rides on trains. I've learned to not underestimate people coming out of reverie, neither in debate or defense. Them not knowing what they are going to do is dangerous. If I cannot restrain the subdued, one of us will get hurt.

A lot of times when I make the suggestion that the rider should pay me for their freedom, they absentmindedly answer. I need consent by them in order for me to leave them alone. If they refuse the ride I have to resort to other measures. If they continue to yes sir me without listening I resort to still other measures. They are stuck trying to remember something that they thought had been important. I try to show them things that are really important. It's hard to convince them to not be entranced.

...

I've chosen to never be optimistic or pessimistic. It's a choice. Good things come my way on bad days and misfortune casts a shadow on bright ones. It's healthier to see the forest and the trees. I can act for anyone that expects a show, but feel strange doing it. I've wondered whether the people looking for a free ride are also looking for a fight. When in the forest and you can't see the trees, you tend to yell. It's visceral. I don't see red when I tackle runners. I wonder if they think less of me.

It's not about being in control of your emotions. To have control you must be vulnerable. You can't be invulnerable and still have your wits about you. If you don't have your wits about, your being suffers. You can be someone's beneficent emissary but never able to reap the rewards. The inner struggle won't allow for thought that anyone cares about what you do. You're in control.

...

Radio stations have adopted fact checkers for their talk shows. Backed up stories are able to be used because of the extensiveness of the internet. With so many articles available the only way to get an edge is with quickness. If you have someone in the booth who can bring articles up to prove your point faster than the caller can put the host on speaker phone to browse the internet themself, you can say almost anything. It's hard to listen to talk shows.

It used to be that if you wanted to be entertained you had to make a conscious effort. People now need to make a conscious effort to define what entertainment is. If you can't make a distinction between work and leisure time, than you will always feel like you're missing out. I keep a tight schedule so I never feel rushed.

...

There is a time limit to my patience for negotiations because I try to see the other point of view. If I feel that we've reached an understanding and are still unable to find a compromise, I get testy. It's not that I feel my intelligence has been insulted, and I respect stubbornness, but the train

has to keep moving. It's better for me if there are no people on it.

...

People on trains when they shouldn't be, endangers the cargo on board. I never got too sick back in the day but the same things aren't being shipped today. Free runners also seem to be less hygienic than of old but maybe I am just a better judge now that I'm removed. If any of the cargo is contaminated it won't be known until it's too late. I need to get the rabbits before they destroy the crop. I try to talk them off of the ledge and back to solid ground. I sweeten the deal with traveling entertainment.

Since I've lost most of my sense of smell and touch, I am not at a disadvantage confronting dirty blips. It would be harder before my senses readjusted and the overpowering odor and greasiness didn't effect me so much. I've been at it for a while now.

...

You can measure entropy in a few things on the human body, eyes and ears, but it's impossible to know if they could be better. Most of my adult life has been spent around machinery. Had I been able to have a street named after me in a small town because of academic excellence, my body may have aged better.

...

It was the look, Bonnie. That one look that was a skeleton key. The look that could shake skeletons from closets. Frighten mythical creatures into hiding. Stop a baby's crying. Relieve heartburn. Cause heartache. Your signature.

The first time I saw you focusing on something I didn't think anything of it. It was when your eyes glossed over that I knew the serious thinking had begun. Early on I once caught you interweaving thoughts. I asked a pointless question and didn't expect a response. What a talent you had. You gave me what I was looking for and so much more. I tried to recreate the experiment later but the pointless question got a pointless answer. I should have known by the eyes. I in fact may be the reason you were hounded with so many queries that led to nowhere. I was usually good about keeping secrets around the hub, but how could I not share secrets about you. We were all proud to know you so of course we got competitive. Someone would say you said this, another would say you said that. Everyone wanted to prove they knew you better than their peers.

The look reminded me of trying to go cross eyed but getting perfectly nowhere with it. I've tried to recreate it whenever I feel inspired. Both eyes are still going inward. I'm not sure what I'm doing wrong. I wouldn't ever venture to say I have half the control you have, but I still think I should be capable after all this time. What was it you used to say? No culpability around capabilities. I'm not ashamed of what I can do. It's what I can't that has me exhausted.

If any of the things I think you said you don't remember saying often, perhaps that will narrow down my identity. If some of your slogans were one-offs, I hope that you found them as insightful then as I do now. Hopefully you appreciated what you said immediately so that you may remember my face. If it came to you later then it is hopeless. I'll always be the stranger who heard what no one else had.

I don't sing much. I have nothing to prove with the sound of my voice. If I did challenge my vocal range and

spoke out loud the words I think up, it would be a very long day. Something so simple to write could need several takes to get the sound right. I could get stuck on trying to sing you catch more flies with honey than vinegar. Tongue twisters and other warm ups would take up space in my head, which needs to be relatively empty in order to find the pitch.

If I ever found success in the eyes of industry executives and got radio play, the listeners would get stuck trying to imitate what I do with my voice. If they happen to think they could do it better and try all the variations that they could imagine sung, and through their cover of the song learn to test out their ability, the cycle will repeat. There's already too many reasons to be original.

...

Whistling provides for just as much thought as inventing lyrics to roll off the tongue, but is not done for selfish reasons. Someone that is spotted whistling will almost never be considered a show off and anyone that is inspired by the whistle will mean no harm when they whistle back. There is no jealousy in the whistling community because there is no opportunity for advancement.

...

Back when I was in the ranks and esteemed, I made sure titles and honors were always given when do. If I spotted a scout that was really pulling their weight, I would let Bonnie or Cole know. If they were already aware, we were able to swap stories and laugh at our own carelessness. Our injustice was swiftly corrected and no more did we commiserate.

...

I know that I've already reached the pinnacle of self-employment. I have climbed all the rungs. At first I wanted to break even. When I was able to do that, I got over the hurdle of being my own boss. There were times when I wanted to give the responsibility to someone else. When I was comfortable wearing many hats, I struggled with selling myself. People think I work less than them.

Good thing about a ladder is that you have to think going down as much as you do going up.

...

With an easily defined hierarchy our operation ran smoothly. It was Cole, Bonnie and I and things couldn't have been better. No blood lines were stepped on since most of us were first generation free riders. None of us had children then. I can't speak for Bonnie but I don't think she has any children now. Hopefully if Cole and his girl have some, they'll take better care of them than they did the van.

I was an only child. I grew into an ornery adult. I don't think it would be right for me to bring children into this world. They are the future and if I'm not around long enough to see it than I will be disappointed. I don't want to be let down by my children.

...

The few youngsters that hung around our organization were more mature than those that were on the outskirts. We didn't punish those away that found a spot in a cargo car we had been eyeing, but we never suggested to them any new places. Those that acted their shoe size during a growth spurt were treated better. They knew which of us preferred certain cargo cars over others and would always ask first for permission from us. If a scout reported that there was a car forty cars up that was packed full of electronics, a civilian who liked a firm mattress would be notified.

...

Scouts can cover a lot of ground. More if they work together. Sometimes a scout would need to continue on their trek so that they can be the messenger instead of handing the responsibility over to someone else. It is kind of like my job. I could train recruits so that they may learn my skills, but if they don't have a way with my clients than it will be all for nothing. Scouts built rapport with different civilians around the hub. Should they be out of breath when they arrive to deliver the message, at least it was in front of a welcoming face who will give them the time they need.

...

We always respected the scouts and their ability to cut corners, so it was bound to happen that we would try to replace them. We tried to log in to the train station's server to do so but were locked out. I don't know if it would have done us much good. The scouts may have already had access to it. A middleman is a mediator. They are not buyers or sellers.

...

If you take pride out of the picture you have a scaredy-cat.

...

The bridge gave out many years ago so they put the tracks on posts in the water. If you managed to open the door to your cell when you were going over the troubled water, you could put your feet in and share it's pain. The trains move at a set speed so you learn pretty quickly how long you can dip your toes in.

A more practical approach to cooling down was to put any object that could do the job into the water so that you would get splashed. Stories were shared back at the hub of all the creative ways we were able to cool off. On particularly hot days it was even more important what car you chose. Those days we would all have the same destination in mind and board whatever train was heading that way.

...

I spent some time in a desert. I wrote letters to be sent back home.

...

We had a no nonsense policy in dealing with our subordinates. If jokes found their way up the chain of command through the proper channels there were no problems. If a new recruit thought that Cole, Bonnie or I's time could be wasted and tried to get a laugh from us, we found the fool that they were supposed to report to. Through the chain of fools we heard comic's views.

Some people think that a joke can get them out of a fight.

I don't mind being a jester for any of my fares if they need me to fill that role. A jester is a reminder that things don't need to be taken seriously. If a chauffeur wanted respect we wouldn't wear the hats we do. Jesters make the best character witnesses.

...

When I'm almost at the location of a waiting fare, I take some time before approaching so I can write on a nametag a name I think the person may enjoy. Their clothes and disposition are the inspiration for the nickname. The customer is always right. The faster I can get them to insult me the faster I can agree to self-deprecate. A tip is a tip whether from a place of guilt, charity, or affection.

...

If someone has knuckles like mine I wonder if their senses are also failing. Walk a mile in someone's shoes and get athlete's foot.

...

I don't trust my voice as far as I can throw it.

...

Hide and seek, no matter how many people are playing, involves only the seeker and the bullshitter. Ready or not. The seeker wins if they prove to the bullshitter that they couldn't be fooled by their ways. The first game was played with only two participants but people started to feel left out.

I can only debilitate one runner's dreams at a time. Any accomplices they have that do not take me up on my offer must be prioritized by the threat they pose to my success rate. If they want to fight, and believe as I do that a punch landed doesn't mean as much if the person isn't focused on you, and they don't gang up on me, I make as quick a work out of them as possible. If bouts are taking longer than usual and one of their party has chosen to run away, I must decide if I postpone the conversation so that I can chase, or talk while I walk.

...

Runners have tried to trick me but I'm no spring chicken. I knew the schedules of the trains before I became self-employed. I know them even better now. Not one, but many, have started running only to hop on a car further down the line once the train starts forward. They don't have as much experience as I do and have to prepare themself to make the jump. I've already jumped onto a car a few back as soon I see them start to make a move. They don't look back before the jump. One did. They tripped and fell and I had to jump back off the train.

...

If the shoe fits, wear it to make sure it's comfortable. If you can't see yourself in the shoe then you're selling yourself short. You deserve it.

...

It doesn't often rain on parades anymore. Some are held in a dome. The dome holds the rain. If balloons didn't cost so much the roof would be opened. I don't spend my money trying to further their cause. I don't need to be pumped full of air.

...

Cyclists are some of the more athletic type that I have to deal with. They don't have a lot of muscle mass but they don't fatigue easily. I've seen a cyclist jump from a moving train, then tuck and roll with a bike in their hands. I usually throw rocks at the wheels to stop them. On foot they are no longer cyclists and begin to fatigue easier.

If you catch a cyclist stagnate chances are they are resting for a reason. Some are open to having a dialogue and very few try to improvise the bike as a weapon. If they've taken a swing at me once, they've taken a swing at me a million times. You can't reason with someone who is constantly looking for an excuse to be tired.

...

I only run on one speed myself but am taking steps to fix that. It's not a problem unless you can explain why it isn't.

...

When I drive I like to look alive. If I swerve at another car and they are able to think me stupid and careless, and pay close attention when passing me instead of believing me to do it on purpose, and purposefully swerve at me should it be their nature, then the streets are safer for it.

I don't swerve when I have passengers in the car because the message wouldn't be as clear. Lonely people can be vengeful if they see there are passengers in the car and the driver is distracted. Why don't they have someone to distract them and such.

...

I consider the work week a good one if it doesn't run over into the next. When you have to set your own schedule you can't call in sick. When the date arrives you have to show up.

If I didn't get out of bed in the morning it would turn into a couch.

...

When you don't believe you're supposed to be where other people think you should be, you try to prove them wrong. You're right where you need to be and don't deserve the credit. The motivational speaker has two functions, the first serves the second. To get away from self loathing they tell strangers what they could never tell themself. If they weren't in it for the money they wouldn't be able to continue.

...

Bonnie could spit in your eye and tell you you're baptized.

...

You'll always be Bonnie to me. I know you went by many other names, some of which I'm embarrassed to write, but Bonnie has a nice ring to it. If one could bottle your laughter and play it inside their head, rather than the ringing that accompanies loud noises, I don't think anyone would be opposed. It would keep one on their feet all day. Trying to think of clever things to say. Getting out of our own way so we could hear the laughter play. It would make a panicked situation comfortable. Your laugh would ease tensions after a shock.

Most of my own hearing is gone now. My eyesight seems to improve though with every word I write. Just like the old days, thoughts of you, lots of vigor. It was good that we were all able to use our new lease on life to the benefit of the hub. It's a good thing the hub's location was a secret or people from far and wide would come to get a new lease on life. Maybe they were already so lucky. You seemed to be everywhere at once.

We all helped out around the hub. Hopefully you didn't notice. I wouldn't want to worry you as to how much actually needed to be done on a daily basis. We needed you for the larger problems. It would have been more of a chore than the actual ones had we had to pry you away from small problems. We needed to have you not sweat the small stuff. Let sleeping dogs lie.

Most of your day to day involved supervising the scouts. Administering might be a better word. Delegating power to delegate. Though the scouts would have anyway. What else were the underlings for. We called you in on the case of the missing cargo car. The cargo car civilian inside. You told us that runner was now in a better place. An operator on a rail yard in some distant land. Do you still keep in touch?

I hope you're starting to form a clear picture of me in your head. It will make what I have to say later all the more easy. Don't worry, it's nothing too heavy. High are my hopes that you'll remember, Bonnie. Heavy is the counterweight that it takes to catapult me into your good graces. A lot must be said. Even more thought of but never uttered.

Soup sizzled over fires in the hub to kill bacteria. We put tupperware lids on top of the bowls to keep flies out. No spoons in the bowl until it's cooled, except for if a fly has fallen in. Then you can get an early start to the meal by stirring with the spoon you've set aside. We all liked to share the first bite together, even though we were all only in it for ourselves.

...

We had telescoping ladders to reach new heights. I and Bonnie and Cole were in the privileged position of never being caught off guard. We were not low hanging fruit. Those less fortunate had to have a means of escape should they have to deal with those who laid the groundwork before me. If you have a ladder than can retract you can move to the top of a building, call the ladder back in, and then decide whether to go higher or cross the roof and descend on to another.

Parts of prototypes can still be found around the hub. I confiscate them whenever they're spotted. I know the ladder and it's application well enough for it to not present a problem for me. If any prey tries the trick on me I close the distance and pick the ladder up with them on it. I make sure the angle is right so the worst that could happen is they fall a few feet into the building. I'm still footing the ladder so they are not in much danger. If they are somehow able to get to the top of the building, they usually don't have the strength to pull the ladder back up with me on it.

I've been halfway up a ladder before and seen the perpetrator through a window running around the floor below. If they make it to the stairs and get out of the building while I'm on the roof, I keep their ladder. Depending on the day and the likeliness that they will reoffend, the chase can stop there. If need be I'll give extra time to a case.

...

Donald was well past his prime when I met him but had eluded me for years. The first encounter he had me

believing he was going to call for a ride and was done train hopping. He gave a different name and not a word of anything he said was true. When I spotted him a few weeks later he ran immediately. I'm not sure how I lost him. I saw him months later. We both knew there had to be a fight. He feigned like he was hurt much more than he was, and slowed his breathing so much you would've thought he was dead. A couple years after when I saw he was still at his old ways I knew I had to finish the job.

Donald now makes a living speaking in front of malnourished teenagers. The pay isn't great but there's a lot of job satisfaction. He says if you get stuck on a problem to move on to the next one and come back later. Smug son of a bitch.

...

If you don't have anything good to teach, don't teach anything.

...

There's a lot of fish in the sea. They don't know that about themselves.

...

Salt was added to preserve water.

...

There was a woman who had four young children all around the same age. The father was in the picture but didn't train hop as she did. I never knew the man. I would always give the woman the same blank expression when I looked at her. For her benefit I stared. If not to inspire confidence to have more kids than to have her fear she was missing out. Not with me necessarily, but with other strangers that she maybe couldn't read.

The children traveled with her on school vacations. They had imagination and the family was able to travel in one car. The way they usually set up was the four children close together to support one another and the woman on the opposite side of the car. The weight on the cargo pushed it closer to the middle so should the train shake they would roll into each other's arms.

I'd like to think I'd recognize the children if they continued to follow in their sibling's footsteps. I don't know what the father looked like. I'm not that good with faces anyways. They all start to look the same or none of them look right. I never learned to sketch.

...

I do repeat clever lyrics back when they're sung but never from off the radio. Directly under Cole, Bonnie and I were a group of people who chose to spend their time melodically rather than methodically. They still provided valuable information to the three of us but got their intelligence a different way.

They always came back to the hub after road gigs. The band's identity was mysterious as they would only be seen at shows and never anywhere else. There are no windows in a cargo car.

They were able to move so high up in the organization because of their success elsewhere. The more they grew, the more they were able to scout, and they were extremely reliable. They wouldn't miss a show for the world.

...

The inside of a cargo car is as drab as the outside. Graffiti helped to liven it up but could only be seen with certain loads. The people stocking the cars were too hard working to change the configuration for the sake of art. Though a Jenga styled building would look interesting it would not be structurally sound.

...

I don't mark up my walls with words or phrases and certainly not drawings. Anything worth remembering will come in time. I do, too, have to have my inventory in just such a way. Once the middle of November arrives all clutter stays as is until the middle of March. The walls stay as is year round.

...

If a groundhog sees it's shadow it is bashful. There are not enough stuffed animal groundhogs.

...

Some running fares, who only later come to their senses, first try to use small children as a bargaining chip. Hoping to appear more favorable in the eyes of me, judge, jury and executioner, if I deem it trial worthy, they say that they are young, beautiful and struggling. They wish for me to pardon their abuse of a free ride. If the child is of speaking age and can almost think logically, but have sway over their parent's opinion anyway, I try to appeal to them. The child later turns on me in the car if I ask the parent to read me a foreign article.

...

I only know how to speak one language. I can understand tone from just about anyone. Sentence structure becomes the same in translation. I can also talk with my hands, but if I were speaking a different language would need to adjust when they were moved.

...

Before there were flash mobs there were mobs with torches. The original mobster was as petty as the latter-day one. It was Cole, Bonnie, and I as a figurehead. We didn't do it better we just did it differently. Our gatherings were more exclusive. Bonnie could have made everyone in a mob feel like an individual.

...

When you're on a train you don't need to worry about the approaching curve. Some of the rail riders should worry but it is not their tendency. There's an assumption that people who live the nomad lifestyle do so to be in control. This is not the case. You are in control when you allow yourself to be controlled. When things are taken care of.

...

When everyone on Earth was on the same page individuality suffered.

...

I don't speak the way I write. I fear that may be the cause of my unconfirmed identity. Hearing you speak was a pleasure. It wasn't very often but there was a small intake of breath before you had something important to say. We did have microphones at the hub and we only asked of your voice during those speeches. Unfortunately I think the microphone may have been placed a little bit too high. To those who knew you, you were easy to be around. Whoever was in charge of mic'ing you up that day must have been shy.

I didn't speak as simple as what one would expect from my face. Nor now do I not always speak in the way the weight in my face would have one believe. I say what I think needs to be said. If I'm not quick enough I won't say anything at all. At least until I have a private moment with the person that had took that moment. I could have had more conversations with you if you had spoken up, and saved me the trouble of having to. Cole could get in a word or two but was never known much to keep the crowd going.

I wrote half of the damn speeches and I can't think of a single word that was said. I suppose the information wasn't for me anyhow. If you do not remember me, surely you must remember the speeches. I understand forgetting me because the thoughts you had were so grand. If you remember the speeches then maybe I can describe myself better.

So the presentations were always planned. The night before the scheduled assemblage, you could find me in my tent writing. It was a few tents down from yours. Yours a few down from Cole's. Mine also. All an equal distance to where we met to swap proverbial notes. Assemblages were held in the center of the hub by the generator. Thanks go to our youth for how we were all able to fit on top of it.

Cole had the floor first. He tested the microphone. He was always alone on top of the generator at this point. Then there were always murmurs in the crowd that you were soon to show up. When you were spotted, a path was cleared and you received thunderous applause as Cole

helped you on to the generator. I snuck up to the stage during the applause. The generator didn't always entirely fit us, so the step ladder was added later.

Two twins were born. One at night and one in the morning. They look the same to everyone else but each other. They practically knew what the other was thinking. They wished to share their secret but struggled in finding a way to do so. They built a tower with blocks. That afternoon they were as excited as they had ever been. The family dog noticed and came running into the room, knocking down the tower.

The proud mother let the dog outside and tried consoling the crying twins. She told them that if they cleaned up the blocks she would get them a treat. The dog pawed at the door from the outside the entire time. The father was talking with one of the neighbors. It was a weekend.

...

Moving from a five to four day workweek would make traveling much more of a hassle.

...

When you have to wear a suit all week you want to be comfortable on the weekends. Don't mix business and pleasure. You don't want to look your best during personal time. Casual dressers in a workplace let their skill speak for itself.

Though I don't own a suit my garb is still tailored.

...

The way I dress now is not the way I dressed then. I was in a position in the organization where I very rarely needed clothes that would fight or run with me. It was Cole, Bonnie and I who were the most distinguished but you wouldn't have noticed the honors unless you were schooled in the game.

The traveling band had their own distinct way of dressing. They say they never stole outfits from the cargo cars and I believe them.

The scouts were the most fashionable. They knew what was in season and what to laugh at. They weren't superficial they just had to go unnoticed.

...

Scouts had to be able to be around crowds. The most talented would insert themself in. When we weren't traveling, we ran no risk of running in to a crowd. Had any of us been getting paid, the scouts should have gotten a bigger slice of the pie.

...

Those who couldn't work were welcome at the hub. It was encouraged that healthy free riders made them feel at home. They cared for us as much as we cared for them. Some of us carried the ones who needed it on our backs. They couldn't see we were heading in the right direction but they trusted us, as much as we trusted ourselves by taking on the responsibility.

Any of the disabled that still wanted to travel were assisted in finding a suitable spot in the car for the journey. This often meant that a few of us would go with the patient and spitball. The patient usually found the spot faster but we helped to get them situated. It made us feel better.

If none of us were traveling in the same direction we would send scouts, or drones prone to gossip, to the destination ahead of time. So that when the car arrived a helping hand could reach out.

...

I preferred to go to places that I hadn't been. I was as hopeless as the rest of them.

...

We had a psychic who practiced out of the hub. She was the only local business we allowed. She didn't serve anyone without our permission. She only took regulars.

Being as aimless as we were, we found whatever she said profound. We didn't know ourselves. She knew every self. I never paid her for any insight. She couldn't keep her hands off of me and was always trying to pull me into her tent. I'd say that she already had her customers but she

would say their fate was already sealed. They understood. You don't see a psychic wrestling with a general without having taken some wrong turns in life.

The psychic's name was Marie but we all called her Venmo.

...

I've went to a psychic since. Different name. Same species.

She can show you shrunken heads. Its a trick with the crystal ball and some cameras. You look into the ball and the reflection is photographed, then put up on a screen. Depending on the size of the screen your head may appear to be normally sized.

She says you can never see what you truly look like. Looking in the mirror you already have preconceived notions of how you should appear, and end up looking so. All the photographs of yourself you've seen also play the same trick. Someone can draw you and it may be the most accurate depiction but unfortunately it's still only a drawing. Nothing to hang your hat on. You can ask to be described in full detail but who has the time. She may have a point there.

...

Cole's girl looked like she had a small head. It was winter when they left and I was too far away to really tell.

...

It was Cole, Bonnie and I that were reported to when boxes of winter clothes had fallen from one of the cargo cars. Not one of our own but an outsider had needed to make room for other things. Not every runner belonged to our organization but we liked to think that all the smart ones did. The runner of no relation was going where ice doesn't even try, with contraband ice that would be considered fly. We kept the waste. In terms of risk and reward, we may have made just as much money as the diamond dealer because the clothes were above the books. They didn't belong to us but were first time fenced objects, whereas the ice may have passed many hands already.

Around the hub you could spot rank easier in those winters to come. It was Cole, Bonnie and I that would have still kept you guessing with our minimal matching headgear. Every other class chose jackets, scarves or what have you.

...

In the winter I drive with the heat on. Only if I have customers, so that I won't have to spend money on cough suppressants.

...

I prefer to fight in the summer. It's always funny to see my opponent take off their shirt and expect me to do the same. I would have before I made modifications to my attire. Now it is like a second skin.

There's always a chance they will run anyway. I don't want to have to backtrack to the scene of the crime to gather my belongings. I usually turn their shirt in to the boss or on coal burning days in to the furnace. If they have a dog I wonder if the scent is picked up through the smoke.

A lot of dogs still turn up to the hub. They may even be spawn of previous guests.

...

If dogs could talk we would be able to tell what a bark meant.

...

Thursdays were the closest to containing the word hub and were special to us. If you weren't one of us you didn't know, and if you really knew you probably didn't care much.

I work seven days a week. Whenever week ends coincide with my schedule, on those nights as well.

...

When people say they wouldn't want to be ya they may think very highly of themself. Them leaving your company will take such a toll on your well being that you are pitied.

...

Imagining Bonnie in her underwear would make anyone nervous.

...

I would be good at public speaking if I were able to choose when I did it. Since it's never asked of me there is not much of a choice. I have to be able to eloquently elate otherwise I'm just as bad as the rest of them.

My charges include those who I have to detain and those that give me permission to do so. The latter sometimes leave tips. The former don't listen to any of mine. If I've got a runner, and if they're any good, they usually are better with endurance than myself. Immobilizing them is top priority. Keeping them in that state is just as important. I usually let my guard down if they are the ones that choose to open a dialogue. It's when they start to quiet that I get nervous. Saving oxygen for a moment they know will come but aren't sure when. I'm too veteran to give them any opportunities while I'm talking, and those that believe they've found one are mistaken. The only way I really get distracted is if something happens that is out of the runner's control. It could be one of the folks that live by the tracks having a fit of hysteria. I could be bombed from above by a bird. If the runner misses these opportunities, and I realize they have yet they didn't notice, I tend to apply more force. There can't be two acts of God in the same day but I still rush to further immobilize the tyrant.

I needed to learn how to not speak of my day job while working at night. At first I found it difficult to not be reminded of the trajectories I've changed when in the car. Passengers previously runners would say some common remark and I'd be sent in another direction on a topic that was completely unrelated. I couldn't be too quick with an apology in those situations. I needed to inspire confidence in my passengers.

Runners that are on the fence about my invitation for a ride are sometimes brought along when I have more law abiding persons in the car. If they are on the fence it means they have already been immobilized. I do this to show the runners that they are more normal than they think. That the law abiding persons aren't so bad after all.

What any of my interactions think of me I can never know.

...

There is a break room at the station. I try to walk quietly in there. I don't switch labels on any of the leftovers, but I do switch their positions with each other. I don't stay in the break room long enough to see any reactions, nor do I gossip with those workers and hear any stories that coincidentally connect back to me. A worker would probably say can you believe the nerve of so and so. They wouldn't even know they were talking about the nerve of mine.

I think they all would be able to agree on most things concerning me. They are the categories makers.

...

Marie Venmo probably couldn't describe me if she looked up from her crystal ball. The only thing in that dark, barely lit room that I could describe would be the crystal ball. If Marie's voice changed I'd have an easier time believing there was more than one of her. It's been speculated about. She does seem to change shades when she's sick and can drastically fluctuate her weight, but I always heard the same voice. It must be the same fortune teller time after time.

...

No one could read a map better than you Bonnie. It was amazing how many runners you had to show how to correctly do so. I'm proud to say I wasn't one of them. Where I was going I never needed a map. Those runners needed a map because they thought they were going somewhere. You showed them how to actually get there. On behalf of all the runners who can't properly thank you, because they couldn't possibly find you, I say thanks. I used to be in a position where showing sentiments like that meant something. Now I'm normal and such outpouring of emotion is commonplace in the working class.

I don't know what collar you would wear. I know the thing about the labels, but buddhism has as many holes as Marie's left sock, and quotes from one of it's holiest can only mean so much. I mean, so what if we were all once runners. I still was able to change, and now the label has even less power than if it were not used at all. I'm sorry Bonnie but I think a label would help you remember. If I can find an adjective, I will attempt to describe myself.

I'm always searching. Searching for that thing that never was but was imagined to be, and in so becomes more than what it could have been imagined to be. Had things went differently around the hub, and you were able to immediately remember me after reading my first letter, it would mean that I was right to take things for granted while I was there. I did take it all for granted but have written my lamentations. Some of which have overflown into these reach outs.

Before I knew the strength of my powers, I was taught a lesson about sneaking up on people. It was to be an innocent joke that resulted in calamity. I snuck up on someone making a griddlecake in one of the corners of the hub. I blame the accident on the sizzle. When I was standing directly behind the cook, they jerked their head back to avoid some grease and took my two front teeth out. They burned their snack as they wasted time asking if I was alright. I said yes clearly enough but they didn't want to

hear my words. There are plenty of difficult interactions because of distractions. I guess the blood trying to rush to my absent teeth made me harder to understand.

The help I got was not from the cook, who I pleaded that they not worry about me and instead themself. I said a burnt griddlecake is almost as nutritious as one that is fully formed. They stayed around the hub while I was in recovery. Who got me to that state was Cole's girl's sister, Cassandra, who had spent some time abroad and traveled our own country, so was able to pick up on accents. She thought I got a concussion because of my concern with the griddlecake and my lack thereof for my own grill. I wasn't rushed to a hospital but we did try to get the on site doctor to rush their other patients.

The doctors usually were good about speeding things up. They eased patients into recovery and by their fourth return visit, it was the patients that were animatedly hurried. The doctor that saw me in half of my christmas glory, though it was a dental problem, arrived right on time. Any longer and the griddlecake would have caught fire. I can't say I had ever seen her before or after that visit. I'll have to ask Bonnie about her should I ever choose to write. Cassandra could help but she's even more accomplished than I, and you don't get to that point without making less time for certain interests. The doctor said I should be quarantined for the madness.

I asked the doctor whether the process could be sped up. She said it could be one for all and all for one, but I would have to be the one asking for support from hubsters. I said I'd do the time. I was put in a tent. Inside of it was the grill that may as well have committed a crime, a scraper that had to atone for the grill, and myself holding two teeth in one hand. Switching hands when I could no longer feel my teeth. I was quarantined. No one could see the bloody hands and I answered to no one.

I was in that tent for three days. The grill was scrapped when the tent was took down. I gave permission to the griddlecake cook to tear it down. They were very adamant

that it be destroyed. I said if it had to go at least they could get some money for it. They said they couldn't profit off of my misfortune.

The money got from those busted up parts never made it's way back to me. I waited too long to put the original teeth back in.

...

The two front teeth in my mouth really are my own. What was left of the originals that was not in my hand, got sawed down so I could have caps put on. They haven't failed me yet. They may have altered my sense of taste but I haven't had to be quarantined again. I haven't been misunderstood. I don't have the company health insurance of my peers. I can't ask directions for a hospital when I'm with fares. I now know not to trust body language of someone that is unaware of you.

...

I didn't know Cole's girl's sister was Cassandra. I didn't know either of the sisters well but they seemed to be opposites. Cole's girl was never around the hub and didn't bother to learn most of our names. Cassandra was a giver first, and an asker of seconds second. Cole probably could have fell for either one of them. If Cassandra was more like her sister, and there was a third, Cole might have chose her. It was never his decision but neither was it any of ours.

...

I have an uncanny knack for spotting families in the backseat of my car. Sometimes the all grown up families share more resemblance than the overworked parents and their energetic child. Either way, I enjoy those fares because I almost always get more of a tip than what they had been discussing. The families try to talk quietly so I don't overhear but they know it isn't enough. When all is said and done, there's usually a little extra left.

...

On average, there are between sixty and eighty cargo cars being pulled by one train at a time. The insides mostly look the same. The outsides of the cars look different on the

surface. The inside of the cars always look different on each ride. If it's a slow work day I pick up on the little things. If I'm aware there's a runner nearby, I seek out the most minute of details. Many a runner has been spotted because of their breathing through their nose.

In order to find the camouflaged I learned to become the camouflaged. I don't often need to employ those skills but it's still good to know they're in my back pocket. I could hide and hope a runner will stumble across my car. If they never find me they'd likely fall asleep. Then I can't possibly detain them. It's just easier to be the aggressor when your job is to play defense.

...

If I had to tally all the lives I've saved from following in my footsteps, I wouldn't get anything else done. Perhaps some of the captured runners did find employment at various train stations. I didn't drive them all that way, so can only hope they arrived by walking, or some other civilian mode of travel. I don't think I could learn anything from anyone who has similar duties to myself. It was Cole, Bonnie and I that headed our organization. There was no second threesome. The band below us were all able to get along and never lost anyone. I don't think they were ever competition to us though. They certainly didn't behave like hold a gun to the head so you'll put a finger on the trigger replacements.

If I didn't have Bonnie and Cole back then there very well may have never been a hub. Like any ideas that were related, this one came from Bonnie's mouth. She wouldn't speak as plainly as she did unless she was using some other's words. In fact, Bonnie may have been silent. That's the kind of impression she leaves on people. You meet Bonnie and years later can't remember what you had for breakfast the day before.

Bonnie probably at least set up the structure for the organization. There were some underlings that never made it off the bench. Underlings that could have been standing next to Cole, Bonnie and I at the onset, but had never stood

next to us since. We were unable to promote those who didn't come to ask for our advice. We couldn't know how their projects were coming along, or even if there were any, if they didn't sequester us.

...

There's a bumper sticker on one of the available cars. It says give kindness, get kindness. It's simple enough. If you are able to part with something then you obviously understand it.

...

There's been talk of overseas infrastructure in the papers. Time is universal. There are no competing metrics for time. Their time is the same as our time. The blinking yellow dash on traffic lights is being considered. How fast it should blink and for how many seconds. They go at a different pace than we do over here, so personally I can't form any conclusions. If the bold yellow fades slower, and before completely dimmed flashes bright again, and drivers know how many flashes till a change, the stoplight may be more effective. Drivers approaching that wish to beat the light, may count the number wrong because they're all hopped up, but they'll learn.

I don't believe the yellow blinker should be thrown out entirely. It would take too much power to flash two lights instead of one. I think it's easier to see yellow flash than red. I can't recall ever seeing green flash.

Stoplights can usually be put at four way intersections. When they are absent they are surely noticed. The rule is to queue appropriately. If a traffic light was put in, I think to keep the integrity of the four way it would need to be clicker operated. The first car to the intersection clicks, the light responds. They click again when they are through. You can't always trust the drivers on the road with you. You can't trust a machine but you know it harbors no ill will.

...

Before approaching a machine you must always remember to check to see whether it is controlled remotely. Forgetting your manners can prove costly.

Should the machine fail your check, and provided it has enough power to move you, if you know what you're doing, can attach it to your belt loop. A drone on your hip is worth two in the sky. The owner will try to wrestle it back from you while you are unawares. Thankfully you need not be aware at all times. Even better should you be a convincing sleepwalker.

Once you have located the handler it is within your right to give permissions for being subjected to. To part from the drone is more difficult than you expected, it's been attached at the hip, and if someone has all that footage it may as well be made accessible. There's a chance they won't release it to you if you give the drone back too soon. Better to sign away than to hoard.

...

Venmo was so in tune with the frequency of the world that she could willfully be incorrect, yet be proved in truth before she could even draw a breath. She became even more renowned throughout the hub once we all got smartphones. For some reason the owners thought they knew more than they did. They in fact might have known more than any of us. Marie would tell them they were wrong though, and state the reason they were. She would change a detail ever so slightly but enough so that what she said sounded unbelievable. It shouldn't have been believed.

As if this wasn't entertaining enough, there were come-correctors who had a webpage with the facts open earlier, that realized they had been tricked and couldn't believe everything that they read on the internet. They would pay Venmo after that. It wasn't a large fee to keep her mouth shut. She didn't always use her abilities, but when she did she could turn a skeptic's view. Customers have left her tent, never straying far from the hub unless travelling, and were unable to believe Venmo was anything other than what she said she was.

Venmo's happy customers drew in what business they could. I don't think she cared one way or the other. I don't

think she slept in that tent. I know I would have been afraid to.

...

Sorry admits defeat. As does thank you. You're welcome is said from a position of power. Excuse me is a ruse. You could say any of the four with a look. I say many of the four as a hook. For though I know what I mean, and now you too, many don't know the ulterior motive behind each phrase. Most words have at least two definitions but phrases are entirely interpretive. Maybe that's why when you spoke of acorns and pinecones it somehow made sense.

You would have made the best bait, Bonnie. We never used you as it, but surely you must have known. We never needed to so perhaps the thought never did cross your mind. If any of your features didn't capture one's attention, your eyes always did. I've got many migraines trying to recreate the look. I know what came from it for you, but am not sure what you used it for. I'm almost certain our motives are different. None of us could even hold a candle up to you. We all may have held lighters up had you ever broke out in song.

Not that there was ever much to sing about around the hub. I suppose you could have sang about how well the organization functioned, if you had thought that anything but normal. You probably inspired many songs Bonnie. I speak differently than I write, and write so that I'll never have to sing. Maybe that is something that can jog your memory. I must have had a look in my eye that said so. Not the look I'm trying to recreate from you, but one of lesser smugness and content. I suppose the look will come when I reach that level. You deserved to be smug and content. We all worked our way towards contentedness with thoughts of you.

I imagine if the look ever is recreated it could only be done in the presence of you. Maybe the look can only be attained through surprise. Perhaps you were always surprised and the inner demons you battled did a number on your eyes. I battle less demons every day. I'd tell you more but not until you remember me. Until then, you don't know enough about me.

It's the faces you remember that affect the names you forget. To see someone's face so clearly in your mind, but unable to look up the address without being looked at yourself. Love at first sight is lost in a second. I've decided to start small with my letter writing. Perhaps writing Cassandra to ask about her sister's name. I definitely don't have the chops yet to write to Bonnie, or any of the investigative work that would entail. It's amazing how fast you lose your address book once employment is involved. If it were still Cole, Bonnie and I, I would be able to enlist scouts to seek. I don't want to trouble my fares none. I can't trust the runners as far as I can throw them.

If sunglasses were in the description a better picture could be formed of Bonnie. Without her eyes covered there would be a million takes. She always chose squares for the frames. It did something for her face.

Bonnie would also be easier to describe if she were wearing a hat. When her hair was free to fall on her shoulders we were all helpless.

...

I've never used wanted posters for any of my bounties. Don't want anyone to know what I'm doing. That there's money to be made doing it my way. I couldn't use an anonymous tip line, in case I ask for too many things and my job description is reverse engineered.

Some runners think they're experienced, and because of that experience, are clever. If they saw their face over a reward they'd surely try harder. I like for my matches to be fair and played on an even ground. Metaphorically. I much prefer darting along the countryside on top of one of the train cars. Doing battle that way.

It's important that the runners are not able to dive off the train in those situations. Those that think they're experienced may get hurt. The less naive may land safer. I'll land as I always do, on my feet, and will have to chase after them.

...

So there aren't any misconceptions, once I have caught a runner I do always offer up my services. There is no malice behind the chase. If I could be faulted for anything it would be greed. Money is no concern but I don't want the young bloods following in my footsteps. If I'm able to help someone and get paid to do it, I'm happy.

...

There was a tree where there is now a stump. The stump is significant because of the tree. The tree was special to all those who saw it. The stump isn't very special to anyone except those that had seen the tree. There used to be rubber skeletons hung from the tree around halloween. You can't hang one from the stump. One could be perched on top but it would be too painful for anyone that remembered the tree. The tree was special for many different reasons. The stump is only special for one.

Jumping on top of the stump changes your perspective. People view you differently. Positively if you have something to say. Negatively if you're stumped.

...

I haven't suggested to runners that I take them on a motorcycle ride. I'm not sure the station has any in the lot. I have suggested they sit directly behind me in the car. If the windows are open just right and I have messed with the settings to the radio just enough for pure cacophony, then I can convincingly create a two wheeler experience. If I stay behind a diesel truck it can be even more convincing. If all of this is as so, the fares hear me ask what they're thinking much more often than if the setting wasn't such. Motorcycle is such an ugly word. I never mention it directly.

I imagine if any of the runners had access to a motorbike they wouldn't choose to ride the rails. I can't say the cargo cars move many freights of bikes, so it would be difficult for the runner to hide one in plain sight. It might make my job easier though if the runner didn't want to abandon their two wheeler.

If a runner didn't want to abandon their two wheeler, and I had already detained them, I would likely say that

they're hurting the environment with their emissions. Try to play to their guilt. Once the respect in their eyes starts to grow, and I know I've got them, I list any smart car models that I know about. State perfunctorily how drastically cleaner they are from a motorbike or an eighty car train. My primary is cleaning the train. A secondary is making motorcyclists smarter. Regardless of if they move more or less horizontally in their vehicle selection.

...

I look less suspicious roaming around the lot at the station if I have prospective fares with me. Sometimes the runners are still a little hesitant to be alone with me in such a confined space, so I take them to the garage. I show them all the makes and models so they can defend themself to their liking. I boast about my skills with some of the newer models. Before they accept the ride I pretend to get a phone call, and then apologize for something having come up. The pay as you go phone that I have is constantly tracking my location. There's a glitch that occurs when I make a phone call, and the last number dialed's location is relayed to me. I secure the number of the potential fare, even more likely rerun runner, and then call them so I can be added to their contacts. I tell them to put in the name Bert. It's a failed acronym that stands for Be Right There.

Once their phone has started to be tracked, I wait and watch for them to leave the garage. Only when they are completely out of my eye sight do I choose a car to take. I then pull out of the garage, find them, and offer a free ride. It makes the fares feel doubly important, after just being ignored for a phone call and then getting restitution.

...

In the backseat of my car there are many photos taken. I always ask that none are of me. If I don't bring it up, they probably wouldn't even consider it. There is a lot of thumb and forefingering, followed by more pictures. I've asked what they need magnified to such an extent. A lot of the responses have something to do with the eyes. If you can crop most of the face out and leave the eyes, what you're

left with is a smoky, mysterious look. Fight fire with fire, your brain can't reason what good eyes are without a face, or at least two sides of a head, so the beholder's eyes remain bloodshot scrolling to the next picture. I don't mind. If they're eyes get too bloodshot their vision may blur and they could mistake the amount on the bill. It would be rude to question the generosity of the tip. The crazed look in their eyes wouldn't make it any easier.

I don't think Bonnie would have ever photographed herself. She definitely wouldn't have wanted to draw attention to her own eyes. As someone who has practiced for years trying to recreate the look that she sometimes gave me, other times I spotted her shooting at other people, I know you don't just give it away once you have it. I never saw Bonnie look in the mirror. I've tried to make my eyes daggers without one but don't have enough trust in the process. How will I know that I'm looking at people the way that I was looked at myself, while looking at people who don't know me well enough to look at me the way that I was looked at before, and had tried to create by myself. I don't trust moving pictures ever since the time of the hub and the doctors. I wouldn't know when to start the video recorder either.

If I ever write to Bonnie, it will be apparent that I've kept my eyes peeled for as long as it would take. That is where I'm at. If my eyes don't get too dry, I believe the look is quite extreme.

...

Your hair was as a beehive though it looked nothing like one. My hair resembles a rat's nest and looks nothing like the style that Skip wore. I have enough hair to part it over but have no one to do it for. Back at the hub I had the same hair but wore it differently. If I can describe myself in other ways, I might be able to force a memory of what I used to look like.

My apartment has three rooms. Three sinks. Not a sink in each room but the basin can be used for multiple purposes. If you ever remember me, and in by doing so realize you're not bothered by me, I'll give you a tour of the place. For now let my words be your guide, however fallible they may be. And what else can a guide be but fallible. Pointing in directions but afraid to be pointed to. Answering questions but afraid to be asked what those questions mean to them.

The bathroom and kitchen have a sink. The one in the kitchen is broken, hence the basin. I could use the one in the bathroom whenever I needed something done in the kitchen. I also could stick paper towel to the bottom of my shoe. Neither are going to happen.

I don't eat as voraciously as I did around the hub. There is no microwave in my apartment, otherwise my appetite might be different. The meals I prepare on a stove by the broken sink in the kitchen. They are simple meals. Not ever any griddle cakes but some meals that require even less. I'm proud to say I smirked when I was sold the stove and asked if I wanted insurance. I got it. Have had no fires since. I'm moving up in the world, Bonnie. Where before I would have believed I jinxed myself, Marie's influence heavy, and likely caught at least one of the rooms on fire, I've had no such accidents.

It was no accident that you were one of the leaders of the hub. I also, but have an impostor syndrome something fierce. Then there was Cole. Later, Cole's girl. The band below and nothing but auspicious skies overhead. It would have come as a big shock when everything changed. I don't blame you for not remembering some of the baser elements.

The pedestrians near the tracks have a good idea what it is I do. I've waved a handful of times but never during a match with a worthy opponent. The runners that I believe will be early adopters and choose to fight another day, not that present one so no need for smelling salts, are given some slack. If I try to wave to country folk and my opponent is skilled, I may put myself far behind the schedule I keep. It is worth waving sometimes at country folk, as it can confuse runners by my indifference towards them. Waving to someone who isn't there, due to the speed of the train, has gotten many runners disoriented.

I'm not sure what the country folk want from me.

...

We didn't build fires too high at the hub. Scouts built fires across the land, with smoke that could be seen for a country mile. None of the cars I've commandeered have caught fire. There is a suppressant system in some parts of the train, though not usually where runners are discovered. I don't play with matches.

...

Screaming William was the name of a drifter who happened across our outfit. He was quick to catch fire. He always claimed it was because he had been struck by lightning. You could ask him when it happened, and he'd have the year and month right but get hung up on the day. We had no way to verify his claim other than our very own Marie Venmo.

There had been a full moon for three nights in a row and Screaming William wouldn't stop talking. It was Cole, Bonnie and I that huddled together and looked at the cold faces around the hub. When Marie finally popped up out of nowhere, we weren't sure if she had been the one to whistle her introduction. She spoke a greeting partway through the whistle. There was no one else around. We didn't see her until she spoke.

She knew what we intended to do. Screaming William was silent while she knew. He may have tried to ask

something to one of us had he been able to move his eyes away.

When all was said and done, we learned that Screaming William had a compass in his pocket when he was struck and has been unable to find magnetic north since. Screaming William can tell you the year and the month. Venmo told us why not the day.

...

Jacqueline Herreira was another traveling salesman. She didn't focus on the same demographic as Sal Travers, but they shared many of the same clientele. She smoked clove cigarettes. She would have burned incense had she practiced out of an office. The smoke smelled more like clove and less like it's other name sake. She didn't have to say much after blowing smoke in prospective customer's faces. Her products were good anyway. We all liked Jacqueline because she didn't change the names of the bags labeled not for resale.

She had a partner named Ozzy Berstanlly. He was more concerned the clientele have an experience than profiting off of the sale. Him and Jacqueline were quite the pair. If they had more sedentary lifestyles they could have moved through the hub's ranks very quickly.

The band wrote a song about Ozzy. It was called Alice der Millionär. Jacqueline made a lot of money when the song was performed one slow night. Ozzy was nowhere to be found. He was as elusive as Bonnie when it came to being photographed. He only ate red meat. He worked out a lot. He was chasing many dragons. He had the right, he was one of the few of us that ever found any.

Jacqueline was more well known but nowhere near as infamous. She did sometimes wear a fake moustache with glasses, and go by Jack Harris. It was only enjoyable for her with a select type of new customers, and some old ones who didn't mind a little play before they pay.

...

I'm able to make better food choices now that I am part of a functioning citizenry. When it was Cole, Bonnie

and I around the hub we did our best to make sure our underlings and colleagues got all the nutrients they needed. Powdered drinks were a staple. We didn't trust bread that much even though it was inexpensive. We were able to get honey but it was burned one too many times and the hallucinations were even too much for some of the experienced-ers around the hub. There were plenty of griddlecake recipes shared. Other than that our options were pretty limited.

Going to restaurants wasn't really an option. Even the band, who were the best dressed of all the ranks and were able to appear presentable, didn't find themselves being seated very often. It wasn't because we were illiterate and couldn't read the menus, though we didn't publish our own literature. Speaking for myself, I avoided them because the food there was too good. If you really start to shrink your stomach and eat less with every meal, when you have to finish a plate someone has set for you, you will almost always get stomach pains.

It's not quite nausea, nor is it cramps, but is almost like your body punishing you for not having ate food as good as this for so long. Added to that discomfort, is that once you are finished with your plate, the pain is mostly while you're eating, you will find yourself hungry within the hour. If somehow I chose to eat again that soon, I was young and dumb, the extra calories will just make me more hungry in about eight hours. Then the stomach pains would come from not eating.

...

They say no pain, no gain. If coming across gains were easy, everyone would do it. If you have no ambition, you'll never be hurt a day in your life.

...

The band said they were painful to listen to at first. Anytime we heard them they sounded together. I liked to think of myself as their road manager. Bonnie would have been manager superior. The scouts did most of the work for the band. The band made sure to send scouts to different

areas so a following couldn't develop. The scouts were good people but the crowds they ran in had awful opinions on music. Everyone has different tastes but not everyone needs to make those tastes known.

I'm starting to come around on sing song alongs. It's too little too late, as they say. I wouldn't endanger my fares by trying to rouse in them good spirits. I don't think songs are meant to be sung while driving.

...

Venmo's tent was a stone's throw away from the generator when it was functioning. We wouldn't allow anyone to attempt the throw, but that would be the distance. It was Cole, Bonnie and I that sometimes would huddle around outside her tent when we conspired. The thought being that if power were to emanate off of her entrance, we may be able to benefit.

Our duties were many but they could all be put off. We at the hub were a self centered bunch. We came together despite our differences. None of us changed much so we all got along.

In the tier directly above the scouts resided the erranders. As you must already know by now, the scouts could have done practically anything. They stayed where they were to make room for others. So the erranders, doing the job a scout could do, would deliver small parcels by the carry load to those of us who were without. They were rewarded by the blisters on their hands and feet. We couldn't be too appreciative, less they become a permanent caste. It was important for them to always feel they could have been thirty seconds faster. They could have waited for the recipient to stop their conversation, instead of interrupting them. Going back, if it were still Cole, Bonnie and I maybe we could have treated them better. They were the tier above the scouts so that they wouldn't complain. I can't speak for the other hubsters. As a whole, none of us complained very much. Those complaints would have fallen on deaf ears.

...

When you know that by bettering yourself you can better the community around you, it's hard to get a good night's sleep. You can put eight solid hours on your resume. Doesn't mean anyone else will.

A rested community is a disabled community. A home of retirees is the workplace of tired knees. Caregivers beg and plead, and bury the lead that they are the ones in control. I think Cole's girl has a relative inhomed. Cassandra couldn't let that on unless it would help her image. I don't think Bonnie's father ever pandered to the sympathetic demographic.

His name was Alex. Alex, father of Bonnie Alexeva, was said to be a magician in the polls. There was no mountain high enough, no valley low that he couldn't scale. His opponents were nowhere near the sophist that he was. They still thought a grain of truth was less than a pound. Alex could talk a turtle out of it's shell. He could lay it on like it was going out of style.

The highest position that Alex Gregornov ever achieved politically was that of senator. It was on the books as such anyway. You couldn't ever see him on c-span but he was in enough commercials to make believe his job was in jeopardy. If Bonnie had siblings that didn't resemble her or her father, I would have bet my life that they were sleeper cells that had adoption paperwork. There are no such familial members that I'm aware of. Bonnie probably wouldn't give them away with her eyes.

...

Some runners fancy themselves artists. Back at the hub we had geeheehenyouwhines. They didn't run when they saw me coming. They were proud of their work.

...

There have been small fires in cargo cars. They were controlled until I got there. Those runners usually are quick to take me up on my offer. They've realized they've sunken to a point they didn't know existed. I am the lure that draws them out.

My wingsuit does have zippers so I can control how baggy my clothes need to be. If the runner starts on a sob story before putting out the fire I'm managing as needed, I detach some extra baggage to snuff it out.

There are two important things to remember when around a cargo car fire. First, it is now a fire, meaning the car is not yet up in flames. Second, there is a lot of smoke being contained in the car. Both can be used to one's advantage in detaining a runner. However, both can hinder your ability to think logically. I'm as quick as an overworked pilot deciding how to act in a situation.

...

I can rigmarole with the best of them, so long as I'm given fair warning. You can encounter the most talented tongue tier, and be completely unaware should you not see the sparkle in their eye. It's not quite the same look I'm trying to recreate. I couldn't explain it otherwise. A jester would have had the same sparkle as they bit their tongue waiting for the king's subjects to leave their presence.

The king would have been just as anxious as the jester but their thoughts in an opposite direction. Before the king could even dramatically sigh, or should they be an angry personality slam their fist, the jester would be on their feet, when so clearly they should not have been. That is the tragedy of comedy. If it's not wrong then it cannot be funny.

...

I've had some funny fares in the backseat of my car. I tell them so the first chance I get.

I allow them their antics so long as they don't hit on something truly brilliant. If I'm holding my sides then there's no way I could hold the wheel. For this same reason you will never hear comedy albums being played in my car. Comedy albums are going for something that many musicians have failed to do. It's great if one song bleeds into the next on an album, but how can that translate into comedy.

A comedy album could work if the jokes were quick and concise. Each track would accommodate five or six jokes. Instead of just the one. I still wouldn't risk listening to

them, but if I were able to over analyze the set up while listening to the content, I think I would be able to control my laughter.

The best joke I've been a part of was, after listening to one of my fares argue on the phone for almost the whole ride, hang up and then bitch in probably the same manner as they had just been subjected to. When that fare left the car, I complimented the next passenger heavily. I couldn't see my babies get hurt again.

...

Sometimes the simplest compliments sound like insults.

...

We all tried to butter Marie Venmo up but she seemed impervious to our hot knives. She did say you shouldn't have often. That was about the only advice that we didn't take from her. We wanted to see what made her tick. She's probably still alive to this day. It's hard to keep track of how many years it's been since I was general of the hub. Not entirely, there were Bonnie and Cole on my shoulders. They might have even carried me more than I they. The shoulder placement I speak of would in some other instances be a decorative tassel, for an esteemed service member.

I wouldn't need to write to Venmo, I need only listen for the wind. Then I'd be in the right head space and what would most likely happen would be she'd find me rather than I her. Of course I'd be the one moving towards her but who would really be in control then. I'd consider it cheating if I asked for Bonnie when I saw Marie.

...

If I had the chance to ask Cole's girl where she was taking my second to none in command, I probably would have told them it wasn't worth going. The only way they could prove me wrong today, would for me to witness them as a runner. Then I could know that it was worth going, if only so they could get back to what had originally caused them to leave.

...

Red skies at night, sailor's delight. Red skies in morning, sailor's sure ornery. Seeing you in the foreground of either would bring a person to bliss. Don't believe I attempt to flatter you, Bonnie. It is that I wish to inform. After receiving such a shock from the hub being broken up, I believe there may be many gaps in your memory. If you can remember me, you can remember them all.

We never went sailing together. Those that do had their own type of hub. I wonder how we would have fared had we been in their shoes. We also could have flown in aeronautic circles. Things could have been different, Bonnie. They could have been how you remember them. Since they're not, I feel sorry for you. If you're trying to remember one of your sailing or flying partners you will have a very difficult time. I was not one of them.

This fantasy that you have created will be hard to break. May not even necessarily need to be broken. I'm not sure what I meant to you if you don't let me help me help yourself. So, instead of imagining me in a squirrel suit or boating shoes, try to imagine a brown jacket and green hat. If you must use the squirrel suit visualization as an aide, please make it brown. Keep the boat shoes if it helps, but picture them anything but green. That color was on my head, not my feet.

I probably could have been your photographer had we went sailing or flying together. Hopefully if you had one they weren't wearing my colors. They certainly weren't wearing any of my medals or honors. I wasn't as decorated as you Bonnie, but I still had quite the collection. I always defended you when others said you didn't deserve some of your accolades. Some made you out to be not as successful as you were. It's hard to believe, maybe harder for me than you, you might have had those thoughts yourself, but not all thought the ground you walked on was made sacred.

Some artist, hollow be thy fame, said it best. Then much like what I'm afraid will happen if I sing along to a song, the rest said it better. Their music isn't the kind that

I'd suggest to my fares. They already know the artist for one thing, better to not ruin that for another.

I am a man on the tracks, who tracks. It's not much for a song. The story can't be consumed without filler in between.

...

I've never been to Phoenix. I hear it's seeing a real resurgence. We knew someone at the hub who went by the name of Feeny. Some good that did them. Can't remember a single thing about them from before.

...

I have a good idea how intellectually compatible the person I'm talking to is. If I say something that they already know, yet have forgot, I keep my mouth shut. I don't want anyone to think I'm smarter than I am.

...

It is easier to pull someone down by the hair than their beard. The runners have chosen to lead a fantasy life, their hairstyle shows what they think that means. It was Cole, Bonnie and I that were as well kept as the rest of them. The whole society must have crumbled when we left the organization. We were the barber's closest confidants. I'm sure he left shortly after Bonnie and I realized Cole had been swept away.

I suggest to suggestible runners that they get a haircut before they take me up on my offer. If they must keep their hair, some people need to, I tell them to wait a couple weeks before they call. I tell them to wake up, get out of bed, and draw a comb across their head. They may find it enjoyable even. Then the sing song phrase would be annoying to them and lead to a haircut. It's important to know the audience.

...

I'd prefer not to need an audience but you can't choose the job you're born in to. The good thing about my jobs is there are no performance reviews. I could take a critical look at myself, but in the back of my mind I'd know it was all

for show. In order to impress myself I would need to undress myself.

...

Runners would sometimes try to make a fort in the cargo cars. If they were any good they would have had a chance at finding employment. The cars are loaded a certain way. A way that even should a runner find a place to occupy, the unloading of the car will not be affected. What comes out last is what was put in first. Unless the dock workers are just as amateur as the runners.

The runners try to move the things that were put in first, provided the car only has a single door. Once inside they may move back what they had moved first. The runner should concern themself with finding a comfortable place, and not being hidden from view. I can't be at every train station at once.

A slowed train is an evacuating train. Runners don't ever fully arrive at a train station, jumping ship at their own discretion. If the country folk wanted something from me they would harbor me close by destinations. I don't ask. They don't wave me on like that.

If a runner has somehow managed to get to a destination without me detaining them, and I'm aware of their challenge, I try to hide nearby bushes. It's not only the comfortable runners that have eluded me that jump to the bushes, but almost every encounter with a runner I've ever had. It must be instinctual. Things with claws usually can't figure for the claw like branches attacking them. I am the exception.

A runner in the bush is worth two seconds of my time.

...

It's a good thing I didn't have the same worries as an adult that I had as a child. I'm thankful for all those things I didn't do that could have affected my adult life. Hopefully what I've done as an adult won't affect what happens to me after.

I started drinking coffee at just the right time to avoid lifting heavy weights too young. I can't quite remember how

tall my parents are but I know that I dwarf them. Perhaps they had different vices as a child than I. Good thing too.

I wasn't the type of student to stick their gum under a desk. If I didn't have anything snapping to say I kept my mouth shut. I don't need a crutch while I'm not talking. My face doesn't need help to be expressive from chewing gum. It is a simple face. It still can convey. It still can emote. I can't show what I'm thinking.

When someone is chewing gum and you ask them a truly difficult question, there will be a moment when the smacking subsides. It is important to catch this moment before it passes. How quickly they resume chewing after having to think of something other than their next bite, will show you how confident they are in the lie they told.

...

I catch runners in lies as frequently as I catch fares in the backseat of my car. If it is a repeat runner, turned first time customer, they are usually more honest with me. There's less pressure than what I had applied to make them see the light. Most of the questions I ask can go unanswered. Such is the responsibility of a host. If you're not moving, you're losing. If there's five seconds of dead air, someone other than the host will try to ignite the conversation. The host is as embarrassed as everyone else when they hear what is said next.

...

You can never take back anything that is said out loud. You can play tape back and talk over it, but you won't always be available to do that.

...

Bonnie's house was the closest thing to a castle that we ever heard tell.

...

I'm writing this on a passport. I go to any terminal that will have me. I'm usually not bothered. I hope in my writing that that is evident. It would be awful to get sidetracked because of a heckler. Worse if they knew what I was trying to accomplish. The simple face of mine, since I've added

weight to it, is wrongly assumed to mask hidden potential. Hecklers that see that I am writing, and with what fury, try to egg me on. I won't let them get me down.

　　...

　　Cole's van is somewhere down track. Cole's girl left a picture of the two of them hanging from the rearview mirror. It is like a fine wine. Extremely hard to come by and passed down through generations. With veneration we should have cherished the picture. It was Bonnie and I that felt the most betrayed. If the picture weren't drained of it's allure I might have tried it in one of my cars.

　　The fares need to know that I am a person just like them. I could pass as Cole, so could be asked about the dame beside him in the picture. Cole's girl. Fares like to let you know their relationship status. It is an easy out for not having to be good at relations. Sometimes I ask if they know who some foreign representative's significant other is, that they're reading about in the paper. Sometimes I hear people drooling in the back seat over the partner they wish they had. Oh, to have that person that is attached to the feature of the article.

　　Since I don't have a picture by myself with another person in it, I'm not asked about the person that neither of us sees.

　　...

　　Coupled runners are the most unstable. Most of the time it doesn't seem like the two people should be together. How competitive they are just isn't civil. One is always jealous that the other is so quick to side with me. I've caught relationships ending. They still were detained together.

　　It is important that I try to mend these relationships to the best of my ability. If not for myself, than at least for them. If things go well and I catch up with them in the backseat of my car, the tip is often gracious because of my role as mediator. Unfortunately they are not repeat customers as a couple. Seeing me again while they were together would put them back on shaky ground.

...

Though runners for the most part enjoy deceiving themselves into believing they are living the train hopping lifestyle that they've heard about, not all are prepared for the complications that brings. Namely myself, and all the opposing forces that want them to straighten out. The naive runners sometimes mistake me as one of them. Even in my days around the hub I wouldn't be confused with the common folk. Since I've added weight to my face it has become more of a problem.

I keep up the charade long enough so that any respect I acquire is not completely lost when I reveal my motive. The runner may be afraid when I present them the alternatives to them hiding in a cargo car. They may feel betrayed. It is important that I gain their favor back as quickly as possible.

...

I've slept in the backseat of my car but never while on the lot. If there were ever a threat of the car being found to be missing, I would take short naps instead of one drawn out rest. The cars are not tracked unless there is my most recent call's cell phone inside. I don't use any navigation tools other than my fare's directions. When they are a hopeless runner, because they are lost, I use an atlas. If my travels were as extensive as they were when it was Cole, Bonnie and I, I'd have torn out all the pages by now. Though the pages aren't perforated they come apart very easily. You can't read a book while you're driving but you may be able to manage a paper.

...

Screaming William would always say lightning couldn't be caught in a bottle. He believed himself to be a vessel unlike all others. He did think you could be struck by a bottle. He sure could talk. If his mouth wasn't attached to his face I'm sure it would have fallen off.

...

I've heard of Dunbar's number. In order for me to put it in perspective, I imagine two runners to every cargo car on an average haul. Supposedly by the time I got to the last

runner I would still have a clear picture of the first. Although how I saw them originally may not be how I left them. So let's say that each of those hundred and some odd people can be remembered for having two faces. The sample size is the same but the rule is no longer true.

If I had to remember all the faces of the runners I'd seen before they saw the light, I'd have an extremely guilty conscience for any of the those I couldn't turn into repeat customers. When they leave a small tip and apologize for doing so, I am almost always correct in my assumption that if I do see them again, it will be on the other side of the track. The runner turned customer turned back runner, only agreed to my shuttle service to appease me. I can't be quite as convincing as I was the first time but the circumstances are different. I start off by asking if they have any complaints about the ride I had given, and if so why hadn't they called.

I've heard a lot of runners say they just can't quit train hopping. A lot say nothing else quite compares. I don't have much of an argument for them. I thought the same way and it's turned me in to the exceptional worker that I am today. I can't encourage them to keep on what they're doing, in hopes that they'll some day be like me. I'm not that close to retirement.

Some of those faces are easier to remember. They are right in the middle of what they looked like before they saw me, and what they looked like after. They are halfway healed. It's not important that I remember any of the faces. My job doesn't change. It is somewhat more important that I remember the tip they gave, so I can prepare for the next battle. It's something in their eyes when they hand you money that doesn't seem quite right.

...

You had an eye for chaos. Both tampering and feeding it. I had an eye for order. Both imposing and hindering it. Cole had an eye for what it took to get the two of us to see eye to eye. We had a good run, Bonnie. Must have been for the better half of a decade. Or better, a decade and a half. Not that years could possibly mean anything to you after the accident. Whatever accident it was. The day you lost connection between some of your brain's receptors is the day you lost a part of me. Would have been the whole thing for it not the letters I've sent you. And thus finding out about your condition.

Around the hub we were trying to get away from the human condition. I wonder if we'd have been successful if we were elsewhere. Now that I'm removed from the hub I can assert that I am still no closer to my goal. In fact am closer to what I have tried to escape, just by the passing of time. No one lives forever, but forever there will be those who live. Man is the measure of time.

If you saw me now you wouldn't recognize me. The picture you have been forming in your mind through my description may not be entirely accurate. It's easy enough to imagine a man in a three room apartment. Throw a green jacket on him and a brown hat. But that was the old me. I now wear a jumpsuit. It keeps the driver's seat clean when I am with fare, what falls onto it falls onto the floor. I used to have more jumpsuits, but they weren't being used so I just kept the one.

If you can picture a person in a jumpsuit baggy enough to prevent anything from falling on to the seat, you've done well so far. Here is where I fear I'll lose you. See the jumpsuited man walking through the apartment, with not a single object caught on his person. Imagine the simplest face you can think of. Add some weight to it.

The country folk claim thirty meters wide on both sides of the tracks as their own. Anything that is dropped in that area they believe they have a right to. I try to keep what's supposed to be on the train, on the train, and anything

that's not, off. I did throw that card reader and gathered the winter clothes. I've jumped from the train myself in pursuit of a runner.

Runners play by their own rules. Which is part of the reason I was able to get good at my job so fast. If there's always a healthy fear of failure then progress can be made readily.

...

I keep a pen and papered pad with me for every interaction. In order to appear professional, I hardly ever write anything down. If my fares are impressed by my memory I don't feel so bad about them not leaving a generous tip. If runners saw me jotting while jogging, my pace not theirs, what's one man's jog is another man's sprint, they would likely think I was working with someone else. I need the runners to trust me so I don't need to resort to detaining them. I can't have them thinking there is a conspiracy. All I want to do is help.

What I do write down in the pad, stays in the pad. It previously had stayed in the hub back in the time before now, and more recently in my thoughts. It was Cole, Bonnie and I that shared our innermost with each other. Neither talked much, which goes to show just how great the hub was running. If we took notes it would only have been when we knew we were overseen. To appear professional. Staying out of sight of the underlings was as easy as it sounds. Marie probably knew what we were getting up to. If she didn't it was for good reason. She kept us informed when things were running smoothly.

...

Purgy could have talked to a duck and been mistaken for a quack. His teachings still trickle down to I and my colleagues. The respect they have for him was born. Mine was learned.

...

If you don't stoke the fire you probably won't get burnt.

...

There were public service announcements around the hub. It was well served to heed their advice. As a public service, advice was given. I don't think it would have worked outside of our community. What various shops were set up around the hub could all be packed and stowed on one's back within minutes of discovery. What they were selling wasn't always illegal. Where they set up shop wasn't always infringing. Those that busted them didn't always have the most credible authority.

It was Cole, Bonnie and I that were above the law of the street. We did pretty well with the pinched nosed as well. It all had to do with communication. Those below us understood that we could never be near the scene of a bust. Cole's girl might have had a few run ins with people who were determined to ask questions. The van they left behind says a lot about what type of answers she would have given.

...

They say scrap yards are heaven for cars. I wouldn't call scrappers angels. They do work without knowledge of the great plan. They can affect the material world. The scrapping industry hasn't been that innovative yet. Angels don't ask many questions either. Angels are sometimes asked how they did it. They can only tell you the first step. Nothing beyond that would make any sense.

Joanne wasn't a scrapper's daughter but she had three of her own. I never made the rounds back when it was Cole, Bonnie and I. We would have had to all go together. When I see her now she always asks if I'm still driving new cars. I'm still yet to think of anything clever to say back. She has a love to hate relationship with new releases. She knows that without them her business, that of raising her children and supporting her loving husband, would need to focus more on other avenues of junk. Which is tough to hear knowing the type that infest those waters. As it is presently, she has to see works of art destroyed. They don't make cars like they used to. She sees the new cars as rubbish. I see them as dollars in someone's pocket.

I won't give the names of Joanne's daughters because I don't know them. Joanne says they're all named after great models. I tell Joanne she always knows what she's doing. I like going back there because of the response I get.

...

The fares I shuttle around in the car don't know how privileged they are. How good they really have it. I always tell them at the end of the ride to demand nothing less than what I had given them on that ride, from any of their future drivers. If they can go from privileged to spoiled before they see me again, I know I've done well. I can keep them at that baseline while they're along for the ride. Having just got things they thought they wanted from the other shuttles, they are always delighted to see the foreign papers. Excited when I skip through every song halfway that was about to repeat the chorus and bridge.

If I see a fare has went from privileged to spoiled, I expect to get a big tip. The fare that demands so much from every ride, since the intent was not originally theirs, usually cannot break from treating others how they would want to be treated.

...

My cardio isn't what it used to be. But then again, neither is the rest of me. When it was Cole, Bonnie and I, we always knew when the next shipment of cigarette cartons would be at the hub. We had scouts search far and wide for competitive prices. They undercut all of them if they chose to take from one of the cars. We three didn't encourage that kind of behavior, nor did we purposefully look the other way. Scouts were just extremely talented, is all.

If cigarettes are currency then an unopened carton is gold.

...

In coins we trust. In cash we must.

...

The card reader may never get fixed. It's not completely broken yet though. For such a small object you'd

be amazed at how massive the dents are. I'd rather have to give someone the change they ask for back when they specify the amount of the tip, than pretend to believe that the card reader isn't working the way it's supposed to. I know what it's problems are, and the function to leave a tip definitely isn't one of them.

The fares aren't too perturbed when I tell them it's cash or the highway. They hope that the destination will accept cards. They don't want to be let out on the side of the road. Wouldn't you believe it, but some of the fares make empty promises and revert back to their old ways. Waiting till the car has almost come to a complete stop, before jumping away from my hospitality and towards the asphalt. There usually aren't any bushes to welcome them. Their instincts may have done them wrong.

I can't do anything when this happens, save remember their face before it had to be busted up the first time. It is a smug face and I should have known what was in store. Chances are they didn't have a credit card at all. They may have chosen the shuttle over the train to avoid having to see me. Or, at least save themself from any of my surprises.

...

Other than when the train is in the vicinity of country folk, I am not much around trees. There was a movable garden at the hub. I was and still am green in green thumbing. The gardener that we all knew dearly was named Chrissie. Her buds were perfect. Her blooms fantastic. She didn't wear sunglasses. That's how we all knew how hard she worked. Flowers normally aren't very demanding, but the way she focused on them you'd have thought they were. Her eyes couldn't help but pick up on small imperfections. Her hands couldn't help but mend.

If she had worn sunglasses, I would have liked to see her in a floral one piece. The flowers would reflect on to the shades, and if she bent over she would be as one. She dressed head to toe in navy blue. She didn't blend in with the flowers. She said she could never be good enough to be

one. Thankfully, she never asked the flowers the questions we asked her while she was in our presence.

Screaming William tried to help Chrissie in her chores. My words, not hers. She wouldn't even call it a hobby. To her it was a calling. Screaming William had also heard a call. He was more outspoken about his revelation. The two got along together though, and once a real friendship had formed, Chrissie claimed it was Screaming William's electric field that was helping the plants grow so well. Screaming wouldn't take credit but it was clear he wanted to. Chrissie was a good person.

...

The stump where the tree had been is an example of good forestry. The house where a tree had not been, yet is now, is an example of diffidence. The owner of the once proper house, now structurally unsound hazard, had an unhealthy fear of God. His name was Brett.

He believed that since the tree had fallen on his house, he could not remove it for fear it would go against God's plan. Brett was so confident in God that he didn't believe he had ever been tested one day in his life. The tree was not a test to see if he'd move it but a sign that God was watching over him.

When the tree fell on his house, he was inside. No one heard his call for help because it took a power line down with it. When police and firefighters showed up at the scene, he refused to leave his house. He claimed there must be much to do inside, and the tree showed just how close he came to endangering himself by going out into the world.

Neighbors paid visits to Brett in the following weeks. They had had enough of talking with the police and firefighters. They brought treats that would have been comfort food, had they only been prepared in Brett's house. Brett had a satchel that he wore around his shoulder, on his back, and whenever he was asked to eat the food, would motion like he was obliging and put the food in the bag. The hugs he gave at the end of the visit were nice. The

neighbors didn't notice the smell off the bag of leftovers. They had grown accustomed.

Brett heard a million reasons why he shouldn't give up. He heard no reason as to why people thought he was.

...

I don't need a million reasons as to why someone should give up the train hopping lifestyle. I need a few solid ones and to not miss any opportunity when it presents itself.

...

The fact that these letters are being returned only strengthens my resolve. Spending so much time around the scouts, I know that if anyone could game the mail system it would be you, Bonnie. I don't think it would be too hard, but you certainly would have been the only one to have thought of it. I swear when I open the letters there's something different. Are you doing that on purpose Bonnie? Opening the letters, putting something inside, resealing, and then finding a scout, never short on stamps and other forger's paraphernalia, to send it off. No offense to your father, or any other in delicate positions, who may have done something similar in their time.

There are mountains to climb and problems to scale. I encounter less problems now then back at the hub, though to the common observer it would appear there were more. Not seeing you is not one of the few problems I have to deal with. The letters are a solution if I ever feel so plagued. I'd like to include more in these letters, if only so that they would be sent with a different envelope that may be more difficult to return. I'm not saying you couldn't do it but it may have to come out of your pocket. Resealing the packages and all.

A problem that I have encountered sending these letters is the question of your literacy. If you have suffered from some sort of mental injury these words may fall on blind eyes. Maybe these words will be the first ones that you learn. My character the first image you can construct from the written word. Being the daughter of a politician you may never have needed to learn the skills required to read and write. A signature may have been all that was asked. If you could read and write before the accident I think you've had, I do not mean to offend.

The most opportunities I ever missed were in math class. I refused to show my work. Now that I'm older, I realize that the greatest works of craftsmanship are regarded as such because of that flaw. Only in the innermost circles, where people know how things are done,

can architectural marvels be esteemed because of the dedication to minute detail. Not because of the brilliance of the whole design.

Brett's house lost it's integrity the minute Brett called it another's. No other than Brett, the creator of his own content, thought the house looked good. None thought it looked right.

...

Bonnie could look at something commonplace in a way so that others would think it didn't belong. For this reason those who waited on Bonnie never thought they were doing a good enough job.

Bonnie was the opposite of high maintenance. It was Cole and I that understood this best. We weren't always gawking at her, trying to figure out what she was thinking. We knew that was an impossibility.

...

As set in my ways I am, I don't think I would change much if I had to go it again. There is a set of philosophers who proffer the theory that everything repeats as necessary until it is done right. A car goes into the garage throughout one's life. When one's life ends, if the car has lasted them through that whole time it does not need to repeat the process any more for that person.

Siddartha saw the cycles that life takes. When he became a Buddha he concerned himself with the cycles of sleep. His eight hours were different from your's or mine. He probably saw more in the moments leading up to a nap than any of us could imagine in a dream.

If this isn't my first go around, I can only assume that last time I had already made it past this point. I would have already detained the same amount of runners, and shuttled the same amount of fares. I think this because I have yet to feel regret in my life. Once that happens, I'll be able to decide if the regret merits a change. If that change will shape the future. And if the future needs to see more of me.

I'm waiting for the time of great stagnation. Only in an extended period where not much happens could one be reincarnated. If things were to move forward, in any account because of you, it would not be possible to arrive to set things right. From the moment you were born, to the moment you came back, if you did nothing to better the shape of the world but the world needed that from you, you will live almost the exact same life until that moment of regret.

...

When I try to recreate either of the faces of the runners I've encountered in my mind, I can form a very good picture of at least one of them. However, I am unable to see the eyes. I think if that were possible it would be detrimental to the health of the imagined. The eyes are the windows to the soul. To see into the soul while being absent of that person's company would not be good.

I can't imagine that the runners are able to form a clear picture of me in their minds. I believe their view of me changes infinitely since the time they first see me to the time when they see the back of their eyelids. Arrogance can turn to anger, despair to adrenaline. How they view me is not how I view myself. Not until they are aware of the skill I have. Then we both are on the same page and have lateral thinking.

...

My fares think I'm a better person than I am because of my lack of job title. I don't try very hard to explain to them that I am more like the other drivers than they know. They see me as a charitable source of good will. Helping train hoppers ease in to civility, and driving well-to-do's to where they can do well. They feel comfortable in the car with me. With other drivers they don't have the same level of trust. They don't confidently know what that driver is capable of.

...

I didn't know what I was capable of when I first realized I had a chance to advertise. When I first heard that I had won the contest, I felt I was undeserving. Surely there was

someone better who could have brightened the city. There's only so many campaigns you can run on a park bench before they all start to look the same. I did my research, walked many streets late at night to see which benches were lit and which not, before I ever even considered the design.

I knew I didn't want to show my face, but I didn't know how to do it. Real estate agents can never quite smile the same for their customers as they can for the camera. I didn't want to fall into the same trap. I sketched what I thought my face might look like and put it on the bottom of the design. In big block letters above that I wrote, here for you, now and for all time. It was simple. Vague enough to be brilliant.

The number for the ad has given me the most trouble. Because pay as you go phones come with a different number every time, I've had to spend long hours at a service desk. The number for my services is, 438-4836-5446.

...

If you see one headlight in the distance where there should have been two, consider yourself lucky. If you see many single headlights riding in a pack, consider yourself spared. It is the lone rider that is dangerous. The loneliest the most so.

To commit to solitude while doors to parties are continually opened takes a certain inner resolve. The faceless rider with a bike that shouts. Without the bike, the rider sits in a corner. With the bike the rider has to find a place away from all corners.

...

The hub didn't have motormouths. We didn't want any unnecessary attention. There were never any loose ends to tie up. There was never an ignorant word spoken.

What we had was Cole, Bonnie and I, at the helm of a ship that has been proved able to steer itself. A ship that that was mostly land locked, save for scouts who were not tethered to just one sea. Without Cole, Bonnie and I there would have only been the band. They couldn't make time

for people they didn't play with. Scouts would have been running around like chickens with their head cut off. Underlings would have taken on too much responsibility and gotten hurt in the process.

I say that the hub could still be functioning to this day but it is with tongue in cheek. Only Cole, Bonnie, or I could truly confirm it's excellence. We three without invitation. I haven't seen the old hub. Bonnie and Cole could be there right now. Cole's girl might have taken my place.

...

There are plenty of drivers that I share the road with. At any point this could change. On my part or theirs.

I've never been run off of the road by a motorcycle. Not even in the most compacted of cars. Sometimes when someone sees a simple face in traffic they absolutely lose it. Having a little more weight in my face has made me less of a trigger for people going from a bad day at work to, what if they don't take it out on me in the street, will be a worse night at home.

...

Marie was the most trustworthy around the hub. Our opinions of her weren't influenced by outsiders. There was no one that could soil her good standing. No one to be smote for calling her a sham.

...

I don't have my own car on the road but am still very recognizable. If anyone asked I'd say my car was in the garage. I make sure to never take part in defensive driving. Still, never try to be first on the highway. In the lead, sure. Never first. Even if I were driving, I think I'd probably see you before you saw me. I don't go out of my way trying to look for you. I've got these letters instead. If I did see you on the street, I'd honk the horn. Granted I wouldn't know what sound would come out, because even though I have some familiarity with the cars I drive, I am not the type of driver who needs to make use of a horn. I do not drive defensively. Any surprises I should have seen coming.

I wonder if it was a surprise to you when I left the hub. You'd have to remember me, and then me leaving to rightly say, so your lack of response is warranted. Also, I'm not the one asking questions. Even if you do remember me, any good standing I may have had will be chopped down when you remember my exit. So take your time Bonnie. You've been given a second chance to do so.

It wasn't that you were ever rushing around the hub, but you were in many places at once. I'd like to say we all followed your pace, but of course we were all really one step behind. First we had to observe before we could act. None of us knew you well enough to know what you would do next, so the moment of observation was critical. I'm not sure if it's a compliment to say you were hard to read, but please do take it as such.

The alpha dog of the strays at the hub always tried to be in Cole, Bonnie and I's good graces. They always found us. We always found someone else to feed it. Screaming William and Chrissie were no help. They wanted the dogs to eat a plant based diet. They wanted the alpha to fast.

When the alpha is hungry they get mean. Screaming and Chrissie refused to see anything but good in anything they encountered. The insects and rodents that destroyed their crop were given alternatives. They may have took both. When the hungry dog is mean it thinks it deserves better

than insects and rodents. Scouts would report back to us whenever the alpha was getting testy. If the dog had been with us for a few weeks, and we knew their eating schedule, we would direct the scout to take measures to insure the dog be fed.

It was Cole, Bonnie and I that called the dogs by the name on their collars. Everyone else had pet names.

...

If one of the fares must bring a dog with them, whether it be a rescue they just adopted or a try before you buy, I insist it not have a cone on it's head. It's too hard for the dog to get through the door. The help the owner tries to give the dog by it's carrying is painful to watch. The dog doesn't want to be held. The fare is barely coordinated enough to get themself safely in the car. It almost makes me want to give them money so they can go back to the veterinarian and reverse the process.

I should have to wear a cone on my head after fares of that sort. Then I'm the one healing and need a restraint so I don't pull my hair out.

...

You can spot a bald runner from a mile away. They almost always are wearing a hood.

I'd go bald if I wasn't always running around. I don't feel tired and my body doesn't tell me I am, but it must be so. I don't have the testosterone to go bald because of my fatigue. Since some runners I encounter are going bald, they must not work as hard as I do. Either in the days of the hub or presently. Perhaps they are unable to be tired because of the threat I pose to their easy living lifestyle. If I can get them on their feet and away from their spot in the cargo car, I say let them go bald.

...

My supervisor at the station says that bald men do it better. I ask what she means by it and she says, pulling off that hairstyle. She's had me going quite a few times.

...

My colleagues at the station say if you're not eating like your dying then you're not living.

...

The representative for the card reader I spoke to on the phone says, laughter is the only medicine. Everything else is a placebo. That's why fake laughter is so offensive. Counterfeit everything else but leave medicine alone.

...

If I have to speak on the phone, I try to do it when no one is around. The people I speak to on the phone are the ones that are usually around. If one of them were around and tried to call me I wouldn't answer. I would call back immediately if it were a first time fare I had just shown the cars in the garage to.

...

If you know that you will get everything done, you can take your time while doing anything. You won't feel rushed. You won't think you've wasted a day. You will no longer look at small problems as a chore, but rather as something that will solve itself if only you take time in your approach.

...

Every time a runner trips during the chase they always look back. I've never seen a dog look back after getting tripped up, unless they caught a snag. Even when it was Cole, Bonnie and I, I didn't use dogs as a tool. I would never get one to assist in me chasing down runners.

If I did get a dog that could keep up with my pace, they would need to be able to land on all fours once thrown. If a runner decides to take the battle to the top of the train, my favorite place for a fight while darting along the countryside, the dog would need to be able to safely land there first, before I made my move. It wouldn't be fair to the dog to put them in that situation. Dogs don't understand the concept of throwing. You never know what a runner will do, and though I wish for them to give me everything they've got in battle, I don't want them to endanger the dog.

...

Isabelle, wife of Sal, mother of Isadora, is who I will go to in the future for marketing advice. Newt, husband of Isadora, adoptee of Isabelle, is who I will go to in the future for in law advice. If you can market towards your in-laws you can understand your own psychological make up. Understand that and you can get what you want out of business.

If Purgy were still around for the Travers holiday celebration, I'm sure he would find me likeable enough to be invited. He would have known a lot of runners. He may have been friends with a lot of country folk. I'd seen Isabelle at the station enough to be able to let him know how much she cared about him. I'd relate how Newt was as stubborn as any family born Travers'.

My supervisor says Purgy was just a legend invented by the Travers family. I don't believe her. Isabelle must have a maiden name.

...

The first time I hopped a train was providence. I saw a girl who my memory can only let me imagine as Bonnie, sneaking into one of the cargo cars. When the car come back to the station, she was nowhere to be seen. I walked a pretty fine line when I asked one of the transit authority where the last shipment had went. They didn't see me as suspicious, even though I had less weight in my face, and told me some news I thought was good.

I watched that same train roll in and out of the station each day, identifiable because of the graffiti on the sides. I never saw the girl that looked like Bonnie.

...

I used to be able to run a country mile. That was before all of the sprawl. If I ever found myself walking along the tracks, back in the days of the hub, there were almost no country folk to speak of. If I had run that mile now, I would pass people who I would never pass during my duties on the train. They are of the standing where to see someone such as myself running among them, they would surely feel

suspicious. Weight in my face or not, the city dwellers aren't as eager to wave to me as the country folk.

...

If hell is a place where sinners are sent, and the devil rewards those types, does anyone ever stop getting what they want. Called to raise up when needed.

...

It's not the heat it's the humidity. Much rather feel my skin start to peel before getting burnt.

...

If Sal went to hell and set up shop, I don't think Newt would do the same. Newt has gone against the reward he married into his whole life. The devil would have to find another thing to make him complacent.

Newt's wares are not out of this world. His merchandise is not special. He sells greeting cards and commercials. His lab is set up at the kiosk. He can print cards on demand. He can sell you on your own idea.

Newt advertises for people who have people going through important moments' campaigns on public access television. If you taped on a cassette, he can transfer the video and have it ready for publication. He can help you make the commercial but it will cost you. He refuses to promote his father in law's business.

...

Isadora thinks Newt has lost a few pounds every night that he comes home. She watches the public access television as much as possible, and her image of people is distorted. Had I had a commercial back in the days of running around I wouldn't have looked much like a leader. I would look very similar to how I do now.

...

I don't want to ever put a commercial on tv because I've seen too many promos lag and glitch. There may not be as many paranoids influenced by tv as I think, but I don't want to chance any viewers believing they're trying to be contacted.

My number is 438-4836-5446.

The grass was always greener on your side. Just outside of your tent was the only arable soil. Chrissie and Screaming had a garden but it was nowhere near anyone's quarters. You deserved the plot of land that you had, and whatever weeds and crabgrass grew did look nice. Just as the old nobility once had lawns to show off their wealth, you had a patch of turf to show off your superiority. We were all afraid to ask you directly how you were able to accomplish such a feat. We went to Marie instead. I can't tell you what she said since it was about you. You'd have to remember my relationship with Marie and with yourself before I could trust myself to let you know.

So things weren't always better from where you stood but you did have a lawn. There were no pinwheels or gnomes outside of your tent. It's what's on the inside that counts. You did have a nice lawn though. Inside of my tent you would have found things to attempt to show that it's what's on the outside that is important. My apartment is a little different. What's on the inside of it is so vast that most of it will never again be shown to the outside. It keeps the place warm in the winter, and me out of it in the summer.

Summer months seem much nicer now that I have left the hub. A beard can only get so long before you realize you've outstayed your welcome. I'm talking about those bouts of time I spent in cold climates. I didn't have a beard then but saw many that froze to the moisture on clothes. I said let my face be the color of a nose that is not warmed by a moustache in sub zero conditions. Red. In the summer my face can almost reach the same color. That is how I then tell if I've overstayed my welcome.

I don't put my tarp down when there will soon be snow. I also don't pick any of my banners up before a storm. I can't choose which ones to give priority to, so follow fare's orders and don't ask of them any favors. It is a busy time after snowfall, and most drivers are too distracted to notice the benches covered in snow. If one of my fares does

happen to see my ad while I'm driving, I play it off like it was supposed to be there.

...

When you know you're good at something, it is very easy to convince people otherwise. The most skilled can act the most foolish. The truly foolish could pick up skills faster because of their way of thinking. A fool would have to tell them there are different approaches to learning. Another fool to dispute. The truly foolish would need to pass both of them to be a skilled fool.

The skilled foolish would never let on, and would take whatever criticism comes their way. Fools are those that punch down at the skilled foolish. Wise are the foolish whose skills are abeyant.

Fools judge according to their own merit. The foolish by another's.

...

The use of the word verily was required when addressing Cole, Bonnie or I. It was our way of taking oaths. For this reason we never responded with the question, really. An example of what any scout could have said at any time to us was, verily I say to thee three. Other underlings didn't have the phrasing down and were hypocritical with what came after the pledge. An example would be, I say to thee verily three. It was Cole, Bonnie and I that were as one when we were together.

There was no punishment for outright lies. We expected them. Sometimes we asked that one shew their work, but that was constructive. Cole, Bonnie or I weren't the ones who would suffer from their mistakes. We could show them how to whittle their cross down. They'd have to take it from there.

Teach a man he bears a cross, he's weighed down for life. Teach a man physics, he's able to help others.

...

I never have to scrape ice from any windshield. Such are the perks of having access to the garage.

...

I've never driven in the desert. I've passed the country folk around there on a train. They've tried to splay their fingers so they could wave. Their hands cracked and bled. The work they are doing, if done right, goes unnoticed. Protect the desert. Just don't bring too many people.

...

If any of my fares have children, not in the car, and they were my last fare, I have been known to make 'on this day' cards. I've guessed wrong a few times, and sent birthday cards to hospitals for fares that had not been with child. It's so hard to tell these days why anyone is going to the hospital. Too many stories about people not knowing they were pregnant until the baby, to believe the cards don't have at least a fifty percent chance of being warranted.

...

I haven't learned how to play cards since my time away from the hub. Any runners that would offer me a game are few and far between. I can't keep count in my head well enough to play with fares in the backseat. My lack of knowledge is not a handicap. I make interactions interesting by my ambiguous ignorance.

Marie would make an awful dealer. If she shuffled the cards they'd all end up with the same face. She had takes on tarot cards though that are, if not original, completely foreign. Venmo said she was born to this earth from the stars, but is a child of heaven. It might have been a bluff had she anything to prove to anyone.

...

The doctors around the hub were not necessarily Cole, Bonnie or I's underlings. It wasn't their prestige that set them apart, but more so our inability to take orders from someone we gave orders to. It would also have been hard to convince the doctors to do any dirt work. Better to let them go about their business, and we ours. Maybe those prescriptionists would have refused our invitation to be subordinates anyway. Still carrying grudges from medical school and seeing mentors as enemies.

Most of the doctors that treated us believed we were stealing from them. Their habits were worse than any they tried getting us to admit to. Their sickness fed off of our own. If the doctors were just able to remember how they treated the last patient they would be able to find their supplies. I never went to a doctor for anything major. Marie said I was fine, and I trusted her word far more than any doctor's.

...

I don't misplace things, I mistake where I put them. To prepare for the day I unravel my jumpsuit and grab my wood beaded car cushion. When asked why I carry the latter around the garage, I say for hail mary, for full of grace. The people asking the questions can see I'm full of it. Perhaps that's why I haven't been able to mimic the look Bonnie could give. My eyes aren't as bright as they used to be. I might be practicing too hard.

...

If your eyes are too bright, people might find it harder to trust you. Sure you seem quick on your feet and have something to say about more or less everything, but some might find that disrespectful. An overfed ego can lead to one believing they make up the whole room.

Someone who doesn't feel like they are being heard in the room, may also have very bright eyes. To find two compatible people, look for those whose eyes work off of each other. When the ego has just about finished their point, the id will brighten up but hold their tongue. If they do not hold their tongue, then person b has also chosen ego, and the two might not be as good of a match as the ego and id they represent. Having this knowledge won't help you in any way, unless you are conceited enough to believe match making is good for everyone.

...

We didn't mind when the hub moved. It made it easier for our secret to be kept. The first time the hub was identified it was because one of the scouts had been on a mountain, and with an overhead view was able to see

where four trains would get in each other's way. Providing a space to be boxed in for us, we with thoughts outside the box.

We were hubsters but that didn't mean we didn't appreciate the open road. Nor did we yearn for miles of emptiness. The hub most resembled a garden. It was nothing like a room. There were four corners but just like a garden, the roots extended beyond what one could see.

The first time the hub moved, Cole, Bonnie and I knew we would lose some people in the process. We devised a schedule for departure, but some underlings were so far down on the waiting list they may have not even been on it. Cole, Bonnie, I and the Band gave tips for how underlings could manage the journey on their own. They were insistent that we meet up at a checkpoint. I don't think they fully understood what we were asking of them.

Hands were stamped with the date that each free runner should depart. Directions to their train were painted on the other.

...

You can't change the inevitable. That much is indubitable. To try, try and try again, expecting different results is lunacy.

...

Screaming William liked the sound of his own voice. He left us with ringing in our ears. What did get through sounded interesting because of it. It was like hearing a prayer before being baptized, losing the sound while your head is dunked, and then hearing the words anew. Screaming always left us with something to think about. He seemed pretty intelligent because of how long winded he was. Someone who needed to be validated that much may not be the brightest, but their opinions are ever changing, which makes them wise.

...

Have you went so long without sleep that your memory has started to fail? In order to be in so many places at once you would have had to have constantly been awake. I don't think anyone could mimic your voice. No ventriloquist could have captured your essence. Most runners had a habit of napping. That was okay so long as they had finished their work so well that it appeared that nothing had been done. If they were lazy and wanted to nap, well they still were able because we couldn't differentiate between tasks completed and left unfinished, but we kept an eye on them. I don't know if anyone ever told you Bonnie, but you could have been a scout.

My relationships with scouts were strictly professional. No one was on your level Bonnie. They were as professional as possible around you. You were courteous back. I never saw you get angry. It's okay to be angry sometimes, Bonnie. I for one am because of the accident that you must have suffered. You can be angry at me for being angry, but no words of encouragement will weather the storm. The worst part is that you can't even tell me what it is happened, since the outcome has left you lacking in some departments. Seeing the letters returned still gives me hope that the Bonnie that I once knew, and she me, is still somewhere inside. You probably look different, so I hope that the Bonnie that I once knew, and she me, is inside of the body of a Bonnie that I never knew, and she not me.

I wear a baggy jumpsuit these days. Used to be a brown jacket and green hat. How I wish you'd remember Bonnie. I wore runners, sneakers as they are sometimes called. Not to be confused with runners, who very well may be sneakers, or prowlers, vagabonds, or destitutes. The laces of my runners are cross threaded. Much like the stitches that runners may get after encountering me. I won't go into details Bonnie, but I am very good at my job.

We had a talent show regularly at the hub. It was Cole, Bonnie and I that were above it all. Underlings dashed and dove to be first in line. They knew we wouldn't be present

for long. The winner got bragging rights, but since free runners are as they are, the winner was gone before any could even congratulate. The winners switched out very often. In the end if one were to try to brag, they'd be hard pressed to find an audience that hadn't themselves won previously.

Some of the acts we clapped our hands for. During some of the acts we cried. They say everyone has talent, but also that good people are hard to find.

...

They say that submersibles will be the future of traveling. I'll be out of a job. They say when the population is ready that the new transports will arrive, and there will be pilots to commandeer them. At first the price to ride will be exorbitant. There won't be any runners jumping ship right away because of the cost, and the security keeping them away. When the price drops, and the average folk are able to purchase a ticket, free runners will try to make like they are one of the regulars. There won't be as much security after it becomes a common mode of transportation. Not much security underground so it stands there won't be much underwater.

If I did have to chase down a runner underwater, or underground because of the lack of security, I like to think we're all in it together, I would have spent all this time writing, preparing. For adventuring in the sea, I would need an oxygen tank, flippers, suctions cups for my hands, and a cutting utensil so fine that what's been sliced could easily be fixed. Once a hole was cut into the submersible I would face a challenging task. I need to get into the sub without disrupting the vessel. If my cut were as perfect as I imagine it would be, I think I would push in on the stencil and once popped out, spin myself around in the water. Finding myself now in the sub and the piece of glass, or what have you, back intact.

There would not be much of a surprise to my entrance. I believe the submersibles will be auto piloted anyway, so there would really be no way the runner wouldn't see me

coming. There is not much room to manoeuvre in the prototype that I imagine. I would use the confined space to my advantage. Jumping off walls to dizzy my opponent. Smashing my hands on the controls so the error message blares loud and obtrusive.

Once the runner is detained, I would leave as I had entered. Popping the glass out and spinning in the water. It does not matter that I leave the runner semi detained. The submersible would have sent signals to a base on account of all the error messages.

...

If I suddenly took it upon myself to police the subway station, I could have a very high success rate but a very low sense of job satisfaction. There are just too many people to not wrongly assume that I'm going after a runner, and not say, a mother of four. Out in the open it is much easier to see who's who. One can never tell anything with the underground.

...

Marie kept a mannequin in her tent. She warned us all not to touch it. Those who did, and later called Marie a liar, for it had not come to life as she had told, were caught up with by any allies Marie had. Any afflictions that were not physical were mental, which ended up being physical. Marie had a broken heart, so knew what it took to break one. Marie had a rage you'd have to see to believe, so she knew how to use it.

The mannequin didn't have a name but Marie told of all the names that personality type may have had. She said the mannequin was an extrovert who wished to make life hard for all those it encountered. A mind so extraordinary the character type could get away with being a prick, and still be revered and respected. Why any of her customers wished to make life hard for themself is beyond me. Marie could have stopped them from touching it, or one of their friends since troublemakers so often travel in packs, but it wouldn't have done them any good. They would learn Marie's lesson one way or the other, and finally stop being

the ones to cause themself harm. They stopped being their own worst enemy once they decided to test Marie.

...

No runners travel with mannequins. If they did they would not get special privileges. There is no carpool lane alongside the tracks.

I've never seen two twin runners. I've seen a runner twice, and when I caught up with them the second time I figured they must have an accomplice, for they had beaten me to a spot. This wasn't Donald. I finished that job.

The only siblings that I was aware of at the hub were Cole's girl and Cassandra.

...

I was an only child. When I was of school age and refused to show my work, my parents knew that one was enough. Every birthday they would ask if I wanted a sibling. I told them that was too heavy a question for my young soul.

...

Life as an enforcer and light deliverer would get lonely to a lesser shoe filler. I've learned that relationships outside of work are not good for me. Now I never feel as if I'm missing out.

...

They say you are what you eat. That makes me more or less nothing. If you are the hard candies that you dissolve to stave off hunger, than I am both jawbreaker and warhead. I don't chew gum when I am with fare, nor do I chew rubber. They call me sir if they are a runner turned fare. They hold me in high regard. If they are a customer that has seen my advertisement they may also call me sir, but usually stop when I ask them not to.

The fares with history as runners like to bring food with them in the car. It is easy enough to say sir with a mouthful. Timed right, by the time I acknowledge them they will have stopped chewing. Those who have found me through my other intelligent design are usually satiated or starving when they enter the car. Them letting me know which, has

sometimes helped my driving. The satiated crack jokes. The starving crack the whip.

If two passengers are travelling together and somehow one is satiated and the other starving, one already has a pretty good idea of how the night will go. To find a starving with a satiated means that one's appetite doesn't always concern food. I playfully tell them to keep their hands off of each other. I'm a good judge of character. If a situation did arise, I've got a contraption in the car that will hold the wheel steady while I slam the emergency break, so as the car skids to a stop I can jump into the backseat and work over the skid.

...

My steering assist mounts to the back of my head rest. It shoots out when I step on the emergency break, so I have to make sure I have already left the seat. If not, I will get hit in the head, probably knocked out, the assist won't grab the wheel, and one innocent will suffer. The skid and I know who we are.

When I am free from danger of my own device, the assist grabs on to the wheel. Claws close where my paws were. Extended off of the claws and back to the head rest are heavy duty supports. I need only slightly move the wheel right after I press the brake, if the road calls for it, and the assist takes care of the rest.

If I were not able to detain the new target in a matter of seconds, I could do enough to subdue them momentarily to get back up front and make any course corrections. I've knocked out many with one hit. The method is simple. There is a greater likelihood of a one hit wonder if the target's mouth is open. Even more so if they are surprised. It takes one quick movement for me to grab their nose and pull it closer to my face. They open their mouth. As I pull my fingers away, greasy from nasal sebum, I deliver a clean clock.

There's no time to accept thanks or congratulations from the other passenger from the back seat. I quickly get up to the front and disable the safety assist part way so that

I am able to steer easier. If I'm lucky, I figure out how to fully disengage the assist before the subdued comes to and becomes a minor inconvenience again. I always have trouble getting the mechanism back into the head rest, but I like to think I'm getting better at it.

...

People were always apologizing when they were around you. Even for apologizing when told they shouldn't. I was your greatest ally in the fight against absurd politeness. Cole may have been just as vocal as me, but could in no way shoot the look I'd give your congregation. Which what else could they have been constantly asking for but forgiveness and leadership. You did well in your role Bonnie and I in mine. Cole was on about the same level. It was in fact you who would apologize to those who were apologizing for being apologetic because you didn't have anything to offer them. I remember one winter we had to talk you out of taking up the hobby of knitting. No one would have been cold that winter but we needed your hands for other things. Your mind sharp. Not fighting drowsiness.

I have bags under my own eyes now. Age starts the race off fast then falls in with the crowd, only reappearing to show that it has won. I imagine you aged very well. No one would dispute your claims otherwise. Unless you haven't aged as well as I'd like to think, losing some of that power that I know you don't want to hear you have, but you did, and so may be in more confrontations. I hope you have allies as good as Cole and I by your side. Not that you ever may have truly needed us, but our work would have suffered even further if there was ever any doubt in our minds. We had to think the way we did in order that we didn't disappoint. Even if in retrospect our train of thought may have been a little disappointing.

I hope that you're not going through any hard times, Bonnie. Even if you believe what Purgy has been claimed to have once said, and that pain is just weakness exiting the body. But I guess that wouldn't apply. Unless you are going through hard times because you are in pain. I'm not sure the two are mutually exclusive, though having trouble with one can usually bring about problems with the other. I am as sore as any person my age is, but complain about it a whole lot less. I think it's important to not show that your pain has yet to leave your body, ergo you are still weak.

You would have looked strong behind a podium Bonnie, and we would have all been in pain seeing you there. A pain born of pride. Our Bonnie, making things happen.

The way I train my skill at forceful manoeuvring is through the use of a heavy bag and a wooden dummy. Both are at my apartment, and are luxuries I couldn't afford when I was in command. The heavy bag is a sack that had been previously used for corn, now filled with bean bags. So many bean bags. So many that if the bag ever ripped it would look like I had a problem.

The wooden dummy is a scarecrow supported in a christmas tree stand. Depending on where I hit the dummy it will spin around. Since the areas I can target are few, once I've hit the dummy and it has started to spin, I quickly hit in the opposing direction. As one may play tetherball with themselves. As I've grown stronger my reflexes have had to grow quicker. I hit the dummy with an open palm.

I hit the heavy bag with closed fist and a few other techniques I cannot yet give away. Though runners will not lump when hit, as does the heavy bag, it is still useful to know what they would look like if they did.

...

The inspiration for my home gym came from the source of almost all my creative influence. The hub. There was a genuine name brand heavy bag at the hub. There was no wooden dummy. The nameless mannequin that Marie said not to touch wouldn't make for a good replacement. Back at the hub the heavy bag was not a luxury I could afford to have. I did not have the means to buy it off it's owner. Nor did I have the tenacity. I wouldn't have been a good leader had I taken the best from those who had less.

The owner of the heavy bag had short hair. Small features. Eyes that squinted at the world. He called himself a coach. We called him a trainer. We weren't in competition. I'm lucky that I haven't found the hub again, and possibly him with recruits with many more years of study than me. I can't say that when the trainer was in his prime I wouldn't

have been able to detain him. I wouldn't try now. Should he observe my strengths and be able to relay them coherently, it would put me in danger in the future. I'm not afraid for my own moves to be used against me, but I know that doing said moves triggers a response not all can control. I trust myself. I can't trust people I used to know that I never had a falling out with.

The trainer liked to be called coach. We all called him Skip. He claimed he was a hop and a skip away from knocking our lights out. We told Skip when he was around the lights came on. The world was his squared circle. Eyes that squinted at the world.

...

Marie would sometimes watch us train. She looked completely different out in the light than how she did in her dark. Whenever we knew Marie was going to make an appearance we gathered volunteers to run security for her tent. We made sure to never offer kleptomaniacs the job.

...

If you gave Skip a fifth of wine he'd train you as long as the buzz lasted. He was angry when he was sober. He wasn't able to get drunk.

...

We had competitions around the hub. Bets were placed. Bookies were born. Rivalries developed as long as the competitors stayed around the hub. They usually left together around the same time. They had learned how each other thought. Learned someone could bring the best out in them. They were strong when they were solitary. Together they blended in.

I never fought in any of Skip's bouts. I never trained with him. I couldn't think of the mat in the same way as his disciples.

In order to place a bet with a bookie, most of which were scouts, one needed to fill out a card. The card had around twenty five different plays. The minimum for participation was to pick five. Most of the plays on the card were fights. The spread was an over/under for how many

rounds. Draws lost. Fights weren't over until Skip said they were. It was smart to bring a bottle after you placed your bets.

I won't say that I ever won money on a card. I will say that I would have invested it back in the hub. The hub never ran better then when it was Cole, Bonnie and I.

...

The bookie would always tell the winner that they had been the only one. The bookie would say if there was a line behind the winnings collector that they were only bet placers. You didn't want to win too often though. Bookies are in that business to befriend losers and disavow winners. Bookie's friends don't get a slice of the pie, but at least know their money is going to good hands.

Anything you could part with you could bet. The bet placer didn't get to determine the object's value. Using cash was recommended. I didn't bet on any card games. I had seen too many winners to gamble on a game I knew nothing about. It wouldn't have been safe.

...

You were never fashionably late Bonnie. If you remember one thing, please remember that. It would make writing these letters a whole lot easier if I knew you were diligently working on a response. The words escape me to describe how hard of a worker you actually were. It's a shame that you may have lost some of that. I've already mentioned that you seemed to be in multiple places at the same time. I will continue to remind you because I think it's an important part of your identity. So aside from your work ethic being shown by you being in places where you were noticed, one also was given hints by the voice you used to conduct business. We all knew when you were talking recreationally versus professionally. One tone cut like a knife, the other like an axe. Not that we minded hearing either, there is smoothing soothing about both sounds to those in the know.

One voice was like a knife through butter. With all the anticipation surrounding whether or not it will be a smooth cut. Your other voice could clear a forest. Perhaps you may have an easier time remembering me through the sound of my voice. This doesn't have to be so difficult Bonnie. Please send a tape recorder in the next returned envelope so that I may send you a sample. I will do my best to describe my character from the noises that come out of my mouth.

My voice is caught in between gravelly and smooth. Mellow and shrill. Odious and pleasing. Before I learned to enunciate, strangers would ask if I was putting on a voice. My dialect is my own and any followers of it have long been forgot. Those at the hub couldn't always understand what I was saying, so it was good you and Cole were around. When Cole left, his voice sounded almost like mine. If only we had caught his goodbyes. His and your's was probably special. I can't give you the details, and who knows if you'd believe me if I did. I am getting somewhat better at developing a story. You might not believe that either.

Hunting was a pass time for many of the free runners at the hub. Groups would go out together, and if the hunt

should be a success, come back staggered. We never wanted to draw attention to the hub. One person dragging an animal was more suspicious than five people dragging fifths of an animal. Most of the hunters were scouts. They knew how to move together while apart. One of the hunting party, if there were no scouts, would find one to let them know if they would soon be arriving.

We needed to have the hub ready for the first of the hunting party, who we were warned wouldn't be returning empty handed. We would move the generator away from the middle, and in it's place put whatever posts we had lying around the hub, all in a row. Rope was attached to the uppermost part of each post. Hooks were used to diagram in the dirt how we would hang the meat. We had tools at the hub, so the rope never broke from the weight since it had been properly secured.

They say a good hunter is successful if they hit on one out of five hunts. Those hunters stop when they get a hit. Our hunters had looser guidelines as to what constituted a hunt. They could go two for six. If one hit, it did not mean that it was time to pack up. Not entirely. If the hunter got a deer, and on the way back got two squirrels, they apportioned the meat so it would carry. Should they have gotten two deer, and had been separated from the party, since they were almost always scouts, were able to signal to their companions they needed assistance.

If you had a hunting party of very fast scouts, they may have called for help and rewarded the respondent with an open fire. The two could enjoy the freshly prepared meal, because they knew they could make it back to the hub before the rest of the meat spoiled. The same fire that signaled the supporting scout could be used to feed said scout.

If the meat had something wrong with it, it was better that the hunters had gotten more than one animal so they had to break and eat the food, rather than hurry back to serve it at camp. We also didn't want them getting sick around the hub.

...

When meat did make it back to camp, there were no arguments as to who was more deserving of the spoils. None of the hunting party ever said non hunters couldn't partake in the bounty. The hunters knew how hard we worked preparing the hub for their return.

We didn't keep leftovers and we didn't keep the waste. Everyone was urged to eat as much as they could and then some. Anything we did not prepare for consumption was brought back into nature. Nature would take care of it in it's death as it had in it's life.

...

All things in nature mimic something else. We as humans attempt to convey we're listening by repeating what we had just been told. It works up to a point until the one person is just waiting to hear the thing they can repeat. It is worse than not listening.

...

Perhaps the mannequin is still where the hub once was. Marie said it was of the personality type to not move without valid reason. If the picture left in Cole's van was in better shape, I would retrieve it and start a collection. If I found the mannequin I don't think it'd be wise to move it to the van. We don't need any more of those types of vans made. Seeing an intact crash test dummy would surely catch researcher's attention.

Trying to save that intact crash dummy from a life unfulfilled may lead to disaster. One cannot know how strong was the magic Marie worked on that mannequin. One can only assume.

...

You could always tell who Skip trained from the hair. You can tell I now think it's fashionable to be in society by mine. We didn't allow combs in the ring. Doesn't mean contestants stopped from trying. I keep a set in the the inside of my jump suit. I never know when I'll catch a fare.

Passengers who are traveling solo and choose to sit in the backseat, have a perfect view of the rearview while I'm

driving. If they haven't said anything about their or my own hair, I casually bring it up in conversation before offering them a comb. Should they not have hair, or are considering doing without it, I offer wax. I would never keep razors in my car. Doesn't mean some of Skip's second chance at life recruits didn't try to bring them in the ring.

...

The hair style that Skip's disciples sported was a comb over. A very dramatic comb over, judged by it's closeness to a picture Skip had of himself back in high school. He said the girl beside him in the picture was homecoming queen. Everyone was intimidated by her, so she had chosen to take Skip to prom. Skip said it was one of the proudest nights of his life. When asked why, he always told us to take a closer look at the picture.

Skip never looked as he did in the picture once he had a fifth of wine in him. For this reason he never showed the picture while he was training. The required haircut had to be assembled on his recruit's own time. I saw bright eyed, glass chinned mop tops be rejected for having a single hair be out of place.

Such were the free runners around the hub at the time, that some students were bold enough to paint the haircut on top of their head. In order to really get away with it they had to use the right kind of paint. It couldn't come off the minute they started to sweat. Those who did choose a more permanent paint were some of Skip's favorites. He may well have known what they were up to, but their willingness to conform to his rules softened him up.

...

I don't care how talented a painter you think you are, my cars would not look better with splotches left in the back seat.

...

What to say about crowded places and all those stranger's faces. Who would have looked upon you just as your friends had. Or those who were able to get close enough to you to consider themselves as such. Or consider them close enough to you to even risk having you in their thoughts. Who knows what kind of power thoughts of that nature actually have. That is why I have done my best to think of you as seldom as possible since I've left your acquaintanceship. It's something about never judging anyone unless you judge yourself. I don't know what position you are in so any thoughts directed your way would be unsafe.

Marie liked to say that thoughts were nature's way of making you feel connected. At the same time the absence of thoughts would make one one with nature. If you are still around Marie, please do not mention my name just yet. I know she would quickly return my letters which is why I have yet to find her address and send any. With you there is still a little bit of mystery. Will the letters be returned unopened, or will the letters have a touch of your hand that will let me know the channel is open?

You probably have children by now Bonnie. I only hope you remember them better than you do me. It's an awful thing to say but it is the only help that I can give. I do not know your children, if you have any, and never knew them so I fear that I will never be adequately able to describe them. Do not be angry at me for this Bonnie. I will tell you how you dealt with any underlings that were not yet tall enough that they should have ever been allowed on the train, or around the hub.

I don't know any of those children's names, just like I don't know your's, if you have any, but they looked up to you just as much as any of the adults. Perhaps even more, but then again they may never have understood exactly what you were, or what it is exactly that you did. Us adults could appreciate you fully. Apart from the little things any adult would do to help a needy child, tying shoes, getting bandaids, reaching for things in high places, you went above

and beyond in accommodating their stay. Their parents you were not so gentle with.

You hired a contractor once to try to knock some sense into the parents. Ordinarily we never would have allowed an outsider in to the hub without first going through initiation, but something in your eyes told us this case was different. I don't know how you ever afforded to have that contractor come to get the parents on the right path, or where you were able to exchange our currency with that of the outside, but the hub is sure glad you did. Once that family left, the hub was all in agreement that no children should ever have to suffer what those children who you went above and beyond for had to suffer.

The distrust for technology that was shared at the hub came from a cyber attack. That is why to this day I still only use a pay as you go phone, with limited internet access, and a flaw in the software that has me redialing numbers. It wasn't just the hub that was attacked, but the whole surrounding municipality. We were vulnerable because we were trying to recruit through covert means.

It wasn't that we necessarily wanted more numbers at the hub. We were looking for people who could prove useful by finding us. We welcomed some runners that found our physical address. We welcomed most that found our internet presence. One had to click on many links and go through many back doors, to even know they were onto something. Once they realized we had set a game up for them, they were more or less hooked.

So the recruiting was going well, and there were many potential scouts setting fire to the internet. Coincidentally, there were some politicians who were trying to do the same thing. It didn't take much for them to accomplish their goal and avert all eyes away from their scandal. They stole as many identities as were available and doxed them to the world. Their tactics went viral.

Years passed and the scandal was forgotten, as was the crime against our personal information. A few of the

politicians, who were involved with both, were scheduled to ride in a parade just a few train stops away from the hub. We gathered as many runners as we could and headed in that direction. When the parade started we blocked the movement of the cars through our peaceful protest. The politicians smiled and waved the whole time their cars were stationary. We were eventually escorted out of the middle of the street. Screaming William and Chrissie were harder to persuade, and though the substance they squirted from their potted plants could not do physical harm, it was psychoactive. Those of us on the sideline were later interrogated by police who we could tell were at their first rodeo.

...

The police shouldn't have experience with psychedelics of any kind. They take bites out of job satisfaction.

...

I don't mind chasing down runners on rainy days. I enjoy driving fares in those weather conditions. My jumpsuit wicks off water during my pursuit. The car rooster tails when I go through puddles and the fares seem to enjoy it.

On those days when I will be taking a car out in the rain and am waiting by the phone, I make sure to always bring some detachable mirrors. The mirrors are put right above the backseat's windows and positioned so fares can see the waves. The mirrors do not block my view while driving. Since I switch them between so many cars I am not questioned by authorities, who assume the design is the way of the future. It very well may be. The backseat mirrors could be angled to play off the ones in the front so that the driver could see what was above them in the sky.

I've never been involved in a police chase so need not pay any mind to any helicopters overhead, but the application could be used elsewhere.

...

Tangoing in rain with runners works to my advantage. The runners that I surprise in their cargo car who had been

sleeping, require extra vigilance on my part. When they arise and jump into the rain, they are still half mad from waking up, and the cold water on their face makes them downright feral. There's no sense trying to talk to them in that state. First I need to damage their armor.

...

If one of the runners somehow gets a shot in on me, or rather hits my baggy jumpsuit, there is a good chance they'll get injured during the throw. Overextending the arm while trying to hit something that isn't there can really hurt. My jumpsuit has never been spread so tight that their hand has bounced off it and hit themselves in the face. If my bouts took longer perhaps I would look into the modification. I don't really need any help from the runners, and I don't want to embarrass any who could potentially be a fare.

...

In the summer you can smell runners from almost a country mile away. Less so in the city. I am never that far out of position but others might be just as unlucky. They would like to be at least a mile away, but if were in my shoes would thank luck for being where they are. Back at the hub we were all used to those smells. As far removed as I am from the hub now, I can still pick up the scent. The combs I offer to my fares could only do so much for hygiene, so I don't offer any to runners.

My nose has never been broken.

...

One of the scouts had a story, most of them do, about a friend they once had that broke their nose so bad they never recovered. His nose was left on his face for aesthetic reasons and so there could be an open casket at the funeral. I can't recall what the scout said his name was but I'll always remember what they said was written down at the grave site. "No regrets. See you when you get there."

...

I don't give much to the runners. A whomping if it be their tendency, and always an offer for a ride. Battles that have occurred while the train was on a bridge over water,

and the water had risen, featured rooster tails similar to those of the cars I drive fares in. Unlike when I am with fare, I don't let the runners know that puddles are coming up, as I might do with a fare so they can prepare to look in the mirrors. Use what poor architectural design has given. If it's a day where I forgot to bring the mirrors, I still let fares know when a puddle is approaching so they aren't surprised when I suddenly jerk the wheel. There's no sense driving through a puddle for my own amusement when I'm supposed to be conducting business.

...

Rodents are a problem on some cargo trains. I wouldn't know if my colleagues hadn't said so. I won't call any runners rodents, though they are pestiferous. If I can't help them to see the light then it is a failure of mine. Not theirs. Cargo cars filled with potatoes and corn, run off from what couldn't fit on a truck, get a bad reputation around the station. Perhaps my eyes aren't trained enough to see what's right in front of me. I don't see it.

What I do see is the devilish runner surrounded by taboo vegetables. If I weren't so good at my job and they had more time in that car than I allow them, it could explain why I don't see the rodents. Why the corn and potatoes are left untouched. The runners eat the rodents. They are what they eat.

...

I hear news about foreign composers and maestros shouted up to the front seat of my car. I hear fares the first time but cut them off repeatedly so I can ask them to speak up. I keep my hands at ten and two when I do. I've asked meaningless questions once I believe they are at a comfortable speaking volume. Questions made meaningless because the fare has no opinion on the subject and only wants to hear mine. Since I am the subscriptionist they believe I'm in a position to be an authority on various subjects.

I don't tell them about the band I used to know. How some could argue from a distance that I myself was a

maestro. I tell them that sound sometimes travels in different directions overseas.

...

I got back the last letter I sent you the other day. There were drops of water on the page. Seeing them almost made me cry. Were they your teardrops or mine? Were they even teardrops at all? Why would seeing your tear drops affect me so viciously? Knowing that you had already gotten it all out should have been a comfort to me. Instead it was a reminder of how openly you cried in public and all of our fear to offer a shoulder to lean on. In short, painful not comforting.

So that I don't misrepresent you, let me rephrase. You were not opposed to crying openly in public. It's not like you could be seen with tears running down your face everywhere you were. But since you were in so many places at the same time, it makes sense that in at least one of the scenes you would be in long face. So that you don't confuse the power of those tears, I will plainly say there was not much in them. You were more likely to get your way by using your look or any of your other machinations. It would be cruel to tell you not to cry, just please use your tears sparingly.

Back at the hub there was only one day I can remember others crying along with you. You all looked like a bunch of infants. It was very strange to see. I don't even know the reason behind it. The explanation I was given must have made so much sense that I didn't think anything of it. It's more important that you remember, but I can't tell you how much so, since I myself don't know. Perhaps if you were to try crying openly in public the memories may come back to you easier. If others were to join in I think you'd be in good shape.

Sometimes a loquacious passenger rambles on. It is not quite music to my ears. The hum is overall pleasant. I don't repeat the hum back to them as I hear it but watch the rearview for small shifts in body language, which let me know when I should tune in.

...

Sometimes I am able to sell subscriptions to fares. After asking so many questions about the news from overseas, they feel invested and halfway committed. I don't profit off of these sales. They are in fact trades. If they have anything that can be redeemed for pay as you go minutes, I further negotiate with the fare. It's good to know that I help my fares seem interesting. As I do myself by selling subscriptions that showcase my taste.

...

It was written in what was half newspaper, half magazine. Wholly unheard of until flipped through in the back seat of my car. Those in hell look up to heels so much they think that is the missing difference. Heels that are holier than thou. In hell they are always one step behind. Able to copy immediately but never produce any of their own. If hell can produce heels then maybe heels can get a shot in at heaven. First those in hell must become heelish.

...

If I am on foot, trying to draw up business with my bench advertisements, and I see a line of cars with parking tickets, I have been known to discover the speed limit for the road they are parked on and add advice to their ticket. After the driver sees that they have gotten a ticket, it is highly likely that they will momentarily be unhinged, and may drive off with a fury. I like to help them, help me, put a damper on their reckless driving. Speed limits are suggestions anyway. I reinforce this so there will be less competition on the roads. It's easy to give advice that you yourself would never follow.

...

There was no maze to get to the hub. No one felt trapped when they went to the hub. We were all trying to get away from something. We all felt we could. No one getting further away from their troubles than anyone else. It was all forward and forward for all.

...

In every interaction I have, I do my best to do my part unto my duty to show life isn't that simple. Every road ends

in a fork and so on. With runners it's pretty cut and dry. They can be my adversary or my friend. Enemy would be giving them too much credit. Though I do never underestimate them. Either keep trying to evade me, or have me always in sight from the backseat of my car.

The fares can choose whether to leave a tip or not. Whether they keep the insights gleaned from the foreign paper to themself or not. If they want to try and have me join in a chorus with them on a song I do not know, played off of their phone.

...

It was Cole, Bonnie and I that stuck up our nose at those who skipped around on songs from an album. Radios were popular at the hub, and we had no qualms with music beggars not being choosers. It were those who had access to the start, finish and everything in between, and still picked individual favorites that we couldn't stand. Trying to choose songs to fit into their idea that they're living in the big picture. The full album would be more relevant to their life.

...

If you can't remember your accomplishments, it's going to be hard for you to find success in anything you choose to do in the future. Even harder if you don't take those people's words about your feats. Believe me when I tell you, that without you the hub wouldn't have run as efficiently as it did. I'd like to believe the same to be true with my absence, but you'll have to remember me first before you can rightly say. What I remember you most for is your work around the hub. You made everything seem effortless, which perhaps why it takes such an effort to tell you something you might have been proud of.

One time you had more money than anyone else at the hub, and when a couple of people wanted to go out for a night on the town, you eagerly exchanged their money so that they could. You were then doubly rich, for even if the exchange was fair you still had more of either currency than anyone else. The stories that were told of that night on the town were told for many nights around that town. Luckily none of them made it back to the hub. We knew their antics anyway. We didn't outright accept all of the things that they did but they were one of us after all. Never you mind those people that were outrageous Bonnie. They can't soil your good name anymore. Let us not soil theirs.

You had comforted Screaming William countless times and even suggested that Chrissie and he team up. For the sanity of all those at the hub, we thank you. Once again, I find myself speaking for others who were at the hub at the same time as I. I believe I am in a position to do so because of the position that I was in then. However, if you don't remember me then you most certainly will not appreciate the sentiment of appreciation so please allow me to get back on track.

You were the matchmaker between many introductions. You wouldn't introduce two people unless you believed they could peacefully coincide in each other's head space. Not all of the matches were romantic. In fact, almost none of them were. For the sake of example, let's say you introduced a scout to a former mechanic. I needn't say anymore. How

they both could help each other out is apparent. So you see, you were very well accomplished. Now even the smallest step in the right direction for you makes me proud. If you fully get back on track, who knows what you'd be able to achieve.

I'm rooting for you Bonnie.

The hub didn't have physical security guards. We had scouts that were quick and effective. Even more so should the band be practicing nearby. Then they would signal to the band to play something everyone knew, at a level to let everyone know. We did welcome a lot of runners to the hub. But, if circumstances were such as stated above, those runners usually were turned away. What would have been a one person job turned into three. When no one was there to welcome the runner, it took a concerted effort to get them to leave. The band played them out.

...

When I am on my way to a fare, all the doors are locked to the outside. For a passenger to get in the car, I roll down the window so they can reach and let themself in. It's an assurance so that I don't stop for nothing. If the fare was thinking of drawing me out to a pick up spot, so they can turn back runner and have a head start only to flee when I arrive, chances are they will have a harder time if their arm is inside the car. I would need to see their intentions before they mine in order to hook them. The second I know their hand is on the inside door handles I would either need to roll up the window, or drive just fast enough that they would have to start running alongside.

If I do get the fare turned runner tethered to the car, it is very important I get them moving fast. If the car goes too fast at first, they may be able to get their arm out. After that though, I need to get them to a speed where if they stop running they still won't be able to fall safely. Should they happen to suffer less injury than I expected, I may need to ditch the car to pursue them on foot. I don't think I would have set up the backseat mirrors for a questionable fare. I

can circle back to the car after I've circled back from the fare.

...

It's hard to imagine that everyone you meet has as many thoughts as yourself. Even during moments of silence in conversation there are still thoughts. Some get offended when they are not being addressed. It is hard to remember that everyone is thinking constantly.

...

If a job requires you to think, you'll never stop working a day in your life.

...

Isabelle never would say much about Purgy. We all drew our own conclusions that even if she wasn't entirely trustworthy, at least Purgy must have been. Purgy must have been a real person, even if Isadora claims her mother is mute. Newt and Sal are businessmen. They don't believe any of their predecessors were as great as they were shown to be. Purgy could be real to them but they don't see the appeal.

I can't blame the Travers family for the tightness of their lips. Though, it is completely opposite from the person Purgy was made out to be. Perhaps if Isabelle had not spent so much time drinking alone at the tracks we would have forgotten the whole family.

...

I have never encountered any of the Travers family as runners or as fares. Never come across faces that bear resemblance to Purgy. It might be a mental block on my part. I wouldn't be able to see them for who they really are if I saw them as runners. I just wouldn't be able to believe it. Prosopagnosiastic insanity.

...

If there is water down at the pick up spot, I sometimes don't have the doors locked. There's no sense in having a potential fare step in a puddle while they are trying to get their arm on the door handle inside. Even if I had judged the fare wrong and they weren't going to turn back runner, and

stop me without getting in, they might give it a second thought after getting their pants and shoes wet.

Unless I am trying to detain a runner near hazardous waste, splashing them usually doesn't do much good. If in the quickness of my movements they are doused by water from my hand slicing through rain, it is entirely coincidental.

...

The only regret that could be pinned on the friend of the scout were for his wishes that a song that meant nothing was sang at his funeral. No one really knew the man that well so the song choices struck a chord with next to no one. The acoustics couldn't have been better on that day. The curator of the pieces aggressively defended her selection.

Maybe the man should have been even more vague with his request.

...

It's easier for me to not have music at all playing in any of the cars, than every once in a while. I know that there is so much to share about music. I'm angry that fares don't open the door at the perfect time when I'm listening and close to revelation. Writing down my feelings on the subject would be too difficult.

I could prepare an album to be played so right at the time I arrive, the fare would hear the part of the song I want them to. If the fare is running late I would have wasted all that time anticipating, and anything I had to say about the new piece would be hurried. If anything even comes to mind. I haven't done this nor will I. When music is produced it is spontaneous. My listening will also be.

...

It was Cole, Bonnie and I that would sometimes sit in on trances. Depending on the customer or act of charity, Marie had some people going more than others. We were allowed to watch as long as we wore masks and moved to the motions Marie had had us rehearse before the performance. Marie was the closest thing to a masktasker we had. If Marie's work was finished, right before she

brought the willing back to the living she played one last trick on them. The story varied but the action was always the same. Marie would wave her hand and ask how many fingers. She then would put her arm into a sleeve on her person, put her fist as far into the sleeve as it would go, flick her finger and pull the sleeve further up. She then would ask the question again.

...

I'm not sure anyone ever gave Bonnie a run for her money. All of Bonnie's assets were liquid. She had nothing solid. She didn't get by on favors. Everyone thought they owed something to her.

...

The doctors had an insignia on their breast pocket. This symbol has been around for a long time. It is said that whoever is able to see the symbol has something activated in them. Should the doctor be able to look down at their notepad and see the symbol while the patient can also see it, so much the better.

Our doctors used this technique back at the hub. Most of us were aware of the trick so a brought a mirror to all check ups. The doctors needed to be able to see their own face during the procedure in case their perception of faces around them had been momentarily altered. Should they need a mirror during visits absent of anesthetics then they may have done permanent damage.

It was still good for them to see the symbol. Who knows what it looked like to them during those states.

...

The generator was used for a few more things than charging the barber's clippers. Many runners had a fascination with microwaves. Such were the times. If one arrived at the hub, we tarried nary and used it presently. The generator could handle two appliances being plugged in at the same time. Those in the barber's chair enjoyed appetizers.

Most microwaves that were plugged in shook violently while the clippers were in use. Better the microwave than the clippers.

...

If one goes without eating for a while their mood changes. Along with everything else in the body. If Simon says to continue to malnourish, whoever doesn't follow the direction has also changed. If Simon says there are fish under the bridge, you should wait to hear if they're edible before dropping everything. Simon will say when to tow the line.

...

There are no kiosks under any bridge. If you look under a kiosk you might find Newt. If you see a kiosk turned upside down in anger, you've probably encountered Sal. Isabelle doesn't think Sal is an angry man. She has turned herself into a petty woman. Isadora left many stones unturned when she married Newt.

...

It is fun to hear two people arguing to prove they have the better point. That is how conspiracies are formed.

...

Most runners do not carry firearms. If it were their tendency to do so, they probably wouldn't be runners. I don't attempt to show threat that I myself am armed. I am not. However, most assume so after taking one look at me. They don't know for what purpose I wear the baggy clothes and so think they are for concealment.

I would never surprise a runner with a weapon. Many may not even be surprised, and could even know how to turn a weapon against me, it's wielder. I don't have the time to practice for a skill that may or may not help me. Better to quickly grab their nose and work from there.

...

Runners aren't surprised after being detained when I offer them a ride in the car.

...

Doctors around the hub would recommend that treats, of the same quantity, also be taken with the prescription. They said it was a good way to manage the stash. If one were to come out of a daze, on account of either one, the prescription or the substitute, they would be able to tell what damage had been done. If the treats were sugar based, an example would be seventy pieces of chocolate to the seventy doctor's orders.

The doctors never recommended anything that they wouldn't do themself. How they never gained near the weight in the face that I did is beyond me. I never went to see the doctor on my own behalf, but rather for all those who couldn't face them on their own because of their iatrophobia. Where this fear came from was different for every underling. The symbol on the breast pocket must have caused them to spiral out. If doctors were in a better state they might have been able to bring them back.

The requests I received to schedule doctor's appointments didn't bother me much. The scouts made things stress free. If I couldn't get a hold of a scout, I'd requisition an underling to find one for me. The scouts were such that they heard my plea before any underlings were ever close to reaching them. It was still important to use the underlings. Scouts knew how to read them and if they were acting in truth. With a higher officer, scouts had the ability to decide whether to act swiftly or take a moment to talk and come up with a plan. With underlings, as soon as the scout heard they were needed for something they took action. They didn't need to confer with those under them who had not yet acquired their status.

...

It's important to give in an inch in conversation. It's important to take what space is given. If one has a conversation and are in a poor position, another can force themself in and take one's place. First they will talk louder. Then they will obstruct the view of the former speaker, so lips can not be read.

To interrupt a conversation is to take food out of the mouth of thought.

...

A few of the cars available to me are convertibles. I never drive with the top down when I am by myself. Only when with fares do I let my jumpsuit's folds blow in the wind. I figure I'll draw less attention to myself if a passenger is in the car. I don't get the most attractive clientele as fares, many are turned runners with before and after faces, so when driving with the top down it appears I'm doing an act of charity. Like the fare is celebrating their last day of freedom or such.

It is important that I draw attention to everything but my jobs. Let those who see my jumpsuit's folds blowing in the wind double take after glancing in the backseat, and think me a friend.

...

I don't play music in the car. I've spent too much time around the band to tolerate any talking over the songs. They said that a foundation was laid and dependant on the song, the singer either sang above or below that foundation. If one were to talk in the absence of singing, it may disrupt the foundation. When the singer reenters the song, the listener may hear them differently. Where before they were on top, now they are on the bottom. Unless the speaker had spoke so that the music was in the background. Then the singer's reappearance, if meant to stand out on the song, would be more digestible.

...

Whenever the doctors prescribed anything they gave a speech about placebos. On every bottle patients picked up was a label. It said, take at your own risk, this may or may not be a placebo.

Some say a person never really changes. Others take it one day at a time. If abusing a placebo, change is born from a lie. On a return visit to the doctor, the patient is visibly self loathing. The doctor can do nothing but promise that with the next visit their reasons for the attitude will be different.

The size of the bottle prescribed may change. The label does not.

...

Not much help in a doctor's office, but a tried and true method of leaving a party is to continuously compliment the cook throughout. Then one can leave whenever they want.

In order to get out of conversations with doctors around the hub, one only needed to get them started talking about their job. They were all free lancers. They had a chip on one shoulder and a bag of multicolored candy sized implements on the other. Get them talking about either and they would rush away to the fountain for youths or become conscious of how much they were letting on.

If a patient wanted to know about the chip on their shoulder, there was only so much the doctor would say before getting lost in their own head. The bag of implements are for those who don't know any better. The supply is more or less endless, as is a fountain.

...

Bonnie probably never touched a candy in her life. Literal or metaphoric.

...

Cole's girl would have told Cole to get off of that stuff, had it been a problem. She seemed to know what she was doing with him.

...

It was Cole, Bonnie and I that could have had a case for being the oldest soul. We all believed that things happened to us right as they should. Stereotyping greatness at all the right times. Realizing why when it was late enough to not wish to change anything.

...

If Cole's girl kept running Cole the way I believed she would, his life cycle as an adult would be such. Bachelor, family man, monk.

...

Doctors said to try to feel good in the moment, so as to not worry about the future. They said in the future you

would worry about how much you had worried now. Neither was healthy.

...

The most nervous about the future around the hub was Screaming William. If he were able to get shocked by lightning every day he would have been happy. The not knowing did a number on him. Only because what he anticipated was, to him, inevitable. Had he never been struck by lightning and still chose to live every day waiting to be, his mental health may have been better. Chasing a dragon which one is unsure exactly what it is, is less tolling then chasing one you're sure about. Once Screaming William had a taste he had a point of reference. Without that first taste he would have been able to settle.

...

Purgy used to say that if the crew gave one hundred percent, they could take the next day off. We followed the same logic around the hub though we had never heard of Purgy. Perhaps that's why his saying stuck with me when I heard it later. If workers gave one hundred ten percent, they would need to come back again to finish the job. The client would be expecting more. I don't know how much effort the scouts ever put in, but they sure were good.

Purgy's occupation was such that if anything less than one hundred percent was given, everything would come off the rails. The train's schedule was such that workers could take days off after a voyage. Purgy's crew never chose to take those days. Purgy was their leader.

It was Cole, Bonnie and I that doled out time off. The scouts never asked for any days. Or if they had, we could never tell the replacement apart from the replaced. Underlings were more needy. They worked hard at finding reasons why they deserved time.

...

Erranders got runners what they needed in the days of the hub. I make small purchases from both Sal and Newt. So there's no competition they can both say that I am a loyal customer. It's easy enough to drop in and spend coins.

We didn't think we needed a vendor. That was why we worked so hard to run them out of the hub. It was unlikely they would find any success in their business, or what were they doing there, but we still couldn't risk it. Marie could tell us if it was an auspicious day, and if we would find any trouble gathering supplies. Cole, Bonnie and I didn't allow theft of the cargo cars. I still don't to this day.

...

For lack of common vendor, when fireworks were brought to the hub there was always quite a variety. Lighting them where we lived was one of the more careless things that we negated the consequences. If the hub were to get busted on a night of celebration, it would have been meant to be. Back in those days we probably would have rebuilt. The wise do strange things to keep up appearances.

...

I will never take credit for the hub falling apart. It may never even have. I would have been king around that place had it not been for Bonnie slandering the title. I'm not sure of the education Bonnie had, but being the daughter of a senator she heard the humpty dumpty nursery rhyme a lot. She said the king in the story was not meant for the role. He didn't train his men, they not their horses, how to assume responsibility in crisis. She thought it was good that they wasted all that time trying to recreate something that was past it's prime. The kingdom didn't deserve to grow. Not one of the king's horses or men stepped forward in the time of need.

...

As a civilization we collectively agree that competitiveness is okay during a nonexistent race. Not everyone participates in the rat race, but most everyone wants to get ahead in someway. So in the nonexistent race, there are moments in life when things are going so good that it almost feels like one is cheating.

...

My eyesight hasn't failed me yet. It hasn't been put to the ultimate test yet either, but through these letters the day may be closer than anticipated. I've imagined our reintroduction thousands of times in my head. None of the times have I been able to find the words to say. Somewhere along all those times imagining I decided to take pen to paper. I've realized I quite like that phrase, even though as you have probably guessed by now these letters are not handwritten. Written by my hand all the same. I would sign my name with a pen at the bottom if I thought it might help with your memory. I don't know how many people you know currently and don't want to push anyone out of favor. Dunbar's number and Murphy's law.

I hope that you have surrounded yourself with good people. Caretakers generally are, but I'm talking about any others. Are there any others, Bonnie? It's important that you mingle with more than the staff. Not to say they aren't great people, those under your command usually turn out alright, but if they refuse to say no I fear you may lose your edge. What is a great debater if they are constantly being accommodated? I'm sure you get enough challenging conversation from your family but please allow me to pitch in.

It's not much of a riddle but it may help to get a crowd on your back. Whether behind you or getting closer all depends on the delivery. Once I have written it down, it's in your hands. You cannot say where you heard the riddle or from whom you heard it from. Any mention of the riddle made not in an offhand way will surely affect the outcome. Be careful who you pose the riddle to unless you are completely sure of the consequences. If someone does correctly answer the riddle, never let on that they have done so. Go ahead with the prepared back up riddle a few wrong guesses after the correct one. If someone happens to guess the answer to the second riddle you must then go on with one of the wrong suggestions. Thank the crowd for their participation and pat yourself on the back for figuring out the riddle. It may be likely that the crowd doesn't want such

an abrupt end to the show. If you're following me so far,
which I wouldn't put it past you, I need not say any more.

The fares that have no direction when they enter the car are the ones who usually have an ulterior motive when asking to leave the meter running. There are no meters in any of the cars I drive. The car weren't intended for my use. I still know what the fare means though.

Since they didn't have a place for me to bring them, I usually drive around until I see an empty street. I park the car and tell them they've got thirty minutes to an hour until I have to pay to park. I used to tell them that it would come out of their fare, but too many were running on me so I stopped.

If a meter checker does come to the car while the fare is away, I pull up one meter. I haven't been faulted yet. By my moving the car I allow for fellow drivers to occupy the spot I was just about to get ticketed for. I have time to argue with the meter checkers while the fare is doing who knows what. If the fare plans on returning, when they come back to the car either to tip or traverse on, I talk them up to the meter checker. If the meter checker likes the fare there is less chance they'll give me a ticket.

The meter checker knows how well I can argue and won't want to put that burden on my fare. If the fare took an extremely long time, the meter checker would have had to follow my car from meter to meter, and at close may be too tired to finish.

...

If you see me walking with a cane you can safely assume that my mind is off the runners and on to the fares. It's not that a cane would slow my pursuit at all, I think I could run just as fast if I held it with both hands horizontally and swung it side to side, but I don't want to be underestimated that badly. If a runner saw me with a cane and then were overcome, they wouldn't respect me because of the deception. I need subdued runners to be able to say good game at the end of a bout, so I have an in

to offer them a ride. If they later saw the cane was in the car, they probably wouldn't leave a tip at the end because of their weariness. They'd have been thinking about how they could have possibly been had the whole ride. When out of the woods and thanking their lucky stars, they'd exit the vehicle in a hurry.

I do keep a cane in the backseat of the cars. I never know who I might be giving a ride to. If they need to use the cane, I'm quick to offer. Otherwise it is on display as a reminder to any runners turned fares that I'm getting older and their time may yet come. I don't expect them to live on the straight and narrow forever. I do expect them to be able to make the smart decision on their own next time.

I've tried to barter with the cane. Only with fares that are much older than me. They take the suggested trade as an insult, before realizing they could probably get the better deal. The cane has never left my possession. Their egos save them from embarrassing me. Those fares usually leave a good tip. They remember when they were young how foolhardy they had been.

...

The only scout I ever underestimated had a wheelchair. They said they were really good with carrier pigeons and so didn't need to use their legs much. I never saw any promise from his interactions with the birds. Their situation was similar to Purgy's. They very well may have been a talent, or they were as skilled in deceit as one can be. They could have been using their legs the whole time, but then to lie so gracefully takes a special kind of person.

How the scout ended up in a wheelchair happened early in their life. It was a simple case of testing authority. They were so young that they still needed to discover their own limits. That age where a child will go hungry because their is a warning on the stove not to touch it. The mother of the wheel about scout had said to look both ways before crossing the street. Scouts had to grow up too and were not born fully formed, so the fledgling only looked one way.

Never made it to the other side. Was pulled back on to the curb by their mother and the driver.

The scout also credited advancements in wheelchair technology to their uncanny ability.

...

When Marie vouched for the scout I stopped giving them thought. Marie told us who we should surround ourselves with. Who we should keep at a friendly distance.

...

Just as you can pinch yourself to see if you're dreaming, you can close your fist to see if someone exists. Only in my wildest nightmares is my fist not already closed.

...

It's easy to tell the people that are affected by night terrors. Bring a group to an art museum. Who ever stares a little bit too long at any one painting is going through some stuff.

...

What limited internet I consume is done at the library. This way if everything goes to the dogs I'll still have a place to do research. I don't have to do much now, haven't looked up Bonnie yet, but someday I may want to improve myself. The library is the last place to be looted, if it at all, and is a haven for conscientious objectors.

I think if some disaster did send everything to the dogs, I would hang up my boots and put all the cars back in the garage. I wouldn't fight as I do now. If I can even call it that. I wouldn't be able to serve the community. The participants in the nonexistent race would now have something to really compete about. Money is no object in a barter.

...

There was a one around the hub who prepared for the dog days. He had all types of things going for him. We would have allowed him to be a vendor, only because we knew he wouldn't part with anything.

He had guns. He had alcohol. He claimed what gatherings he had were parties. If there was music it was

live. The generator wouldn't be able to handle the clippers, microwave, and also speakers.

He liked to take a shot of one then take a shot with the other. He said that one shot didn't affect his capabilities and only gave him a little boost. We all knew that one shot boost just lead to more shots. He was really accurate in the beginning. So of course he thought things were too easy. Took another shot to see if he was just as good as anyone else when inebriated. Finding he still could compete, he'd keep consuming. The playing field never evened out.

He wasn't ever the last one shooting. Those left were impressed amateurs. The sound of their guns couldn't wake him after one of his victories.

...

We didn't print our own literature at the hub. If we had, some of the people I've spoken about would have names. Documents landed one a fine with Cole, Bonnie and I. Marie would have let us know if we were ever in any real danger.

If one of the runners did write something of note, I never heard about it. Judging from the way many of the underlings talked I don't think their writing would be free from spelling errors. I don't think they talked as such to give attitude. I genuinely think they thought words were spelled the way they sounded. You could tell from how they talked.

If what the runner wrote achieved any kind of literary success it would encourage others to write lazily. The last thing we needed around the hub was lazy writers. Picking up a pen never crossed my mind until I was out.

...

A lot of knowledge was lost when the hub disappeared. If I ever find it again I'll have a busy day. I don't think it could have continued operating under my nose this whole time. Who would have replaced Cole, Bonnie or I anyway.

...

I don't think the band ever achieved any kind of envious neighbor success. They still did alright though. The foundation they spoke about could not be heard in any of their songs. It made listening to other artists very easy.

Had we had a formal goodbye I could have asked them why there are songs at funerals and not in the birthing room.

Bonnie might have the answer.

...

Cole's girl's van has a cassette deck. In order to find a cassette you'd have to hit the deck.

In remembrance, I've been thinking about finding the hub and organizing a mass gift drive. Cassettes last longer than canned goods. The experience anyway. I would then bring all the cassettes to the van. Systematically throw them about while sitting in the passenger or back seat.

For now the van remains bare, except for the picture of Cole and his girl.

...

Bonnie aged better than any picture.

...

The man whose house has a tree parked on top of it would probably appreciate the state of the van. He would love for the van to be swept away because of some natural disaster. Maybe someday the tree will roll off his house. Maybe someday the stump where the tree was will start growing sideways.

...

If I'm trying to turn a runner into a fare and am almost at the close of the conversation, usually in my favor, I quickly get up if we had been sitting, to still show threat of my mobility. From there I move around the cargo car and pick up an object that the runner probably hadn't even noticed. To show my awareness of the surroundings. Then, and only then, will I use my final persuasion techniques to try to make a customer. I always hope for their sake that they say yes. I can't be wasting too much time on any one runner.

The scout who was in a wheelchair never needed to show threat of his range of motion or awareness of his surroundings. If he had found himself in a situation where

he needed to do so, I'm sure he was quick enough on his feet to think of something. Scouts usually are.

...

It was Cole, Bonnie and I that were in charge of any rescue missions. Sometimes an underling would be stranded and unable to find their way back to the hub. It was our job to make the call whether or not to give them a way home. Scouts were under orders in those situations to give the underling some time to see if they can't figure it out by themself. Scouts relayed that the underlings were lost in the first place. The best ones were never seen by the underlings.

So if a scout returned to the underling after receiving our orders, the underling was given a few shortcuts to find the hub online. We couldn't make it too easy. But they had worked for us, so we felt they deserved at least somewhat of a break. The scout would give them the first few websites that would head them in the right direction.

The underlings that we had accepted into the hub who first found it by way of the internet were given different directions. They hay to keep up with the scout. Depending on how many days journey it was, the underling would attempt to meet up with the scout at checkpoints at the end of each day. The scout was not to tell the underling the checkpoint for the next day. If the underling failed to keep up, there was a chance that an onlooker might take their place. That was fine. Normally the scouts aren't noticed, but in those cases they were performing at their colleague's level. They would put more effort into shaking the onlooker.

...

New recruits were judged on a case by case basis. Pick any adjective to put in front of the word case and one of the recruits would have embodied it. It wasn't that there were very many applicants. It's just they were all wild.

...

If we could see the whites of your eyes we knew we were close enough to hear what you had to say. I feel somewhat sorry for those who had to hear your words from a distance. As good as scouts were I think most of the message would be lost in translation. We couldn't have you speak through a megaphone at assemblies. Your voice didn't project in quite the same way as your eyes. When we three would stand on top of the generator it was often Cole or I that would have to shout the points you failed to get across. It was hard for us to be accurate since there were so many other distractions and your way of speaking very unique.

You probably had more one on one consultations than any of the doctors. Probably were more help than them as well. When runners would say they were going to see you, they would say that the meeting was someplace up up high. Did you turn them on to that phrase? Is it supposed to mean something to us that are not in the know? I took the majority of my meetings in the place where we three would convene. Occasionally, if I were operating alone, discussions would be had in my tent.

There was a time in the very early days of the hub when meetings were recorded. We actually stopped the practice on your suggestion, based on Marie's advice. We didn't want to draw attention to our spot. If a scout or underling were to be discovered with notes, and Cole, you or I weren't there to settle the situation, who knows what may have happened.

Sometimes I still recorded the discussions had in my tent. I never used names and the meetings were always so agreeable that on the transcript it would appear as if only one person had been talking.

Runners haven't calmed down much since the days of when I used to run with them. Those that I deal with now don't know I was as wild as them once. I took it as far as it would go so they wouldn't have to. I try to show them the light. They show what precautions I need to take to diffuse

their particular situation. If the interaction is wild from the start, I subdue them just as fast as any tranquilizer could. Fight wild with science.

...

There were no elephants around the hub. I never saw any being transported on a train. They say that elephants can remember other elephants years after, even if they only met them once. They must be interacting with each other differently than humans do with their own kind. Words obviously don't help anyone remember anyone else. If the conversation is stimulating enough, it is amazing how easily one can forget the name of the person they had it with. Too many words were used. Possibly too many other names referenced.

I'm not sure which of the six blind men would be able to figure out why the elephant's memory is so good. It may be one thing or it may be the whole. If six blind men walked up to a human and couldn't figure for what it was, it would be the fault of the human for not helping them. Elephant's memories may not be as good as they seem. Both elephants work together to reestablish the bond they had started to form.

If a human can't remember someone, that person is often offended and it may be harder to reestablish that bond. I like to think that I would recognize a good majority of the people that were around the hub. Scouts not included. To assume I could recognize a scout is both arrogant and ignorant. I would probably have an easier time remembering underlings if I had Cole and Bonnie by my side. We humans need many prompts to be the best we can be.

...

The smartest animal around the hub was the dog. The dogs were low maintenance. A smart stance when subject to a master. Not that any one of us owned any of the dogs. They still tried to curry favors. Favors are easier granted when they are not often asked.

...

Sal wished Newt would do him the favor of working for him. As an added incentive, he would be getting paid. I'm not sure why Sal wants to be so buddy buddy with Newt. Newt's got the best friend he could have in Sal's daughter.

It's not my place to say if Sal was what Isabelle needed him to be. It depended on when you asked her. Why anyone asked was usually because they knew Isabelle's past.

...

Any runners turned fares can't hide their pasts from me. A past is created for me, when random fares decide to call the number on my advertisement. My face isn't very marketable but I still obtain some customers this way. The fare, upon seeing my face and number, assumes that I specialize in transportation. Until the sweepstakes suppliers put their name somewhere on the advertisement, I appear professional. None of the fares need to know I was sponsored and didn't face the daunting years of trying to break even.

Letting the fares make assumptions about me helps my business. It is amazing how easily one gives away money when they believe they are in a position of power. I don't need to be smart. I just need to be helpful.

...

I either help runners help themselves or I force them to.

...

Some runners think they have all the answers. They aren't too much trouble to deal with. If I can get them to believe I think they're as great as they think they are, I can usually get them to think I'm better than they think I am. Once a runner's ego is sufficiently stoked, and they don't think I'm half bad, it takes very few words thereafter to get them to see the light.

I still pump runner's egos up even if there will be a fight. The harder they throw punches the quicker they tire out. The harder it is for them to think rationally, the faster their subconscious will take over. My fists are always closed

during night terrors. Hopefully they escape me in their dreams.

    ...

I couldn't listen to music in the car in case I might tap my foot. The band said that tapping the foot is a good way to keep time. If a fare was in the car, I would have to make many decisions as to whether to tap the brake or the pedal. I'm not saying I couldn't do it, but I do want to get the best tip I can. Jerky driving is frowned upon. In a perfect world, everyone would smile at sharing the road.

If I were parked waiting for a fare to perhaps return, so I can get paid, and tapped the brake pedal they may think I was signaling to them. I don't want the fares to feel that rushed. Because the cars I drive are usually newer models, my car could be mistaken for one supposed to meet up for a drug trade. If the dealer was behind me and saw the brake lights flashed, there's a good chance I would be an attempted target for a robbery.

If I tapped the gas pedal while waiting at a red light, because of the music, and my other foot was on the brake, still tapping but much slower to a different rhythm, any cars next to me may think I want to race. If a fare was in the car and wanted to see it, I would have no choice other than to play, so I can get paid. If I weren't mentally prepared for a race right then I could lose, and no generously sized tip would comfort me.

If a fare wasn't in the car and I was propositioned for a race, I'd have to decide if I'm up for it by whatever song was on. I could make all the moves like I was going to race and if the song changed before the green light, I'd be at a disadvantage. My brake foot would need to change with the song, so if things went wrong I could blow right through the red light. I'd need to decide if I should let up on the brake pedal and move my gas pedal foot over there to lead. If this happens I won't have lost the race but will have forfeited. They would accelerate while I was tapping my foot on the brake. They'd be far away while I jerked my way through the intersection.

...

They say you catch more flies with honey than with vinegar. If you butter someone up they'll stay buzzing in your ear. A dinner winner is buffeted with requests.

...

Marie would ask that any of us sitters please come back for a patient's next consultation. It was Cole, Bonnie and I that sometimes had this pleasure. During some of Marie's trances the seeker would fall asleep. On the return visit, Marie asked that any of us sitters that could, please go pale when we heard the apology. They always apologized to Marie on the return visit.

It was when they said sorry for falling asleep on you that we were asked to act. Marie recommended we bring new recruits along to hear the sentiment and see our reaction. She said that her customers had no reason to feel embarrassed. If they should, we knew they wouldn't last long around the hub.

...

Sometimes I encounter a runner who tries to explain their present situation is as it is because of their past. They wish to get a free pass. Anything they say can, and was, used against them before. They believe now that since they know they've changed they can get away with a lot more.

Doctors around the hub liked to give their back stories. Not so detailed that they mention where they were trained or by whom, but how they obtained their knowledge. Whether any of their other patients considered them knowledgeable is unknown. I found them to be smart but wholly unorganized. All their thoughts led back to prescriptions.

Some of us around the hub were able to take these prescriptions to pharmacies. It depended on the state of the doctor when they wrote it. There were times when the doctors' handwriting was so awful that we knew we'd have to go back once they had plateaued. If we weren't able to get the prescriptions filled at a pharmacy, we had scouts find work arounds. The scout's knowledge came at a price.

It was Cole, Bonnie and I that advised underlings on their own financial situations. It was Cole, Bonnie and I who could be seen positively one moment, and loathed in the next. It wasn't our job to be a poor underling's friend. Our job was to get them where they needed to be. Get them to a place that would have them.

...

I never really knew about holidays until I left the hub. We had small gatherings. We had people who called things parties, who weren't themselves party people. I always had a tough time with introductions at the gatherings. I over think what the first thing I'll say to someone is and what comes out is usually a greeting for a time of day it isn't. Good morning doesn't sound right spoken on christmas eve.

...

Neither humans or apes live long enough for one to revert back to the other. It is what it is.

...

There was one entrance to the hub where bicycles could get in. Screaming had a way with the dogs. Chrissie's garden was a ways away from where Screaming thought he had the best chance to get struck by lightning. It was Cole, Bonnie and I that would sometimes sit on stoop like platforms with the dogs and wait for Screaming William. It didn't take many times doing so before we realized how good the dogs had it. We watched other bicycles go by and the dogs were usually unfazed. But the excitement they showed when Screaming tucked his shoulders in to get the bike through the alley was something else.

The dogs knew what they were waiting for. Most people around the hub had no idea what they themselves were.

...

I intercepted a mail carrier the other day to interrogate. They told me the address I was sending to was nonexistent. He said that I would have been able to know that had I only checked online first. I still believe the letters are getting to you but I have put another address on the back of this envelope. I imagine the mail carrier would check the back, similar to a person who has just read a confusing note is apt to do. Checking to see if there were any other hints given that may help them surmise it's meaning.

Do you remember all the different links and empty shopping cart pages that needed to be opened in order to find the hub's online presence? It's okay if you don't, I was just hoping that you may be able to put yourself in my shoes and fill me in on any blanks. Up until now I have not asked for any help in locating the hub. Perhaps it is not yet time to do so, but should your memory fail again and my question somehow remains, when you offer me the help that I desire I will definitely not refuse.

You always seemed to know when the appropriate time to ask a question was. What an appropriate question would be to ask. I think through doing this you discovered the perfect time to offer someone help. You knew when to be cold. I always liked to think you knew what you were doing, but now I guess I'll never be able to know. If you remember one thing about me, and it's not that I offhandedly asked for help, I hope it's my smile. I think if you could remember that, all the rest would come easy, since I was grinning from ear to ear whenever I was around you. So if you can remember a smile that shadowed you, you'll be able to look ahead.

It's all ripples Bonnie, isn't it? I think it's more important that you remember small things first so you aren't sent back to the place you're trying to escape. If stress was what caused your memory failure than I need to take precautions so that it won't happen again. If I give you too much detail all will be lost. Not enough, and it will never be found.

When it was time to eat around the hub, we needed to wait for the food to cool. If it wasn't canned it was on a kebab. Both can get very hot. We never checked the internal temperature of any of the meat. We figured the heated up can or kebab would release chemicals to kill any unwanted bacteria.

If you couldn't shake a stick at it we didn't eat it. The whole dominion over all animals was a little extreme for Cole, Bonnie or I. So we didn't take those teachings literally when we ate.

...

There were no preachers at the hub. We set the bar high. Just out of reach.

...

We allowed underlings to warm their hands by any fire that was used for cooking. Otherwise it was usually, go get your own fire. If someone wanted to wait by a cooking fire, they were asked to help. They didn't have to, but anyone near the fire with idle hands had to wait for everyone else to eat before they could be served.

Everyone had to give up something at the hub. If you wanted the comforts of home you couldn't eat like at a restaurant. If you wanted to be first in line, you better have made sure you were far enough away from the fire.

...

When Marie put persons in trance, she often liked to play jokes. All were funny. All were unsettling. She would ask participants if they thought her tent was too cold, too hot, or just right. She knew what head space they were in and how they'd answer. If they were feeling cold, she'd call attention to one of the participants, before inviting other participants to warm their hands by them. She said to put hands around their belly and feel the heat radiating off of it.

She said it was a spirit that warmed them up.

...

There has been talk in the foreign papers of people who believe that they are living in a simulation. They are classified differently than the general public by

professionals in the medical field. I believe that if they believe, then they are deserving of their distinct classification. Only if in a simulation would one choose to live with that handicap.

...

In every interaction with the general public I have, I try to see my favorite person in them. I cannot do this with the runners. I can with some fares. I look for certain tendencies in the runners but have trained myself to see them as lesser than. I could choose to see my favorite person in some runners during the opening dialogue or the rest period after a bout. I'm not yet disciplined enough to do so. I treat them as I treat fares whom I'm trying to get a big tip out of. The selling point is different but the sale remains the same.

...

The band would always say to jump in any time to listeners. I tell my fares the same thing. I don't play music in the cars.

...

It was Cole, Bonnie and I that saved our spit when discussing music singles. Had there been more bands around the hub than just the one, we would have had our own charts. We didn't have vendors so the metric couldn't be sales. I can't see any unknown band charting better than the band we knew.

Marie had a trick that she would play on participants in a trance. I think Marie was the perfect bill of health despite all appearances. She would start coughing. What this sounded like to participants I do not know, but to us sitters it sounded genuine. Building off of the cough she would gradually start to release phlegm from her mouth. Bear with me, it was just one of her tricks. The cough would get so fierce that spit would shoot out of her mouth at least a foot. Never less. Sometimes more. If she really tilted her head back she could project it quite a ways.

As a sitter, it always brought to mind the image of someone pulling their jaw apart and a smaller being inside showing it's contempt for being trapped in the most

expressive way they knew how. I don't know what spitting Marie looked like to those in the trance.

...

It was as quiet at the hub as it is when I'm with fare. Any conversations were conducted with somber voices. Marie said we'd understand more that way. Something about forcing your voice to sound one way reveals uncontrollable expressive body language. The most effective was using a funeral voice. One becomes rigid yet so full of life.

...

I don't mind the quiet in bits and pieces.

...

If I've led you to believe that I am always quiet when sneaking up on runners, I am sorry. Distractions are just as important as the strange way that I've adopted walking before bouts. Just as important as me pulling the nose of the opponent in order to achieve a quick victory.

My go to distraction is reflecting light off of a small mirror at a runner. The minute I see a runner open a cargo door I know the game is on. From there the light is meant to debilitate, not blind. I need any of the runners that will turn fares able to see their wallet so that I may get a generous tip. Usually when they open the cargo door, they'll like to stand on the ledge for a few moments and survey their surroundings. I don't give them the chance.

I have never driven a runner turned fare to an optometrist because of cataracts. The light is meant to incite curiosity. If they wonder about the source of the light, perhaps their mind is such that they will give my offer some thought. When I finally emerge from the source of the light, the runner may still be seeing spots. Again, I have never driven any runners turned fares to an optometrist because of cataracts. If they are unaccustomed to altered states, no matter how mild or intense, they may quickly see the light and allow me to shuttle them around.

If they need to be detained, the advantage I have over them because of their spot seeing is minimal. I can't feel bad about a quick victory.

...

I don't wear any insignia or medals, as Cole, Bonnie and I all had in the days of the hub. I don't need any runners to respect me that much. Back at the hub, since the structure of our organization seemed to be so loose, underlings needed to know right away who was in charge. Since most matters went through Cole, Bonnie or I, and the scouts had more important things to do then cater to underlings, we needed to appear presentable.

None of us three were more decorated than each other. Though the symbols and medals were different, the meaning they were supposed to convey was the same. Work hard your whole life and someday you'll be rewarded. Others will know you are a hard worker in other ways than seeing your mangled body and deteriorating health. They may ask how hard you worked to get that sort of recognition, but will never question if it was deserved.

...

The only credits a fare needs to see is my driver's license. If I were as decked out as when I was younger, fares may believe I'm working with others. Most of the fares were previously runners and are very conspiratorial. I don't want them pushed away because of my ambiguity.

...

The dogs were smarter than most of the runners at the hub. They rarely got injured, and if they did they knew the right people to go. Some of the runners went naively time and time again to the same prescriptionist doctors. Dogs would lick their wounds. Runners would be in for a surprise when doctors tried to lick theirs. The doctors said waste not, want not. They knew their clients and the regimen they were on.

Not all runners went to the wrong doctors. Marie wasn't a doctor but could tell us if we needed a second opinion. Sometimes she would say all we can do now is wait.

If one asked Marie for how long, she'd say perhaps they did need a second opinion.

...

It's not the size of the dog in the hub, but the size of the hub to the dog. Any dogs around the hub adapted so well that their paths were as the crow flies. They wasted no energy. We wasted none watching them.

...

If I had ever learned to play cards, I'd have another avenue for persuasion. I may need to lie to the runners during the initial propositioning for a game. Promising if they win I won't try to get them off the train. I might be able to make some spare change off those runners but any time I'm not selling hard, I'm losing money in tips.

...

I am motivated by compassion when showing runners the light. Though the terms I left the hub on were ambiguous, I bear no resentment towards the new generation. When it were we three, Cole, Bonnie and I, we still thought our goal was commendable. If Cole and Bonnie were around today they may think my new one is not. I can't live with that doubt so I make sure to overcompensate with the direction I'm heading.

...

If I ever do choose to gas up the car, I am subjected to scheduled programming at the pump. It has been this way for a while now but only recently have they introduced sound to the video. I gleaned more from when it was silent.

It has continued to be surprising ever since the first time I saw day time talk shows being played to the general public at the pump. No longer were the shows only meant for those at home during the day, who if they went to the pump it would constitute them getting out of the house. Unless things have changed, those confined to their living quarters seldom see sunlight.

I never would have dreamed seeing the things I've seen at these stations back at the hub. There are too many things to complain about. Too many things to thoroughly enjoy

because of that disdain. What has stuck with me from my handful of times running errands for another, is when a couple was on the screen and one of the pair had their hand resting on the other's wrist. If the one wanted to show intimacy and the other didn't accept the hand hold, leaving the hand as is could only have been done on account of the camera. In almost all other situations if the other didn't accept the hand in their own, the one trying would pull their hand away. A conversation could be had later.

...

The band said they would show you music as a pick up line. Each individual member had their own take after. The only time I didn't see the band together was when they were picking up.

...

You were the perfect bill of health, Bonnie. In fact it was by you that we measured all other ailments. Rather than a scale of one to ten we used a mood indicator of how you might feel in certain situations. So a one would be you taking a dog for a walk. A ten would be you putting that dog down. We still used the numbers, but imagining you in regular scenarios did help to ease patient's pain. Please do not think that you were ever exploited Bonnie. That wasn't in our nature or yours. If you had been an underling, I'm sure there would have been another You, who from their position could help ease our pain.

Not to say that anyone would have been able to replace you, but if someone were just like you then it wouldn't be much of a replacement anyway. So don't feel bad about your imaginary adversary. Unless all your memories have been extracted and are being used to be used against you, or perhaps us all, such is the extent of your reach, you have nothing to worry about. And if that is the case, I believe you gave consent and your ultimate motive is yet to be revealed. But why the secrecy still, if that is your plan? Surely you would want to include me, your old friend, in on project doppelganger. No, this is not a request to put me through the same procedure you went through, it is merely an observation leaden with guilt.

Out of all the expressions that you were able to manage with your face, I don't think guilt was one of them. It was as if you knew that things would always work out for you. I pray they still have, even if I am yet to understand exactly how. A sign that you are doing well would go a long way for both myself and your caretakers. We are here to help you Bonnie. You don't need to put on your weary face. Your leery face. The face that can open doors and let others know to close them.

The face that with each passing day I may remember more incorrectly. Signs that you have opened the letters provides some clues as to what you may look like now. I myself wear a jumpsuit daily. No medals or honors on the shoulder or breast as there had once been. Not that there

would ever be more than what you had sported back at the hub. It's not a competition, Bonnie. At least not until you are a little bit closer to where you were. That Bonnie was competitive. Think of yourself in competition with your old self, so that if you fail we will be certain we can move on.

If the doctors were just able to get out of their own way they would have realized their folly. Their entire state of being rode on substances. They were never without them long enough to rightly say any truths about them. So long as they stayed on their medication, the runners were able to benefit from their own.

Whenever the doctors tried straightening out it was hell for their patients. When they were both occupied, the consultation couldn't go smoother.

...

Scouts never sent a steed in their stead. It probably would have been slower.

...

The foreign papers warn that when things change into something else, they take on the new thing's enemies. I was a runner. Now I take on runners. We took on runners at the hub, but then I was a general. Or at least one of three.

Marie told us the story of neanderthals and sapiens. She said at first the neanderthals didn't want to mix with the sapiens and feared that they would lose their identity. It wasn't theirs to give. It was theirs to lose. Some sapiens and neanderthals did interbreed. Other neanderthals didn't like that. No longer concerned with their identity, they were now afraid to chance losing their power. If all but the elders were the offspring of the two mixing, it would leave all but the elders vulnerable to attack.

...

Out of we three, Cole, Bonnie and I, I assume Cole was the eldest. He left the hub first. Speaking for myself it seemed to be a thing one grows out of. I wouldn't say the most mature all left the hub, what kind of an organization would we have been had they had, but it seemed that not

many of us passed a certain age. Not defined by date of birth, but rather by experience as a runner.

...

Doctors would pump patient's egos for two reasons. To facilitate the medication's maximum effectiveness, or to get them off the placebo.

...

Marie said if you looked at any portrait long enough the eyes would start to shift down. As if the painting was bashful. As if the painting was scheming. If any of us looked at Marie long enough she would say, try to take a picture, that will last longer. Marie was never photographed. Those who tried did spend a long time in their pursuit.

...

Had I not discovered new tactics to uncover runners, I would have spent the rest of my life clawing at cargo doors to get them to come out. I've told you about the trick I play with the light. As played out as it sounds, certain smells can draw out the hidden. Every runner is different but most respond to liquid smoke being burnt on the outside of their door. If I had received a lot of tips before these encounters I may choose to add other seasonings. What's important is that they open the door. From there I need not be so creative.

The job is simple. Get them off the train by any means necessary and into my car using any necessary means. Such as treating the potential customer with respect, after all the dust has settled. Showing them I'm intelligent and will make smart driving decisions.

...

When I left the hub I left a lot unsaid. What I did say was to preserve my tent exactly as it is. The runners may have done so anyway. Their motive being for a memorial. Mine was because I believed there was still potential in myself. If the tent was as it was when I was leading, and improving every day, then in the future it would be seen as a place of power. Not to say there isn't power at memorial sites but those that go there have thoughts going in the

other direction. Not necessarily playing the victim but not accepting the compliments of how strong they are.

...

I prefer to shuttle fares at night and accrue promises during the day. I spent too much time around Marie to not half believe in the power of the supernatural at night. I don't believe in the supernatural but the night is still mysterious. If I were in my tent or apartment at night, anything could be happening outside. Better to be in a car where any threat could be dealt with.

...

Not eating breakfast puts me in the perfect state to sell hard and fight harder.

...

Sometimes when I'm about to apprehend a runner it appears they're washed up. The cargo car door open, and them sprawled about like they were carried to the car by a wave of bad decisions. I only throw pebbles at these runners to give them a chance to wake up. Perhaps angrier than they would have had I not made an entrance.

...

I was given ten canvases when I won the survey taking contest. Due to various weather circumstances I am now left with three. I've bought appropriately sized canvases so that I can copy the original but haven't found the time. Haven't found an artist who could make it. Haven't decided if it would even be worth doing.

My turnover rate for runners turning fares is very high. Those fares also tip better than their counterparts. Both parties see my professionalism a different way.

...

We didn't print our own literature at the hub but did draw our own caricatures of faceless people on matchbooks. We made our own matches. Our own books. The faces always bore resemblance. Marie had the final say as to what got passed and what didn't. She would touch up on our drawings so that the hub couldn't be traced, should a

stray matchbook fall into the wrong hands. The caricatures became legend anywhere nearby a train's route.

They were traded. No two were alike. Marie helped with that. There were no names or stats accompanying the drawing but runners came up with their own. Just as they had with the dogs. To collect five of the matchbooks with similar drawings was quite an accomplishment. The matchbooks were only produced when needed. This made them collectibles.

...

The matches were made with wooden dowels, potassium chlorate, glue, and red phosphorous. Scouts informed when underlings were running low. Scouts informed when accidents had occurred in the match making process.

...

The characters the caricatures were based on were larger than life. Since so few had access to the hub and our standard of life, the character caricatures themselves became larger than life. The face of Skip was thought to be a business man. Thanks to the comb over. Tales of his successes were told to distant runners. He had come from the streets and learned everything he needed to know to succeed through running. After he amassed a small fortune he decided to go back to his routes. They said he could still be seen riding in a dining car.

People thought Cole was a farmer. Screaming William an architect. Chrissie a no-nonsense nun. Bonnie wasn't drawn. She asked to be many times but no one wanted to cross that line. She said she wouldn't get offended but we were almost all offended for her even asking. Marie was never photographed.

...

Flood lights are a feature around train yards. Had they been so available or easy to fix in the days of the hub, we may have had trouble. Now I encounter them whenever I'm taking a car out of the garage. The brightness brings peace of mind to drivers returning to their cars. It makes me look

less suspicious when I'm tying my shoe. If I need to tie it to buy myself some time. If the garage were dark and I tried to buy time by tying my shoe, it would certainly look strange. People can only assume how good someone else's vision is, so if they thought I was as blind as them in the moment, they would be leery of my actions. If they saw I was acting unusual, and thought my sight better than theirs in the moment, they may panic.

...

Should a runner decide to take a battle to the water, they must act fast. Only in extreme circumstances can a runner go more than one round with me. Unless they are by water when they choose to open the door, and somehow see I've been tracking them, they will not have a chance to swim.

My jumpsuit puts me at a slight disadvantage upon immediately entering or exiting the water.

...

I imagine you're living somewhere remote now. Not that that could ever truly get you out of the spotlight. I'm sure in your solitary you are recounted as being in just as many places as you had been when you were out and about. Do those stories still show you in a positive light? Has your constant presence become burdensome to beholders? All I'm insinuating is that times change, even if people don't. So those same people in different times can seem like different people in familiar settings. You may be the Bonnie I remember, but times are different so it's very unlikely.

By that same reasoning, if these letters aren't read within the window of time that I expect them to be, they may be useless. Letters only change the more you read into them. People can't change but one's understanding of static people can. If your life's work is to be a regular person, you are unfortunately on a treadmill. When that treadmill is unplugged you will have gotten what you've asked for. We are not those types of people Bonnie.

Though we did everything we could at the hub to go unnoticed, we did have aspirations of a different kind. It is not ambition that drove us to the hub. Ambition drove the unworthy out. If we could just manage to get by, it was enough. We didn't choose the treadmill but the hamster wheel instead. We propelled ourselves forward. If we slowed, it was not a permanent cool down but one where we could come back stronger. Everyone at the hub looked out for themself. Everyone at the hub was one step behind you.

Those who did not know you, said they did. Not knowing you showed weakness. All knew of you. None grew on you. That in itself is commendable. I myself always had a soft spot for those who were drastically different than me. It was a kindly arrogance that allowed for diverse promotions. Too many cooks in the kitchen will ruin the stew. You can never have too many cooks doing prep work. We fed you the ingredients you needed to cook up something good.

Although the band would say jump in at any time, Skip like to be asked, can I go in coach. He would give his mentee

the once over, and if their hair passed inspection, would allow a tag out. He said there were no winners in his ring. The excessive tagging had fights going on for days on end. Between the practice and the matches, I don't know where any of the recruits had time to groom.

...

Skip always had a mint in his mouth. Sometimes when he was really involved and screaming like a maniac, the mint became a projectile. Much like Marie's trick. The fighters had footwear and if the mint wasn't crushed, stuck to the bottom of their feet. Skip was quick on the draw, so as soon as he saw the mint fly he popped another one in his mouth. The ring was littered with the things. Some fighters gained an advantage by manoeuvring their opponent on to the mints. It's hard to fight when you can't find your footing.

I keep mints in the car, not in my mouth. Every newspaper is bundled, and during the bundling the mints are placed inside. When a fare discovers them, they always ask if I'd known. The answer is always the same. They always offer me the tin. I refuse and tell them to take as many mints as they'd like. Usually these fares hand a generous tip over with the tin at the end of the ride.

...

I think I've spent all the money I'm ever going to spend on mints. If you spend what others would spend in a lifetime on a product quickly, you have the rest of your life to know you won't need to spend any more on it.

...

If it were only so easy to keep the doctors away with one apple a day. Unless the apples were that of old lore, and were psychoactive. Then the doctors would be occupied for at least a little while. Until they came back wanting more. If you give a doctor an apple, they'll ask what's for dessert.

The doctors may have been better served had they followed their own advice concerning rations. Perhaps they had in their not choosing apples. Honey is easier to portion.

Though there is a greater chance it will be sampled. Both the effects from the honey and the apple are not immediate.

The doctors usually did not use holistic medicine. Scouts first told that there were other doctors that did. Ergo the honey reference.

...

Bonnie wouldn't have gotten stung collecting honey. She may have been kidnapped.

...

Three were we and that seemed to be the magic number. Our organization lacked nothing but trivialities. I believe we three were the cause. I was the figurehead. Cole could be confused for me. Bonnie was everywhere but somehow always around. Apart you could barely get us in the same room. Together, you wouldn't be able to get us to leave.

...

Cole's girl's sister Cassandra spends many hours in rooms with mocking windows. She is the businessman randoms thought Skip to be. She is tactful. She is taught.

...

I conduct my business indoors, outdoors, from behind doors, and during car rides. What business I have thinking it's a small world is imposed on me by the absence of evidence that it's not.

...

When ever you feel lucky it is important to bottle your emotions. Can your intuition. It is more often that one is wrong than right. Wrong then right.

...

The only participation trophies handed out around the hub were from Skip. They were combs. His recruits were required to actively participate in their grooming. Your participation trophy was key to getting in on another fight. Though fighters were able to tag out, Skip kept a watchful eye, and all those who tried to pull one over on the old man were dragged from the ring. Physically scolded. Verbally

abused. Skip gave some warnings, some second chances. It was Cole, Bonnie and I that had the final say as to whether they were allowed to stay at the hub. Skip's standards were ever higher, so he had no problem when we showed our power. If we didn't get them, Skip would on some technicality.

I receive my own trophy after driving some fares. If they were a runner that bent to my will, for their own good of course, the tip they give at the end of the ride reminds me I'd be crazy not to play. My character has shown through so brilliantly that it enables the runner, who once thought they lost after being subdued, to realize they are now better off. It is not out of charity that they tip. It is their trophy to give away. It is mine to lose.

If a fare has chanced to come across my advertisement, and finds themself in the shuttle that way, their tip tells me to keep promoting. If they don't tip at the end of a fare, I assume it is because they are a very busy person. I don't need that kind of clientele. A busy person would be fine and may need transport for meetings, accommodations, and dining. A very busy person may not be in town for long. If my promotion was more successful, I could be as busy as the very busy and be known for reliable transport wherever one happens to be. I need them as clients as much as they need to see my simple face.

...

Bonnie could make the hair on any animal stand down. Marie, up. The way Marie coughed playing her trick, you'd think a cat's hair had done more than stand up. Chrissie and Screaming were better with the animals. Marie didn't have time to explain why the animals behaved differently towards us. She did once nurse a crow back to health. The crow would come back and visit Marie Venmo.

I never saw what she fed the crow. I don't know that anyone else around the hub ever showed their palm to the crow. Whenever we did show ours to Marie around this time, she'd always ask where our bird in the hand was. She didn't receive many visitors when the crow was around.

Marie was competitive with the crow, and for a time downright mean.

...

The crow chose it's cage. Not that I have anything against Marie's tent, but out of all of our's it's a strange decision.

...

Every tent had a cot. I got my cot early on in my career and it lasted me through the years. Even in my apartment I sleep very low to the ground. They say sleeping on wood is good for your back, so the thin planks under the mattress serve a double function. For my health and for my sanity. The baggy jumpsuit could lead one to assume I have bad posture but this is not the case. Rolling over onto a plank almost feels the same as the metal bars of a cot.

Every runner had a different story about where they got their cot. We enjoyed swapping tales because we knew we were probably the only ones on earth doing so. Since I've left the hub I've heard no shop talk about cot swaps. Yes, some were traded. It added another element to their stories. Judge not before you judge yourself I guess. My cot probably could have been mistaken for a hamper.

...

Until products began to be launched, time was of almost no importance. But gone are the days of randomly dropping in to solicit a sale. Fair warning is given that you will regret a future purpose. You've been given time to think about it, now think of how much of the time it won't cross your mind.

...

The question was often posed in the days before the hub, the ones of school, who one would sit down to a meal with. Religion was separate from state. The schools were run by the state. Had they been connected, the question wouldn't have been able to be posed. One is not supposed to covet their neighbor. Citing your new knowledge after would also be difficult. For some reason the question was for anyone throughout history.

When it was with which living person, students were often tricked into committing to a trade. To burden the young with idols so early on seems like a crime.

...

If I were able to talk with one of the greatest minds I believe they'd find me to be annoying. There's no way I would be able to speak articulately. When someone can't, they can't even say bear with me while they try an explanation. It would be no fault of theirs that I was star struck.

Time would move too fast if I were in the presence of an achiever. A succeeder in goals unattainable. I would lose a step the next day with fares and runners.

...

Underlings knew a trick to gain favor. I would do the same if a fare turned out to be one of the aforementioned envied great minds. Whenever an underling would finish the conversation they modestly self deprecated. If you didn't know what they were doing, you'd think they went the whole day without making a mistake, but had plenty from the past under their belt. They were quickly apologetic and acted as if they couldn't be convinced in our brushing off the matter. The next time they appeared, they put in extra work and helped out without being asked. When they repeated showing their folly at day's end, if others beside Cole, Bonnie and I were around, it was said that despite all their problems they were still a good worker.

...

Good workers weren't as rare around the hub as one might think. It was an attitude problem that had them leave their job. Most runners were as skilled as they come at working through fatigue. Always having a little in the tank up top should any problems arise. Because runners were so confident in their work ability, they had no problem taking large chunks of time off from socially acceptable jobs, so they could find themself on trains.

...

Doctors would recommend that a journal be kept while on the medication. Asked that the journal be brought for future reference. For both the patient and the doctor's experience. So the doctors kept two journals. One for what was prescribed. The other for it's effects. This was before the days of Erowid, but not very much so.

You can't blame the doctors for wanting to escape. Everyone else around the hub did. There were some sober runners. The doctors never could help them much. The doctors couldn't read them, so consultations were short.

...

Marie never turned down a superstitious customer. How they turned up after a visit was entirely in her hands. If the person whose palm is read can't read it themself, Marie could change destiny. Since they didn't know how to read the tattoo on their palm it didn't matter how many times they were asked about it's significance. Marie telling them what it might be gave it power. Whether what she said was what was written down is unclear. However, her customers clearly thought it truth and adjusted their lives accordingly. Seeking out ways to prove she was right, if only to boast about her later while among friends.

...

Forgive but don't forget. Remember that hindsight is always twenty-twenty. Carrying spite in your spine causes flashbacks. All helpful things to know when you're in my line of work. I can't be angry with runners for trying to pull the wool over my eyes. Back in the days of the hub, if I were ever close to being apprehended I would have done the same. Though for I to be in their role, someone would have had to been in mine. If I ever found a runner who bested me, not through deception but physical skill, I could imagine someone taking my place. When retirement does finally come for me, it will be on that day. I won't be able to detain that runner, and since they'd have to take all the fight out of me, they would probably stick around after the encounter. I wouldn't be able to change their plans and get them off the train. If this ever happens I will pass on my

knowledge in full. Until that time, I write so that that day will be possible. If I were a better writer that day would come sooner.

...

You used to read stories to the illiterate around the hub. Those same people were the best judges of books based on their covers. They all had nicknames. Maybe you'll remember a few. Here are the ones I can recall. There was Sappy, Young Dolt, Beeseal, and Hardy. They were all around the same age, and it must have been their generation that had put them at such a disadvantage. I always encouraged them to go back to school, if only so as to not hear your voice in a cadence that was not natural to you. Not that there was anything wrong with the way you read aloud, it just didn't have the same power as your god given voice.

What I did like about your story times was that you were extremely creative in the re-tellings. It wasn't goldilocks and the three bears, with you it was ginger and the three tech ceos. You were ahead of your time. Had us folk on the sidelines to your story time been paying more attention, we could have later averted certain disaster. Though we did have an internet presence for the hub, I for one was unaware of just how vulnerable we could be because of it. Just like in your story where Ginger hacks each ceo until she finds just the right schematics, our own discretion and overachievedness made us a target for attack. Do you remember when our internet presence for the hub got hacked? If your plan is what I think it is, then I know that it still haunts you to this day. I understand why you had to change protocol after the attack, but you can trust me with the new directions, Bonnie.

I am still your most trusted confidant. It may seem hard to believe because of your condition but it's true. In fact, our relationship is such that that information would never be shared with anyone but you. Shouldn't have to be shared with you, but things happen and people need reminding. I will take the secret, that you and I have secrets, to the grave with me. To the rest of the world, you and I are strangers. That seems to be how you want it. I am in wait.

When fares ask how much they owe, I always start low. I raise the price by five until I see the fare's tell. Once the price is agreed upon I raise it another five. I usually get five less than what I ended up asking for. I need these fares to be repeat customers. When they return, they usually give more than the total they had been thinking about leading up to the ride. After reflection, they realize I deserve more than I asked for. On these return rides when they ask how much they owe, I tell them five more than what they paid last time. They almost always give ten.

I'm more concerned about the tip from any fares I believe are on the verge of running. The amount shows how soon I can expect to see them on the train again. An extremely low or high number means I'll see them sooner than they'd like me to think. They go low, trying to show the transaction was completely normal. Going high, they try to butter me up. A fare could turn runner after leaving an average tip, but will likely see the light on their own when they discover they can in fact play by some of society's rules.

...

Doctors make the best diagnosticians. Not any that were around the hub, but somewhere. Marie was a better judge of disease than any instrument of prescription. Marie made time for the sick. Doctors made one sick in time. If a patient kept a journal, the doctors could usually get them better. This even allowed for them to make better diagnosticians.

A patient's journal could remind a doctor of one of their own past experiences. That, until that point, they weren't sure if it really happened. Even if the doctor couldn't help the patient, the patient could always help the doctor. The journal also helped the patient deflect advances for friendship from the doctors. Doctors would have loved to have someone to do experiments with. Both the doctors and the patient knew that they wouldn't be able to write those experiences down in the journal, which was the only thing keeping the doctors competent.

...

Newt has started working part time at Sal's kiosk. He told me it was the only way to get his father-in-law off his back. Sal was constantly trying to get Newt to come in. Now that he has, Sal doesn't have much to say to him. I think Newt made the right decision.

Isabelle talks much more than Sal. One drinks, the other doesn't. Isabelle hasn't been sober one day since Purgy passed. Be him a fictional character or her actual father. For a long while, Isabelle was quiet when she drank. Sal was more outspoken back then. With Purgy's passing he had an opportunity for his wife to see him as even more than what he was. Isabelle barely even noticed him.

After a few years, Sal began to quiet down and Isabelle piped. She was at that point in her drinking career where thoughts were actually profound and stories captivating. She should have taken a break right then. She didn't. Now, many more years later, she falls back on those same thought patterns in conversation. They are now old and dull.

...

Sophists know when to take a break from drinking. They use the substance to pick apart people's armor. I don't think they count drinks, but they know when they've reached the point of diminishing returns. If they kept on, their arguments would lose wit and become mean. Stopping at the right time allows them to interrupt when needed, to get their opponent off the path they're on. Allows them to hear which words their opponent favors. Allows them to make assumptions about their opponent's microexpressions, and use those against them.

...

I think when it hits you Bonnie it will happen all at once. Memories will flood your consciousness and you will know immediately who I am. Know who you were. Know what that meant for the two of us. How your past has interfered with your present. What's passed, your presence. When you can understand all this, please don't forget me.

When it hits you Bonnie, you'll no longer have any use for these letters. They will however finally have some sentimental value. I imagine when you are reading these your expression is much like mine while I am writing. Always on the verge of revelation though restrained because of it's proximity. Taking all the steps necessary to achieve a breakthrough except for the last one. The crucial moment where one steps back for an objective view. To keep on reading or writing without reflection defeats the whole purpose of the exercise. It is an exercise, Bonnie, and the sooner you realize your sedentary stance on life is base, the sooner you'll be able to reach new heights.

There used to be an old way of thinking which stated that even when inactive, you are still active in your inactivity. In order for you to be the Bonnie of old you need to shed the moss you've gathered and start making new plans. A life lived surrounded by my letters and not much else except for your caretakers is no way to live at all. Sure, if you can remember me and the things I write of you, you can do away with much of your idle time, but there is even more. Don't you want to be seen everywhere all at once, like you used to? Don't you starve for the attention you received as a stranger of the people? I don't miss the spotlight myself Bonnie, but I do miss standing on top of that generator with you and Cole by my side. It didn't matter what we said as long as we said it with the right inflection.

It was Cole, Bonnie and I that were the glue which bonded the hub. Apart we were a lesser adhesive.

When Cole left, the hub suffered. Cole was good at what he did. Like the scouts, and all those who took pride in

the hub, he did things so right you'd think that nothing had been done at all.

...

What fares can't read in the foreign papers, they can describe. Most of my knowledge of overseas comes from the political cartoons that are seen. In the papers where there are no such drawings, the photographs explain why. There is no room for an artist's interpretation in those editions. Too much else is going on.

...

When I left the hub it was with feelings of shame, remorse and guilt. An undercover had broken through our barriers. It was the first one to have done so. Last one that I had the privilege of knowing about. I wasn't asked to formally resign from my position. Many around the hub probably didn't even want me to. They weren't in my position. They couldn't have known the toll it took.

I don't blame Cole or Bonnie for my mistake. It was not ours to share. I had brief conversations with them before I left to try to understand what happened. Cole wasn't around but was the voice of my guilty conscious. I tried an exercise that Chrissie had said can help with grieving. I sat in an uncomfortable seat and imagined Cole sitting across from me. Of course I delayed truly doing the exercise and spent some time catching up. When I asked what he thought I should do, to stay or to go, he said it was a decision I'd have to make on my own. Though his girl had made it easier for himself.

I won't dare write what Bonnie said. Just as I would never label her and limit her potential.

...

Every garden I pass, I think of Chrissie. How if Screaming ever got what he wished for while working with her, the plants would have been scorched. Chrissie must have thought she was never in any real danger. Except to her sanity. Once Screaming got going it would be days before he stopped talking about a subject. Years and maybe never, till he stopped talking about lightning.

The problem with Screaming William's speeches were that he remembered everything he said. If what came out of his mouth didn't match what he had planned in his head, he would break off and correct his mistake. He may not catch the mistake right away, so could be finally reaching his point, only to leave it unsaid so he could unsay what he had said.

Chrissie repeated some of the funnier things to the flowers. She didn't want to give Screaming the wrong idea by laughing outright.

...

Bonnie had a laugh that could inspire whale songs. Get baby birds to leave their nest. Turn a frown upside down.

...

Any runners invited to stay at the hub had to pass the tribal connection method. Only in the most extreme circumstances did we have to move the hub because of a runner that failed initiation, and we thought might fail by the oath they swore before it. I will not hate that I am vetted not great. First words the oath made them say. It gets better from there. If I ever find the hub, I'll speak it's entirety again.

Tribal connection method involved extensive studying under all runners at the hub. The recruit was supposed to shadow any members that were not travelling at that time. Taking notes of why that person deserved to be there. Why the recruit could easily replace them. If the recruit was very persuasive, we were able to thin much of the herd. There was no worry that our waste would run off and reveal our location. They were as reliable as ever, just no longer new.

...

I believe I made the most of my time at the hub. How could any of that time have been wasted while we were around you? Hopefully the lessons we learned were intended for us. You and Marie had a funny way of teaching us things. And though there were some that said you had way too many useless talents, there were others, such as myself, who thought those people just couldn't see the big picture. You were talented Bonnie. Believe that.

You had all us ducks lined in a row. If your singing wasn't cutting it, you'd try a dance. From a dance to a thumb-wrestle. There was no one whom you couldn't exceed their expectations. You were more than a mother or father figure. There used to be a word for it but in this time of political correctness it would be heresy to say. Either way you reigned supreme. If you told us to jump off a bridge, you'd see we were already in the water before you finished the order.

Now with all this power, don't confuse yourself with that word that escapes me. You had limitations as well. After all, what good would you be to your followers if they were in the water and you still on the bridge ashore? That's where Cole and I came in. You needed a buffer between your extremes. Your ideas could usually go either way. Whether you intended for the lesson to be taught through failure, I am still unsure, but I do know that in either instance we came out better than how we had went in. None of your plans proved too disastrous. Not that you could feel remorse for something you don't remember doing, but I do believe it's important to tell you that we were always more or less alright.

Your mistakes were quickly corrected anyway, because of the amount of eyes on you. You couldn't draw a breath without someone wondering whether you were about to choke. Strange that you never had a moment of privacy while in a position of power, but you didn't seem to mind. I tell you that I would never have been able to do it. If someone even walks too close behind me on the street I just about lose it.

It happened once. Two recruits in the same class making eyes at each other only greenhorns can make. They both passed the initiation and were married in the ceremony that followed. After recruits pass the tribal connection method there is a celebration. These two recruits got married during then.

Everyone around the hub would go to the celebration. Everyone was thankful they were still around. Happy for the recruit turned hub runner not finding them totally useless. Not envious of the new runner's talents because they must be similarly matched.

There was no reason for any runner to be married. We still let the recruits go through with it.

...

Since doctors were so casual talking about prescriptions, it made some runners completely unprepared if they were asked by anyone else. For a period of time we were losing runners because they didn't know how to keep their cool. Around that time the question became standard for any interview conducted by law enforcement. Have you taken anything.

No would have sufficed for an answer. Even an admission would have been better than what some runners did. Believing that a sober person would truly feel insulted by the implication, since it would say something about their intelligence, they flipped their lid in response. Shouting utter nonsense at the officer. Admitting to things the officer, no matter how much experience, could even have thought up.

Scouts let us know who wouldn't be coming home for the night. A few weeks. Months. Ever.

...

Just as the band would say jump in, Skip wanting to be called Coach and asked by his disciples if they could go in, Cole, Bonnie and I also said something repetitively. Let's roll out. Since running the organization was such high stress and required much brain power, it was good to be campy when

we could. Sometimes when I'm getting my jumpsuit ready in the morning I can still hear those words. Let's roll out.

I do unroll my jumpsuit each morning and roll it up at night. If it was a messy day, I wring it out. I used to have many jumpsuits and because of their bagginess, used them for insulation. As I was able to acquire more junk to keep my house heated, I needed to find another purpose for the suits. Early on in my career I wore windbreakers. I switched to the athletic wear and never went back.

Early on I thought the windbreakers would instill fear in runners. Most know what a windbreaker signifies and those that don't surely know the sound it makes. The windbreaker was my trumpet into battle. I didn't stick with it long enough to require a reputation or a name. I was making good money in tips from those first runners turned fares. I spent excessively preparing for that first winter. I was in a jumpsuit by spring.

...

When Cole, Bonnie and I said, let's roll out, there was always a joke whether we should ask Marie to come. We all knew there was no way she'd leave her plot of land. She still spoke of the fold, the void, the black, the blue, the dawn, dusk, canoes and other various things taboo. Roll could have been as in whirlpool. Marie might have had a good answer to our bad question.

We said let's roll out, then all rolled up in different places.

...

Marie was Cole, Bonnie and I all rolled into one. We could never get that out of her. I suppose it didn't matter as long as Cole, Bonnie and I were all around. When Cole's girl took Cole away, we tried to get Marie to summon up the placater in herself, and counsel as Cole would have. Marie did the voice and told us that that would have to do. We couldn't argue with her, so Bonnie and I practiced imitating him ourselves.

So Marie was Bonnie, I, Cole remembered, and Cole contrived, all rolled into one. I imagine when I left, Bonnie

sought her counsel again. That would have made her Bonnie, Cole remembered, Cole contrived, I of the past, and I of what I seemed, all rolled into one. Bonnie wouldn't have been able to argue when Marie said the imitated voice was the only help she could give. Because Marie was Cole, Bonnie, and I incarnate, any arguments would lead to nowhere. Marie may have been able to see us for who we were, but being shown that simply through seeing her was lost on us.

...

When I'm with fare, if encouraged, I say my pleasure after they have thanked me. Encouragement is shown through sincerity in their gratitude. It is truly a pleasure to have them in the backseat rather than stuffed somewhere in a cargo car. I've been around enough liars to know sincerity. If the thanks is a ploy to get me off their trail, I usually tell them to call me if they need to talk. It's a strange thing to say after just giving someone a ride but even stranger that I insist.

I don't answer when they inevitably call. They call because they believed their deceitful thanks worked, the call furthers the deception. I redial that number then take my number offline until I have them back at where we started. Them subdued and promising a request for transport.

...

The dogs around the hub made snap decisions. Most dogs do. It was Cole, Bonnie and I that had to train the underlings to act in any other way. They weren't on the same level as the dogs and needed more time to make good decisions. Not that any of us had the right to judge whether any of the dog's decisions were good or bad, but the underlings were of our dominion.

It's easy to tell when a dog is going to react. Harder to be right in those moments when you're unassuming. Underlings had tells as well. Scouts related what they were to Cole, Bonnie and I. We hadn't time to spend learning the intricacies of those who could someday be us. Scouts were

harder to read, but unless they were running a competing organization, were entirely loyal. Scouts could be depended upon.

...

Sometimes when I'm with fare I try to get a reaction. They have to be a particularly bland passenger to receive the treatment. So far in the ride showing no interest in the foreign papers, mirrors if it's raining, mints, or any other objects of interest in the car. Focused on me as if something really can be seen in the eyes of the driver.

When I'm aware their eyes are on mine, I pick a field to survey and stay inside of that. It could be fast food that draws my eye. I will stare straight ahead but then look at any fast food stops on the route. Look for a little too long. The change these fares receive from these temporary releases usually turns up again at the end of the drive.

It's not always fast food stops that I attempt to draw attention to. Sometimes I know a fare is bound to tip well and I need not revert to such measures. Then it could be realty signs, this season's political candidate, what have you.

...

The doctors told patients to name their journals. A lot chose the six letter word, higher. It was a choice on a list the doctors said could be used for inspiration. Higher was what everyone wanted to get. Hired was what many runners became after they understood their journals.

When on medication it felt like so much was just out of reach. If only they could get higher.

...

Those with short term memory believe that, concerning money, they always even out.

...

My colleagues may very well have short term memory. Perhaps a lack of long should their car occupy the same spot in the garage for a while. I never put the cars back where I found them. I probably could by moving the car that had taken my spot, but having too many cars running at the

same time would draw unwanted attention. To this day I still shy away from spotlights I didn't set up myself.

...

I hope I make my fares proud to have me as a driver. That would get me more business. I hope runners that I apprehend are proud to have only suffered as much as they did by my hand, until they saw the light. I hope those around the hub were proud to have me as one of the three commanding party. If others are proud to know you, you can keep on living your life unchanged.

Trying to do things you think will make others proud, when you are not grounded, will be a waste of time. Your time and theirs. You will lose sleep trying to follow an example, which is set by following some other example, and so on. Unless the person you are trying to make proud is confused in what would make you proud of them, accidents will happen. Every person's idol is different.

...

The last thing Skip said to me was, the train is supposed to arrive early tomorrow. I wonder if he knew what my plans were. I didn't say many goodbyes to those around the hub. I felt like I would see them all again. I never thought my resignation would be permanent. I still could go back. The hub could still be around.

...

Skip would never believe what can be done with hair transplants nowadays. His recruits probably know. Having to be so obsessive over your hair for that long a time must surely have been detrimental. They probably notice every person's hair they see. Feeling lost away from Skip, they may even ask to inspect it. You can take the drill sergeant away from the drilled, but you can't take the drilled away from the drill sergeant. Through their quest for the perfect hairstyle they surely would have come across an ad for the transplants.

...

During the goodbyes that I did say when I left the hub, I made sure to tell the person not to get up. Since everyone

was so good at what they did that you couldn't notice anything had been done, most of the time you'd catch runners sitting. I told them not to stand because I wanted them to be as much at ease as possible while they still could. In a matter of days or weeks they would notice I was gone. If the scouts didn't tell Cole or Bonnie first.

...

The undercover that found their way into the hub had tattooed his initials on to his fingers. That should have been the first sign of trouble. His initials happened to be the same as an acronym for a law enforcement agency. I won't say which because he may still be undercover. The hub might have turned him into a runner. He may have taken my place. His superiors may have forgotten about him.

I don't know what he had on the hub.

...

I've started to be recognized at the library. The name on my card is different than what I went by at the hub, but I still respond to either. Some patrons believe I'm the accomplished writer that my work ethic shows me to be. They like to look at me when I write, but the moment I look up, they fail to meet my gaze. I don't know if they have plans to steal my passport. If they want my brain.

...

I would store food and supplies in the library if the world went belly up. Any library would do. Any disaster would send me there. If my use of technology weren't so limited, I could probably find a better place to do research. Not a better place for storage, as the masses are online and life hacks are very popular.

...

Brett, with tree on their house, and Screaming William, have both done all the research they will do in their lives. They both believed they were shown a sign. Let all other believed to be signs lead them from now and ever on.

...

The band didn't play for money or fame. The band played because that's just what bands do. If they hadn't played they'd have frightened their fans.

...

I only resort to fear tactics when those of laughter don't work. They both come from the same place. If I can get a runner laughing perhaps I won't have to introduce a chelsea grin. It's important that I reel the conversation back a little before offering them a ride. I can't have them laugh at my suggestion. Hearing, wait, are you serious, is painful.

If a runner has no sense of humor, which must be the case because I used to be quite entertaining around the hub, there's still a chance I won't have to resort to fear. There also is kindness. Which is very easy to show to someone who doesn't think you're funny. Kindness born from pity. If only they felt as good as me. Then they would have no problem laughing at my jokes.

When I do have to resort to fear, I do my best to not instill it too early in the confrontation. Every runner is different and using fear is a gamble. I want the playing field to be as even as possible. Fear can either back the runner into a corner or give them false confidence. Though in the moment of fear, that false confidence is as real as anything. If the runner is smart enough to be disciplined, and still can think logically while seeing red, that confidence can be disastrous for me. Could be. Never has been.

...

I've been able to contain myself in these letters up until now, but no longer. The last letter was returned and I could sense that you had shared it. The signs that you had opened it were there just like all the other times, but also those from a different person. The undercover no doubt. What did he have that I didn't? Was it his humility? Was I too unassuming? A face too simple to be revered? I don't harbor any ill will towards the under cover. I am shocked to discover there is some towards you. I thought what we had was special.

The first time we met you said not to get hung up on the details. I took that at face value and it never troubled me much. There were so many details after all. I almost immediately knew everything there was to know about you within a week of having met you. Information didn't travel that successfully around the hub about anything. Did you start the hub? Why were Cole and I in upper management? Who is the undercover? Had they already been there before us?

I followed the postal worker on their route today. Rather, I followed many postal workers on their routes today. You wouldn't believe how many different hands my letter was passed between. The last letter, mind you, not this one. I believe when you get this letter tomorrow you'll be greeted with a special surprise. Although if you've read this far then it's already happened. Well, at least you know that everything worked out. You won't have to worry about returning any more mail.

Here I go again telling you things that you already know. It did help before though didn't it? Sorry if any of my previous letters seemed cryptic at the time. Obviously you know why that had to be done.

I'll see you when I see you Bonnie.

The undercover that found their way to the hub would not have been a problem had their intent been good. I refuse to believe us runners were doing anything wrong.

Why it was wished that our merry troop broken up I have no idea. Those are the facts.

I thought he had found his way through various click bait articles, called something else back then, and back doors from there on. If his superiors knew about us and gave him direction without having him earn it, we would have been able to tell. What this runner did was trial by fire, as all except the original founders of the organization had done. When he arrived through the cracks in one of the trains creating the hub, the one a bicycle could fit through, even scouts were impressed. We believed what we had online would lead runners to a different entrance. He really understood the hub.

It was either Cole or Bonnie that disguised themself as an underling and greeted him. Assuming the manner of speaking of them who weren't quite there yet. I left so quickly I may have the details wrong, but in the retelling of the first encounter he was said to have said very little. Perhaps the story I'm told is different to soften the blow on my ego. Once I left the hub I never could quite get back in the confidence of any scouts. I had a talent for picking them out of crowds, but it was impossible to sustain because of their own willpower. The undercover may in fact be more eloquent than myself and underlings are afraid to break the news to me. Especially so because I don't think they have yet understood that I have left the hub, so think I can lose my position.

So, the quiet undercover was immediately liked around the hub. From where I stood, he seemed disciplined. That was more important than anything around the hub. We asked that many interests be held in one's mind. Without discipline one could not accomplish things around the hub so well that it appeared nothing had been done. The quietness meant no nonsense. Tattooed on his fingers were his pledged initials.

He shadowed underlings, scouts, dutiful runners, and Cole, Bonnie and I. Even we three were not above reproach. Perhaps he did find a flaw in my programming and

somehow I knew it, and decided to leave early. We didn't lose many runners after he gave his reviews. He was quiet. Disciplined enough to not spout nonsense, to we who were hungry for it after being around Marie for so long. I obviously didn't read my own review. Didn't dare to open Bonnie's file. In Cole's were as many words as either of them had probably said in their whole lifetime. The undercover probably didn't say much when wearing their other uniform around the office. They wouldn't have been picked for the job otherwise. The loudest person in the room is the most antagonistic. Being too antagonistic would blow their cover.

At the initiation ceremony the undercover gave a short speech, even brief, about what direction he planned to take the hub. If he had written more critical reviews I assume his plan wouldn't have been able to work. It did sound feasible. I did not see what ever came of it. After his speech there were scouts around the hub who signaled the undercover was now one of us. They performed a sound off from each cardinal direction, sneezing in turn. It wasn't quite that simple, nothing about a scout ever is, and before the sneeze there was a yawn. We didn't mind the scouts showing off.

The scouts were spread out around the hub. While the speech was being given, one of the scouts was able to produce a yawn. From a distance, another scout caught the contagion. As did another close by. Then one other a ways off. Until every scout that was present had produced their yawn. The speech ending coincided perfectly with the cessation of suspires. The first scout then sneezed, and all the others followed suit in turn. It really was something to see. I should have known then that my time at the hub wasn't for long.

After the initiation ceremony was the celebration. There were no marriages on that night. There may not have been any marriages since. If the undercover is what I think I've made him out to be, I'd advise to hide all daughters and wives. I've never seen anyone other than Isabelle drink as much as he did during the celebration. He still was quiet.

Even after almost every underling encouraged him to another speech, he was quiet. I should write to Bonnie and find out why. He was the man of the hour but his thoughts were of days, months and years ahead.

...

Just as I will retire once I am bested, I will likely stop driving if run off the road. Fares seem to have something to say if I drive defensively, so I don't give them the option. I drive like I own the road and until I am displaced will continue to do so. I've gotten a bit more careless since I've began writing this, recording what I can't remember from the day at night, taking notes about the fares just as recruits had when they shadowed, and stopping short at red lights to give me extra time. At this point in my career, the tips don't seem to mean as much.

...

The hub is calling. It says, take your time so long as you don't waste any more of it. A noble cause. An inevitable outcome. Ever since I caught myself in the act the other day, giving preference to the past and future instead of the present, I've realized I no longer can sit on Skip's proverbial sideline. No longer record these thoughts so I will know how to move forward.

I know what I must do.

I will get there pretty soon.

...

If my supervisor had been a micromanager I never would have been able to work the way I have. I didn't ask for much in my informal climb on board interview. I said I needed to be able to see the forest for the trees. The pixels to be fine enough to see the big picture. My supervisor asked me to stay on topic. We always had a good relationship after that.

...

My locker was with all the other lockers. Not with the one that was separate. That was Purgy's. I imagine if any of us are ever memorialized we could get our locker next to his. Go through the wonderful transformation of man to myth

to legend. Never to be forgotten because the lies told have no way to be discredited. The truths so mundane they are not even believable.

...

I don't think Isabelle ever stopped drinking. Sal went against the advice you never go shot for shot with a girl twice your size. Isadora and Newt's relationship is on rocky ground ever since Newt took up part time work for his father in law. He had to pick the lesser of two shoe flies buzzing in his ear. Only Newt knows if he made the right call. When Newt does know, it will unfortunately be too late. Such is the burden of social economics.

...

I could have sworn I saw the scout in a wheelchair on television. A day time talk show to be more precise. Everything was going well. The host was as lovable a fool as you could find, the audience could read and respond to lights, and our old friend the scout was grinning from ear to ear. I was curious, and I didn't want to leave the car because I was blocking the license plate, so I watched some more. The smile was as powerful as Bonnie's look. His was mischievous.

The self deprecating jokes were going over okay, all things considered, the audience, the lovable fool for a host, but the shots taken at the aforementioned got the show pulled right from the air. Right off the screen at the gas pump. I didn't think they were all that bad, and what wasn't bleeped out sounded insightful. The last thing the scout said before the blackened screen was, if he knew that losing his legs and being resigned to a wheelchair would mean he wouldn't be able to get away from this disaster of an experience, he would have chosen death instead.

Leave it to a scout to still be the resource I need, this far removed from the hub. It was I who gave a generous tip to the cashier after I filled up. She asked what was so funny but I didn't do justice for the story. In between my laughter she could only make out, wheelchair, disaster and death.

...

When I left the hub it was the last time I ever asked Marie for advice. She said that both the undercover and I would never be able to find peace while the other was around. That it had been a long time coming. I think Marie's words are the reason that to this day I look for a rival in others. Had I known then what I came to gradually figure out now, I may have put up more of a fight to stay at the hub. Had I put up more of a fight, I may still have been stuck in my ways.

Ironic, that in order for me to see the light I had to fight. I give runners many options as to how to see the light. Fighting was only one of them. It wasn't even my preferred method. Some runners could sort of fight, but all runners could sort of talk. Fighting against someone who doesn't know what they're doing is not very fulfilling. Waging battle of the intellect with someone who will do anything not to fight is more rewarding. Also, if I know they are apt to conversation, I can expect a tip when we meet again. If they choose to talk, there is no way that I will disappoint.

...

Fares that are without direction are starting to influence me. Where once I knew exactly where to bring them to insure a generous tip and more rides down the road, since I've become distracted I've found them finding their own voice and giving guidance. Maybe I just didn't hear them right the first time. The fares are starting to teach me things.

Not things that I was prepared to learn, such as their interpretation of foreign news or their observations of what's going on outside of the car, but what civilians actually do from day to day. When I left the hub I knew I would have to make up for lost time, but if I've been doing it all wrong, I think I may have added to the deficit.

Fares do not always want to be driven to and from home. Aside from work those are really the only two directions I go. Whenever I stopped at their destination, I never stopped to see where I actually was. The fares

seemed to be without direction, because to them I was a loading screen. The start or end of some chapter.

...

Runners turned fares could also have mistaken me for a loading screen. Thinking they were just out of the woods by accepting my offer for shuttle. Realizing that what comes after always seems more difficult than what came before.

Perhaps I didn't need to resort to such drastic measures to get runners out of the dark and into the light. I'll always keep to one however. Never give the runners names.

...

It was Cole, Bonnie and I that had access to seating plans, and therefore the names of everyone around the hub. Just like how Chrissie said to visualize a person to help with grief, Marie had a similar technique. So we kept a map of where everyone would sit around the generator in the center of the hub for lengthy speeches or other small gatherings. Marie said that if we stood on the generator and could imagine all the people around us we would be able to achieve an altered state. Like how if you can visualize those of the round table, and then yourself sitting with them around the table, you've already won half the battle. If we could get to that altered state, our speeches would become the stuff of legend.

...

I still find matchbooks of the hub's old character's caricatures. I confess that I still go to where the hub once was, in case things have went back to the way they once were. Now that I am removed, the stories I come up with for the people I used to know are as far off from the truth as any other normal folk had once assumed. Skip wasn't as old as he looked and very well may have become a successful businessman.

I've tried to find the hub through the internet. I confess that while writing I have gotten sidetracked because of what has been put down to paper. I've went on as may unsecured websites as I could find. Clicked on many links for

items no one could honestly want to purchase. Searched for any names used at the hub. Names like Cole, Bonnie and Cole's girl. I was bested by the undercover and never may have caught up. If I have been replaced I would like to know.

...

Around the matchbooks I also find small vials. Ones that have a capacity of two milliliters. Ones that used to be passed between two hands. Asked to be returned if not completely satisfied. Doctors could find a use for them.

I am lucky to say I have not needed to make any use of doctors after leaving the hub. I imagine I'd fail a button downed's protocol during the consultation. The doctors around the hub went by a different book. I imagine I may scare a doctor from the straight and narrow. A certain rapport was built with the doctors around the hub. Carrying it over would at best get me asked to never return. At worst, get the police called on me.

...

Stained glass no longer bars windows.

...

I haven't tried discovering what organization the undercover worked for. Since I believe they did all the legwork on their own, I choose to do the same. Of course if I still could exercise the hub's power, I would. But if I could, I wouldn't be in the situation I'm in now. All the steps covered for self actualization but stuck in the moat outside of the castle.

In a predicament slightly like the nursery rhyme with a river and a boat. Replacing the word merrily for verily. Gently for otiose.

...

The day after the undercover's initiation and the ceremony on that night, the morning was perfectly normal. Around the time when most runners would succumb to their hunger, rather than waiting about an hour for it to pass, and were gathering food, the undercover was talking diet. The tenacity. I couldn't stand aside and let him spoil all

the meals we previously had worked so hard on. It is not like a leader to be confrontational with a subordinate. Interrogative, sure. But not supposed to do what I did. That was the day I lost my role as leader.

When the dust had settled, I realized that the undercover was no ordinary come in off the street runner. Not yet discovered they were undercover, but certainly not like the others. I took him up on his suggestion for what I should have on my plate. I should have known then I was in trouble. Even in the days of the hub I sat down to eat no more than twice a day. Definitely never at any times other than night.

I can't remember exactly what was said while we ate. There was a large crowd gathered around us. I remember someone shouting tell us more. That was when I noticed all the people behind me. Positioned there so they could have a better look at the quickly gaining esteem guest. I tried to shoo them away but they said if I didn't like it I could leave. It wasn't at that moment that I did but it wasn't long after. I was without Cole and Bonnie by my side and didn't know how to react. I had never been spoken to like that by an underling. Never did the underling have a bigger audience than me. I was losing control and losing it fast.

None of the runners behind me left. They were now to stay in the undercover's care. I tried to still look regal as I finished my plate, but from behind I swore I could hear murmurings and laughter. The undercover wasn't phased in the least by the whole ordeal. Just as how I thought I would have been.

...

Marie said if you can't put on a happy face, you have no hope of ever putting on one strong.

...

I left the hub abruptly. In the same vein so too will this book be finished. Cole and Cole's girl left the van because they didn't need it anymore. In homage to ideas I think are great, I will try to honor them in my own way. This manuscript will be left in the van. The van will have changed.

The picture will be in the book. From then on the van will stay the same.

Those who find other copies will likely have been able to find the hub back in the yesterdays. I like to still think I can string others along to a goal only I have defined. Maybe through reading this, others will find the hub. They'd still be able to find me at where it used to be. I wouldn't ask for help in finding it's new location, if there is one, but wouldn't be opposed to small bits of food. I'd have to be coaxed out of the corner after scurrying away. I can't hide in plain sight like the scouts used to. I can't act casual in a conversation unless I'm trying to sell.

...

Scouts must know my whereabouts and my goings ons. Perhaps I'm being tested and upon my return to the hub will be rewarded. Maybe this manuscript already has some attention. It could, on release, reach the eyes of Bonnie and the rest of the crew. If this is the case, this space could be considered wasted. So it is not, a message for the scouts. And on the seventh day, god rested. Only a scout could tell the rest of the story. No scouts have yet done so. A few must have been there. Any day now the rest of the blanks will be filled in.

...

I did try to say a formal goodbye to Marie before I left. She had a new crow. I got as far as I ever got with her. That was enough.

...

Though I haven't been bested by a runner, something still must have happened. When I started writing I didn't ask what for. I had given so many what for's I forgot to take care of myself. I've still won many battles since ink has blotted the page but I wonder if I hadn't lost one before that. If my memory for all other things is only because it's lack of one specific. If I lost the fight it would surely show where the inspiration came from. A place of terror.

...

Perhaps a fare sneezed scopolamine onto me, and has been instructing my dissertation. Something must have happened. It can't be that something happened at the hub and then nothing after that.

...

After my meal with the undercover, the group behind me started to chant. Those same initials that were written on his fingers. How I wish I could remember the organization. I'm not sure why they were chanting but it soon broke into song. Listening to any music around others since that day has been next to impossible. I didn't know the song. Can't remember it now, but I know I didn't like it.

The undercover had a great voice, and I'd be able to compliment it even more had he kept singing. Instead he asked Bonnie to dance once the chorus was reached. I didn't even know Bonnie had been around. Bonnie might have even been singing. I was out of my league. A leader shouldn't have taken it so personal. On that day I was no longer looked to for leadership.

...

Bonnie could twirl, like during dizzy bat, and an observer would feel drunk.

...

My sober drunkenness turned ugly. It was no longer Cole, Bonnie and I. It was I, myself and the agent of anger inside.

...

If I ever do return to the hub, I won't be able to say hello to everyone. Unless I have not been tested and my return will not have me see my old honors and position. If my return puts me on the bottom rung, I won't have to worry about slapping an expression of leadership on my simple face. I would be able to greet one and all.

...

If I ever do reach the hub, and this book those there by providence and scout's intervention, I believe the transition will be seamless. I won't be asked of where I've been or what I've been doing. They will all know as well as I.

If I can't immediately assume my leading role, I'll have a lot of hands to shake. If I do rejoin the ranks of the three, the undercover replacing Cole and not myself, I have many thoughts for moving forward. I'm sure I could smooth things out with the undercover and Bonnie.

I've got to find the hub.

...

And just like that my work has suffered. My own tricks used against me. The scouts must have had something to do with it. No one has read my work. Runners couldn't yet know. Competing drivers weren't supposed to move in this early. The advertisement sweepstakes survey wasn't set to occur until the end of the year. I have been displaced. Replaced. Erased. What was left, gathered and disposed of, just in case.

I have bested myself by estimation of others. No reference point for myself. Lost, found, and told this was my new home.

...

The cars in the garage seem to move whenever I take my eyes off them.

...

Runners are traveling with cargo car doors open.

...

Who'd have thought I'd hear the sound before I got the look. After years of straining my ears against the screeching of the trains to try to hear the hub, now I cannot escape it. If Bonnie was plagued as I am currently then I may be closer to the look than I think.

...